18 February 2015

CW01560335

The
Postmaste
Mistress

To Claudette

With best wishes

Ruth Fifield

The Postmaster's Mistress

RUTH FIFIELD

PARTRIDGE
A Penguin Random House Company

To order additional copies of this book, contact
Toll Free 0800 990 914 (South Africa)
+44 20 3014 3997 (outside South Africa)
orders.africa@partridgepublishing.com

www.partridgepublishing.com/africa

CONTENTS

DEDICATION

Elena's story is a tribute to those who sacrificed their lives for the greater good, that the survivors of the Second World War might be given the chance to add their word to a wholesome human tale.

Seventy years after the cessation of that titanic struggle, may people of goodwill apply the lessons learnt then, in a world evermore fraught with terror and conflict.

PROLOGUE

Having an interest in local history and Port Edward in particular, I wanted to meet Elena. I had been told that she was a fund of local history but one can't simply 'phone someone and say, "Please share your stories with me." When a young friend was looking for someone to interview for a school history project, I grabbed this as a pretext to contact Elena. I 'phoned her on a Sunday evening and caught her in a rage. Elena doesn't dislike many people but she'd just had a run-in with her least favourite person, a man she describes as a Nazi, a self-confessed Vlakplaas (the infamous apartheid detention, torture and execution centre) operative. In her gravelly voice and thick Italian accent, she was threatening to put the evil eye on him and offered to teach me how to do this. I was thoroughly entertained and thus began our friendship.

We spent many afternoons piecing together her history. It quickly became apparent that there was much more to her story than just a record of local goings-on. In any event, if the two of us want to continue living in this town, most of the local stories couldn't possibly be printed.

She introduced me to a cast of fascinating characters, events and places which I found compelling. Above all was her enduring love affair with her husband, George. Her story also provided an insight into the contribution made to South Africa after the Second World War by new European immigrants.

Gradually we became aware that a book was evolving. It's been a journey for both of us. I am particularly grateful to have got to know this warm, vibrant character, who, at 93 and growing increasingly frail, is still interested in the world, helping out wherever she identifies a need, sharp-witted (although she complains of a failing 'floppy disk') and gregarious.

CHAPTER 1

That a girl infant, born into a privileged European family between the Great Wars, should find her destiny on the southern edge of Africa, the raw south coast of KwaZulu Natal, can only be explained by love.

On the 25ᵗʰ of April 2007, when Elena was eighty-six, she flew back to Italy for what she said, would be the last time. The date also happened to be her sixtieth wedding anniversary.

I pictured her floating above the clouds, comfortably ensconced in the efficient Germanic care of Lufthansa. I saw her looking down at the world and thinking about how different this day was in comparison with her wedding day so long ago: no hurtling about to be at rendezvous points on time, no noisy troops and clattering, crashing metal or screeching trains, no panic. But also, sixty years on, little euphoria and anticipation and, undoubtedly, a great sense of loss.

Elena, however, is a survivor and no sentimentalist. She had decided that at her age she couldn't cope with tourist class and booked business class instead. Her choice of airline was Lufthansa, imagining that German efficiency would contribute to the ease of the trip. She also asked for a wheelchair to speed things up and cause everyone less inconvenience. The VIP lounge appealed to her as did the Chivas she was going to order in the lounge before boarding. Managing the entire flight without a chance to have a cigarette was the most daunting aspect of the trip.

And off she went. Her dear friends, Margaret and Arthur Harris, delivered her to Margate Airport from whence she flew to Johannesburg for her connecting Lufthansa flight. She had her Chivas in the lounge but was not allowed to smoke. Before she could order another drink, all the wheelchair

1

passengers were pushed outside to a waiting area where they were left for a long time with absolutely no attendance.

On the plane things weren't any better. Her seat was very comfortable but once the stewardess had tilted it back for her, the woman didn't come near her again for the entire night. The man in the seat next to her had embarked, adjusted his seat into a fully-reclined position, covered his face, and didn't communicate a word throughout the flight. She could get no response from him to help her adjust her seat and so she was stuck in the same position all night.

The first time she could get to a loo was when she arrived at her sister's apartment in Florence.

So much for Lufthansa, German efficiency (which it certainly was, but with one of those humbling, ironic twists life tends to broadcast), and so much for my romanticised picture of her luxurious and nostalgic return journey.

Despite Lufthansa not quite achieving the mark, the contrast between this journey and Elena's wedding night remains enormous.

The planning and preparation Elena and Margaret put into this trip took months. They even went on a shopping trip to renovate the contents of Elena's cosmetics case.

That night, sixty years ago, was spent on a troop train crammed with servicemen finally leaving Europe after trying to mop up the war mess. On that wedding day there had been no time for make-up. There hadn't even been time to don the beautiful pale blue, wool dress into which so much planning had gone and which had its own tale to tell: the wool had been produced at the Cape, imported into Italy by the Marchesi family, whose son, Bruno, long carried a torch for Elena. The fabric was given to Elena with great affection by Bruno, specifically for her wedding dress, when he finally realized that he didn't stand a chance.

Elena was the sole woman on that troop train. The only concession that was made to her female gender and to their honeymoon status was that George managed to wangle a coupé, but that was where privilege ended. The train was as neglected and battered as the rest of Italy. The paint was peeling, the woodwork dull and scuffed, and the leather seats cracked and spilling horse-hair stuffing, so irritating to tender flesh.

Their luggage was tossed aboard, Elena was unceremoniously shoved in and George slammed the door as the train jerked forward. Collapsed on the unyielding seat, they looked at each other and began to laugh.

There was disbelief that they were finally married and that the very process of getting married had been so dogged by the bizarre circumstances of the preceding two days. There was relief that they had actually, and finally, triumphed over all the vicissitudes of the years of their courtship, of the previous few months, the last two days, and every hour of that day. Then there was humour in their laughter – the sheer fun, despite the panic, of their race to the altar and then to catch this abused, war-worn, noisy train.

Always, there was humour! And this being their honeymoon, of course there was more than humour. One glimpse into the iceberg-blue of George's eyes transmuted the laughter into an altogether different joy. Those eyes had been Elena's undoing from the very first moment that she had met that penetrating gaze, one which she would never be able to resist.

Being George and Elena, they, naturally, enjoyed another twist to the romance and passion of the moment. It was deliciously spicy to make love in the turmoil of a rattling, lurching troop train, bursting at the seams with rowdy, bawdy men. Locked in each other's arms as the train clattered and swayed its way over bridges and through tunnels, their love-making took on a new dimension. Already familiar with one another's bodies, together having disposed of Elena's inhibitions, born of ignorance, and secure in knowing that officialdom could never part them again, they discovered an unexpected and new level to their intimacy.

The next morning, as she and George were disembarking, she was given a rousing cheer and received many raucously-concerned and ribald enquiries about her health and the peacefulness of her sleep. She had the grace to blush but complained in private to George that those cracked seats had been hell on her derrière.　　　.

The comparisons between that night sixty years ago and this night of her return flight to Italy, are perhaps too great to comprehend. They're not only about the physical differences in transport technology and fashion, but the whole world is a different place in moralities and pace. For Elena, this trip also held immense poignancy – the biggest difference being that her beloved George was not with her. On that night so long ago she was still very close to the start of the romantic and loving journey which sustained her for so long.

The wild train ride wasn't, of course, the first adventurous journey Elena had undertaken in order to be with George. A year earlier, in 1946, she had made the journey to South Africa aboard a Liberty ship but, life being life and Fate having a mercurial temperament, George and Elena's plans had gone badly awry.

CHAPTER 2

Elena was born in Holland on the 27th of November 1920, to a Catholic mother, Lucia Husker, and a Jewish father, Barend van Praag. Of Lucia's and Barend's four talented and individualistic children, she was the free spirit.

Their firstborn was Natolia, who was named in memory of her paternal grandfather, Natan. She was born on Valentine's Day in 1917. Toly was very serious and academic and excelled at her studies, becoming an accountant, lecturer and teacher.

Next was brother Orso, born in 1918. Orso took his name from Barend as 'orso' means 'bear' in Italian and Lucia's pet-name for Barend was 'Bear'. The family's nicknames for one another are revealing of their affection and informality. Apart from calling their father 'Papa', the children also called him 'Papalino' or 'Little Father'. Lucia was called 'Tazio' after the Italian racing driver Tazio Nuvolari, because she drove so badly.

Orso was bright but not particularly excited by scholarly pursuits and a great trial to Toly who undertook the supervision of his academic progress.

Then came Elena who could never sit still and whose school career was pockmarked with repeated years because she couldn't achieve the required standards of behaviour.

Agnese was born in Genoa on the 31st of December 1924. She studied law but her real vocation was care-giving and she continued her hospital visiting until she was eighty, at Santa Maria Nuova. This institution was founded in 1288 by Folco Portinari who was the father of Dante's beloved 'Beatrice'. It was also the hospital where Leonardo da Vinci gained his knowledge of anatomy. The marble baths in which the corpses were stored for dissection are still in the basement of the hospital.

Father Barend was born in Den Haag in Holland in 1882 to a Protestant mother and a Jewish father, Natan. Despite his mother's Protestantism, Barend always regarded himself as fully Jewish.

He was a very active and carefree boy who loved nothing better than a good joke. One of his boyhood jokes was made at the expense of a woman who worked in the local butchery. She was notorious for her foul temper and that made her an even more tempting target for the irrepressible Barend.

He had noticed that she had tiny feet which inspired him to ask her if she had trotters. She said, "Yes," to which he replied, looking pointedly at her feet, "Then you must have a great deal of difficulty walking!" It took a second or two for her to make the connection and Barend bolted for the door before she could negotiate her bulk around the counter. Meat cleaver in hand, she yelled a stream of disapprobation at his retreating back.

Barend fostered a sense of humour in all his children, encouraging practical jokes, an appreciation of the ludicrous and ironic, and an ability to laugh at themselves. He was often in the midst of their horseplay and the planning of their next caper, much to Lucia's chagrin. It was in Elena, though, that his lessons found the most receptive ears.

As a boy he also loved sport (especially soccer and fencing) and this, too, was a love he would one day encourage in all his children.

Barend's father owned a printing business which Barend was expected to enter after school. This held no appeal for him and in 1900, when he was eighteen, a friend called Wilming offered him the opportunity of going into the ship-building and navigation industry in Genoa. This company was known as 'Italian Navigation' and built ships for the Italian government. Barend jumped at this chance and gained very valuable experience in the shipping industry, experience which would accompany him all his life and which led him into all sorts of unexpected ventures and misadventures.

During this period in Genoa he seems to have cultivated the company of a large group of artistic friends. In 1910, when an indigent young sculptor needed a model for the sculpture he wanted to enter into a competition, he couldn't afford to pay anyone to pose so Barend offered his services. According to a paper, written by Ines Marcelli and Marica Mercalli of the Central Restoration Institute in Rome and presented at a conference in Jerusalem in 2008, the city council of Genoa declared an open competition for the best draft design for a monument celebrating the expedition undertaken by Garibaldi and a few loyal supporters in 1860. The number of his supporters eventually grew to the famous 'Thousand'. The expedition set sail from Quarto in Genoa and made for Sicily, which was the starting point of their Italian campaign and which finally resulted in the Unification of Italy.

Barend's sculptor friend, Eugenio Baroni, won the competition, beating fifty-three other entries. The judges were amongst the most highly respected painters and sculptors in Italy at the time and included Leonardo Bistol, whom Eugenio venerated and who had greatly influenced his work, along with Rodin. This was certainly heady stuff for Eugenio and even Barend. In addition to the artistic achievement, it was immensely exciting, and a great responsibility, to create a statue to Garibaldi, the hero and darling of most Italians.

On winning the competition, Eugenio was required to create a mould which was then cast in bronze by the Pasquali Steelworks in Pistoia. The statue consists of a central male figure standing with his arms at his sides and hands in determined fists. The chest is thrust out and the whole figure shouts power, dominance and determination. The pose is reminiscent of a ship's figurehead. On either side of Garibaldi lie prostrate male figures representing the Thousand. Their postures suggest various emotions from adulation to the writhing agonies of death. Their faces, too, cover a gamut of emotions, the most haunting of which is the expression of the figure at Garibaldi's feet. It is a mask of horror with empty eye-sockets and gaping mouth. Behind Garibaldi are more male figures reaching up to, or supporting, the wings of the female figure of Victory which surmounts the whole statue and who has her linked arms stretched above Garibaldi's head, suggesting a victory wreath or benediction.

Eugenio's inspiration evidently came from a patriotic hymn by Luigi Mercantini 'The Tombs are Uncovered, our Martyred Heroes Arise'. It is this connection that Eugenio used to justify his use of naked figures when he was accosted by disgruntled veterans of the campaign at the unveiling ceremony – these grumpy old men didn't want themselves portrayed in the nude.

In the Central Restoration Institute paper, the authors say that the statue was unveiled to much fanfare on the 5th of May 1915. One of the speakers at the unveiling was Gabriele D'Annunzio, a leading Italian poet and novelist. It was he who used the occasion to plead for Italians to join the First World War. This is precisely what Eugenio proceeded to do.

To what extent he was influenced by D'Annunzio's speech is anybody's guess. According to the website of the 'American Friends of Italian Monumental Sculpture', he was awarded the Medaglia di Argento for valour at the Battle of Monte Grappa. His war experiences, however, left an indelible scar of pessimism on his psyche from which he never recovered and which had a profound effect on his work. His postwar work is regarded as revolutionary in laying foundations for the development of Art Deco sculpture, but because the imagery which he incorporated in this work is so tragic and dark, it was not popular or commercially successful and commissions were sparse. It also didn't help that his war experience had left him with a deep suspicion of anything which smacked of Fascism.

It is extremely regrettable that Eugenio's Art Deco work is being so sadly neglected and is in such great need of restoration. However, our Barend's statue, Garibaldi's Monumento ai Mille, is in fine fettle having undergone a major restoration in September and October of 2007. The restoration was an involved, collaborative affair amongst researchers into the best possible way to preserve bronze used in public, outdoor monuments and especially the corrosive effects of sea air on such works. The project also served as a teaching workshop for art conservation students. The research and work focused largely on the figure of Garibaldi.

So, it is Barend who is the central male figure of the statue which still stands in Genoa today. Hence Barend is immortalised in all his naked glory, to the great amusement of his children. Barend was also tickled by the idea that it was he, a Dutch Jew, who became the proxy for the adored, rambunctious Garibaldi, architect and hero of Italian nationalism!

Barend's artistic friends seem to have been an important part of the family's life, cropping up wherever the family happened to be, or whatever their circumstances were.

He returned to Den Haag and his family at the outbreak of the First World War and was again employed in shipping. This employment resulted in two major events in his life.

The first occurred when he went to Germany on a business trip. The Netherlands managed to retain its neutral status with great difficulty through the First World War, and this explains why Barend was able to conduct business in Germany during the war.

On one fateful trip he was arrested as an Allied spy. He was thrown into a prison called Zenner Lager, having been informed that he was to be executed by firing squad. His insistence that he was a Dutch citizen fell on deaf ears. The intransigence of the Germans bewildered him. No matter how hard he tried to squeeze information out of them as to what had led them to believe that he was a spy, he could learn nothing. He also couldn't come to grips with why they were expressing such disproportionate pleasure at having captured him. Plunged into gloom and desperation, he spent the days prior to his execution sitting on the edge of his bunk with his head in his hands. It just wasn't possible that his life could end in such a farce.

In preparation for his execution, a few days prior to the event he was asked what his last wishes were. He replied that he had always wanted to die dressed in a white suit! Perhaps he thought it would take them some time to find a white suit. Possibly it was his irrepressible sense of humour turned black and bitter, or sheer bravado, that led him to come up with that idea. What the German reaction was, Barend never said.

Somehow a message about his predicament reached the Dutch Consul. This man rushed to Zenner Lager, arriving the day before the execution, and testified to Barend's innocence. When Barend was unceremoniously hauled out of his cell by his very disgruntled guards, his first thought was that his appointment with death had been brought forward. To be told that he was free to go at this eleventh hour was staggering and a shattered Barend gratefully submitted to the Consul's care. It was from him that he finally learnt the details behind his incarceration. It turned out that the Germans had been looking for an English spy who looked very much like Barend!

The second important event was meeting his wife.

In the course of his business activities Barend often had to call in to the telegraph office at the main post office in Den Haag where a pretty young telegraphist, called Lucia Hulsker, sent his telegrams for him. He was genial, outgoing, suave and very funny, and his invitations to 'walk out' were soon accepted.

Lucia had been born in Utrecht in 1888 to a staunchly Catholic family. Her father was the organist and choir master in their parish. He died when his eight children were very young, leaving his family extremely badly off. Lucia's mother's brother stepped in and arranged for the children to be educated at Catholic boarding-schools in Germany. This was where Lucia completed her education. When she returned to Holland she went to work for the post office in Den Haag.

Both families were horrified at the blossoming relationship. When Barend proposed to Lucia, neither of them bargained on the reaction of their families. Barend's mother could cope with a Jewish husband for herself but the thought of a Catholic wife for her son was just too much. Lucia's family was equally horrified at the thought of their good Catholic girl having anything to do with a Jewish/Protestant family. Their families cajoled, threatened, begged and reasoned but neither Barend nor Lucia could be swayed.

Nothing had been resolved with their families by the day of the wedding and neither family had even begun to relent in their condemnation of this union. When the determined and ostracized couple set off from their respective homes on that day, the only acknowledgement of this important day which they received from both their families, was a view of their erstwhile homes with the shutters firmly closed against them and their wayward decision. Closed shutters were a time-honoured sign of mourning.

They were married in a civil ceremony with no one but the officials present.

Lucia's mother eventually relented and Lucia was restored to her favour. Elena has photographs of the old lady taken on holiday visits to the Van Praags in Italy. Elena also remembers visiting her maternal grandmother in Holland. She doesn't remember much about the rest of Lucia's siblings or their relationship with her mother apart from one nasty experience.

Lucia and her children, whilst on holiday in Holland, went to pay a call on one of Lucia's brothers. Elena was just a little girl at the time. She can remember climbing a flight of stairs to the dwelling and a large, slovenly-looking woman appearing at the front door. There was no sign of Lucia's brother.

This woman shouted at them that no cursed Fascists would ever be allowed into the house! Elena's uncle had thrown in his lot with the communists and the Italian Van Praags had been labelled and condemned. Lucia, in her dignified way, didn't try to put up an argument and she turned and ushered her children away. As young as she was, Elena can remember her mother being very cut up about the incident.

CHAPTER 3

Despite the worst predictions of their relatives, Barend, Lucia and their young family found great satisfaction in each other's company and soon prospered in every way. Their economic prosperity was especially boosted when Barend became a port captain in Rotterdam.

Rotterdam was an extremely important harbour because of its strategic position on the Nieuwe Maas, a northern branch of the Rhine. It had grown enormously in the latter part of the nineteenth century, especially after the unification of Germany and the industrialization of the Rhineland. A great web of ports had developed and it had become known as one of the best equipped harbours in the world. However, the First World War did bring great economic hardship to Rotterdam. Despite this, the Van Praags lived very comfortably in a large home with the convenience of horse-drawn carriages and plenty of staff. Lucia was also able to employ qualified nurses as nannies to help her when her children were tiny.

Fate (and perhaps the curses of their angry families?) came very close to intervening in the secure and contented family life they were creating when, in 1918, Lucia, Toly and Orso fell desperately ill with the Spanish 'flu which dispatched so many. Orso was a very young infant, and although he, too, recovered, his health was never strong throughout his life and he always looked a little frail. This was attributed to the desperate struggle he had had to survive as a babe.

In 1921, when Elena was only a few months old, Barend decided to return to Italy in pursuit of new business opportunities. This was a most fortunate decision in the light of what was to happen to so many Jewish families when Hitler and his Nazis over-ran Holland in the Second World War.

Initially, he spent some time with his sister, Tante Sus, and her husband in Abruzzese where his brother-in-law owned considerable property. Thereafter he travelled to Genoa where he stayed with great friends who had two sons and two daughters. Agnese still has the letter they sent Barend, giving him directions to their home in Genoa.

Some years later, this family was devastated by the death of their elder son who had been sent to Naples and who suddenly, at the age of twenty-one, died in the bath of a heart attack.

Thereafter, for years, the Van Praags went to see them every evening. This came to an end in 1939 when the entire family, including all their in-laws, made their escape to the USA. Barend and Lucia obviously had a capacity for solid and loyal friendship.

Barend had preceded Lucia to Italy and she left Holland when Elena was seven months old. This wasn't a journey that Lucia relished with four young children, to a country with which she wasn't familiar. Neither was Lucia able to speak Italian. Her ordeal was made a little easier because Elena's first nanny accompanied them to Italy. However, the nanny returned to Holland a short while later and Lucia was obliged to find an Italian nanny to replace her.

This seemingly simple task proved a bit more complicated than Lucia had anticipated. Firstly, there was the language barrier. Then there was the cultural barrier. Lucia had very particular ideas about how babies should be handled and some of these were very strange to the Italians she interviewed who also held very firm opinions. One issue was that of potty-training, but more of that later. Eventually she found someone who seemed able to follow her rudimentary Italian and hand signals.

Elena blossomed in the care of this Italian nanny. She was a bubbly, happy, alert baby who slept well and glowed with good health. There was a problem, though. Lucia complained that Elena was an exceedingly unpleasant-smelling infant and she couldn't work out why. The doctors Lucia consulted couldn't detect any problem. The puzzle was eventually solved when she discovered that Elena was having her diet supplemented with a traditional Italian peasant baby food – bread soaked in olive oil and garlic! Unfortunately for Elena, Toly and Orso must have been privy to the discussions on their little sister's 'problem' and must have ragged her about it because her comment on Agnese as an infant and a little girl, was that she always smelt so good. Would a child remember such a thing without good reason?

Elena remembers the family always having a maid, a cook and a chauffeur, all of whom were Italian. Their nannies seemed to have changed fairly regularly and were from various countries. She remembers a very nice Polish nanny, a French nanny about whom she can't remember much, and an awful German Fräulein. All the children came to loathe her because she was such a martinet. The nursery was run with military precision and discipline. Spillage at the table was the result of poor discipline; a food stain on a bodice or shirt was a sign of weak character; a scraped knee was carelessness and a personal affront to her care; outings caused such tirades and stress for everybody that they were hardly worth the trouble. Lucia was not one to give up easily but she could make no headway with the woman. The Fräulein didn't last very long but she did leave a lasting impression on the children: a deep distrust of Germans. The positive contribution all these nannies did make to their charges' development, was the children's grasp of European languages.

Lucia's attitude to her servants was markedly different to the attitude of most Italian employers of domestic help. Although there was little social fraternizing, and no concept of the sort of equality that would have master and servant breaking bread together, they were always treated with respect and dignity. The tradition in most Italian homes was for the family to be served first and then the servants to have the leftovers. Lucia, however, insisted that the cook dish up for the servants first, and only when they had had their meal, was the family served. This was regarded as very odd by the Van Praags' Italian contemporaries.

The staff had to wear the traditional uniforms of cook, maid, chauffeur and butler and Lucia was a stickler for neatness. Some of the maids were very young and had little idea of grooming and decorum. Lucia soon sorted this out.

One young woman, Gina Morcio, who was employed as a maid, was an orphan and when she was to be married she had no family support. Apart from always being concerned about the welfare of her domestic workers, perhaps Lucia's experience of her own wedding day, devoid of family blessings and good cheer, motivated her to arrange the girl's wedding and a small reception.

It must also be admitted that Gina was a great favourite with the whole family and especially the children. She was a very cheerful and optimistic girl and she possessed a remarkable talent which gave her immense prestige with the children: before coming to the Van Praags she had worked in a circus as a contortionist! The children's favourite trick was to see her fold herself over so that her feet rested on the floor above her shoulders. Being babysat by Gina was better than any outing. Often at their bedtime she would put on a show for them. They spent many hours trying to emulate her. Perhaps it was her influence that inspired Elena's love of gymnastics later on.

The children enjoyed the excitement of planning the wedding and the thrill of being in on the choice of a wedding dress. The frock had to be suitably pretty and romantic but a traditional gown would have been daft. It was a rare treat to have a brand-new dress so it made sense to choose something which she would be able to use again and again. Lucia took the lass to her own dressmaker and even the fittings contributed to an all-round growing sense of occasion. The cook took care of the catering and the whole staff helped with preparing the dining-room with flowers and Lucia's best china and napery.

On the wedding day she was seen off from the Van Praag apartment by over-excited children who danced her across the terrace and then, with faces pressed to the railings and arms reaching through the bars, they waved her off in the family car, accompanied by Barend and Lucia.

After the Catholic service, the family, all the servants, the groom's relatives and the couple's friends, gathered in the apartment where Barend toasted the pair and wished them on their happy way.

When Lucia heard that Gina and her husband were expecting their first baby, she bought Gina a beautiful wicker pram and had it delivered to her home. Gina told Lucia that she had been looking out of a window when she saw a man pushing the pram along the pavement beneath her apartment block. She had been filled with envy and longing that she could have such a magnificent vehicle for her babe. When her bell was rung and she went to answer the summons, she couldn't believe that the pram was being delivered to her. Elena remembers her seated in their sitting-room with her very round tummy and fizzing with excitement and gratitude.

The Van Praags' first home in Genoa was in a block of four floors built in the 1800's, each floor being a separate apartment. Their apartment was large by any standards and included six bedrooms, two bathrooms and an impressively grand terrace. Barend brought his by-now-widowed sister and her son to Genoa and they lived in the apartment above the family. His sister was able to supplement her income by having two English lady boarders.

Barend's sister, also named Elena but known to the children as Tante Sus, had been engaged to a general in the Italian army in Abruzzese. This was Generale di Corpo d'Armata Paolo Berardi who went on to have a very distinguished and challenging career during the war. He had a brother and when she informed him in a row one day that his brother was far nicer than he was, he said, "Well in that case, why don't you marry him?" which she did.

This wasn't such a bright idea either, as he had an addiction to morphine and after leading her a merry dance, he died of an overdose. Thereafter she had very little that was good to say about Italian men and the girls grew up with constant warnings about the dangers of having any dealings with them. Elena remembers her as having been very pretty, very plump, and prone to histrionics and hysteria.

Her son, Rafaele Berardi, was about ten years older than Elena and Elena doted on him. He spent hours teaching her to dance when she was a little girl. He was also a great inventor of games for his cousins. She has a delightful photograph of herself at about seven, in which he had dressed her up and posed her, sitting with legs crossed, on top of a pillar. She is wearing a nattily-tilted beret and has a cigarette in her mouth - and looks like a very accomplished little tart-in-the-making.

The Van Praags occupied the ground floor. This meant that the children had the freedom of a garden, could have a dog and could even keep chickens. They always had at least one cat and Elena, in her old age, is still passionate about cats. Joy, Elena's Port Edward neighbour Margaret's cat, used to visit every day and share an afternoon nap with Elena. Joy was not too fond of Margaret's grandchildren and when they came to stay she would move into Elena's house. After Joy's earthly departure, Elena wasn't going to have another cat until a cocky little bow-legged grey tom infiltrated the household. He supervises all comings and goings and makes his disapproval of Elena's smoking very clear.

Elena's first memory dates back to the apartment in Genoa when she was four years old. Her parents were out for the evening at the opera and her aunt and cousin were babysitting. Suddenly the world seemed to be shaking itself to bits: an earthquake had hit Genoa. Her aunt proceeded to have hysterics and her cousin, who must have been about fourteen, had to take charge. He decided that the safest thing to do was to get out of the building. This was easier said than done because the terrace was enclosed by a high railing fence and the gate was locked. He had to get three frightened children and his wildly flailing, sobbing and hefty mother over the fence.

He managed all this successfully and there they were, standing in the street, when Barend and Lucia returned. They had been held up at the theatre. As soon as the shock had hit the theatre Barend had realised what was happening and told Lucia to stay seated. She was seven months pregnant with Agnese and he was aware that the audience was likely to make a mad dash for the exit where they would probably bottleneck anyway. They had remained calmly in their seats and then left with dignity and limbs intact. Barend's reaction to this event would become his hallmark in protecting his family: stand back, assess and then take decisive action.

Agnese was born at home two months later, with very little fuss. When Lucia went into labour the children were packed off to bed in the same way as they were every other night and when they woke up next morning, there was Agnese.

The children's first school was a little private Swiss school where they were taught in French. The school was in the same street and Lucia could watch her tumble of children race from their door right to the school gate. The building was set in a garden with a fountain which delighted and intrigued them. A favourite activity before school was for the girls to dip their fingers into the water and then let the water drip from their fingertips, making 'water nails' as Agnese called them.

Elena and Agnese both recall their first teacher, Signora Bolla. She was elderly and had never adapted her dress style from her Victorian youth. Her skirts were always long and her blouses pleated and ruffled at the neck. Her formal manner was forbidding and she struck mortal terror into the hearts of her young charges. However, this didn't curb their liveliness and both remember having to stand behind the red velvet curtain which covered the glass doors and which served as the 'naughty corner'.

Madame Peruset was the French teacher as well as their botany teacher. She was inspiringly elegant and very kind. She delighted in showing them all sorts of plant-related intrigues such as how to skeletonise leaves by placing them between sheets of blotting paper and then beating the pages gently with the bristles of a paintbrush to get rid of the green flesh. Elena has a beautiful gilded skeleton leaf which her great friend Eleanor brought back from Aspin in the U.S. for her as a souvenir and which she treasures as a memory of Madame Peruset.

It was to Madame Peruset that all the children went whenever they had a loose baby tooth. As long as they presented her with a clean handkerchief, she was happy to give the tooth its final tug and they were very happy to have her do it. She didn't hurry the job as she believed that the tooth had to be pulled vertically so that the next tooth would grow straight. As a reward for their bravery she would present them with a little potted plant, along with the tooth wrapped in the handkerchief. She was a spinster, despite being called

'Madame' by her pupils, and not very well off. Lucia often had her to dinner and the whole family seemed to have had a soft spot for her.

Their maths teacher, and the only male teacher, they found frighteningly gruff. Elena claims she was so frightened of him she wet her pants on one occasion. There was a dispenser of distilled water in the gym to which the children were forbidden from helping themselves. Never daunted by rules, Elena was having an illicit drink one day when he silently crept up behind her and shouted in her ear.

He could swear volubly and his favourite expletive was "Sacra li poppet!" The poor man was also seriously disadvantaged in dealing with a bunch of Italian children: he had a hunch-back. In Italy a hunch-backed woman is a sign of good luck, confirmed by touching one's nose. On the other hand, a hunched man is regarded as bad luck, which is warded off by using the sign of a curse – the index and small finger pointed at the ground.

Once the junior primary phase was over, they had to go to a recognised Italian school where they were compelled to study Italian plus another language. This second language was French, until Mussolini chummied up with Hitler and their second language became German. Amongst other subjects, they had to study Fascist history and do Catholic Religious Studies.

They also had to pass 'Behaviour' in order to be promoted. This was Elena's nemesis. Astoundingly, she failed an entire academic year three times because she couldn't retain the necessary credits for conduct. One year she managed not to blot her copybook until the very last day of the school year when, 45 minutes before the end of the day, her exuberance got the better of her. This kind of discipline code beggars belief in the 21st Century.

Barend never smacked his children, much to Lucia's disapproval, but this must have been one of the occasions on which he used the only comment that could really upset Elena: "You are the first nail in my coffin!" He seems to have reserved this comment for Elena alone.

The twenties were prosperous years for the Van Praags. Barend, with a partner by the name of Venturini, owned four ships. Elena can recall the names of three: the Afrodite, the Antiope and the Atlantide, the last-mentioned also being the name of his shipping company. Barend also invested in a number of properties.

Their second home in Genoa, at 4 Passo dell' Acquedolto, was a penthouse high on a hill overlooking the harbour. The apartment was circled by a glorious patio with a pergola and flower-filled planters. Barend owned most of the building and installed Tante Sus and her son in the apartment below. This building was older than their first home in Genoa, having been built in the fifteenth century. It had a wide marble staircase and an enormous bath carved out of marble and situated, very oddly, in a kind of cupboard jutting into the passage. The bath was far too big to fill to any satisfactory depth and didn't retain any heat. It was so big and heavy that it had to be broken up to be removed and the 'cupboard' was converted into a bedroom.

As the household continued to include at least three staff members, there was little that was required of the children in the way of chores. Consequently, the girls grew up with no idea of how to cook and clean but a fair idea of how to organize a home – experiences which would handicap and advantage Elena in the life that lay ahead of her.

This comfortable and idyllic lifestyle was, however, dealt a shattering blow by the coming of the Great Depression. There was no escaping the economic ramifications for Barend's business and no way that his family could remain unaffected, regardless of how hard he tried to shelter them. He did his level best, though, to protect everyone who depended on him.

No matter how dire things became, Barend kept on his domestic and business staff. He went to great lengths to keep his ships going and to retain his crews. Harbour taxes had to be paid and each ship was crewed by thirty-two men who had to be remunerated. Barend promised his crews, come what may, that they would continue to be employed. The men decided amongst themselves, in order to prevent having to retrench anyone, that they would take pay cuts. The married men went on to half-pay and the single men took a quarter of their normal wage packets. Barend guaranteed payment even when the ships had no cargo. There were long periods when all four ships were in harbour and no loads were available.

As much as Barend was struggling to keep things going in the business, Lucia was battling to keep things going at home. No money was coming in and their savings were being eroded by having to pay wages. Firing the domestic staff would have reduced wages and Lucia had the added responsibility of finding food for her family and her employees. She could have complained and resisted Barend's decision but she never did. She stood solidly by Barend in his mission and did whatever she could to support his stand.

1932 to 1935 was the bleakest stretch and within this period there were many times when they reached desperation point. Commodities like butter and jam became absolute luxuries.

It was during this time that Lucia began to hone her skills at making do and scouting for bargains. If she heard that jam was available cheaply at some point in the city she would set off in search of it no matter how far she had to walk or for how long she had to queue.

At one point it became evident to their acquaintances that their clothing had reached the end of the line and, good seamstress that she was, even the redoubtable Lucia couldn't hide the fact. Someone brought them a donation of clothing for which Lucia had to be grateful but was, nevertheless, mortified that they had reached the point of having to accept charity. Her private comment was, "We're not poor! We're in a depression."

A family rule was that they were never allowed to dunk their biscuits in their coffee. However, there was one occasion when Barend broke this rule. They were all seated at their dining-room table, which had been set, as always, with a white cloth, a full complement of cutlery and crockery, including the finger-bowls, but there was nothing to consume but black coffee and stale bread. Barend looked at his slice of bread and then at his cup of coffee, and announced, "Soppen, soppen, in de caffelatte!" followed by them all dunking their bread in the milkless coffee. There was laughter but Elena happened to look at her parents during this exchange and noticed the tears in both their eyes.

Barend often came close to losing courage but the feisty little Lucia continued to support and encourage him. There were times when she feared for his mental health and worried that he might attempt suicide. She took to accompanying him to his office every day and meeting him again after work. She never let on to him what her motive was and he never forgot how she had stood by him.

The time came, eventually, in about 1936, when Barend came home one day and announced that they were back! He had full cargoes for all his ships and they were ready to sail.

Barend extracted a great deal of fun from the company of his children. Elena informed him one day that he really wasn't a proper father. When he asked why, she told him that proper fathers were supposed to shout at their children and beat them regularly, neither of which he ever did.

He was also responsible for teaching them the art of the practical joke. Lucia had baked a cake and put it on the sideboard in the dining-room. Barend summoned his offspring and together they polished off the cake, cleaned the plate and put it away. And then all of them sat back and enjoyed Lucia's confusion as she looked about, returned to the kitchen, came back, shook her head, and repeated the whole exercise. Eventually she caught Barend's eye and the game was up.

His practical jokes did come back to haunt him on occasion. It was he who taught Elena to smoke when she was about fifteen. Every now and then she would cuddle up to him and tell him how wonderful he was as she picked through his pockets for cigarettes. She would then leave the room and return with a lit cigarette. When he demanded to know where she'd got it, nothing delighted her more than telling him that he was her source.

Lucia was the disciplinarian and could be very icy and strict. However, Barend and she did seem to support each other and they had mastered a technique which came in very useful in controlling their children. Whenever they wanted to discuss anything without their offspring knowing what they were saying, they would draw on their telegraphy skills and tap out messages in Morse code to each other with their dining forks.

Barend was passionate about sport, especially soccer and fencing. When Elena was about ten he decided that they should all learn to fence. This included Agnese who was only six. He kitted them all out and even had a small foil made for Agnese. Of course she couldn't duel with it but she could learn and practise all the moves with it.

Their fencing coach was an elderly man who still hired himself out to fight affairs of honour. He was, however, too old to do the actual dueling and used to make his much younger assistant-coach fight in his stead, a bizarre and idiosyncratically Italian arrangement on every level. Years later, after the war, Elena was to meet up with the younger coach again at a time when he was trying to re-establish himself and needed a venue to conduct his classes. She was able to provide him with such a venue in the building where she was employed.

Also when Elena was ten, Barend sent Lucia and the children on a three-month working cruise on one of his ships. A cargo ship couldn't carry passengers without having to pay much heavier docking fees so they were all signed on as deck-hands. This was no honorary title and they all really did have to scrub decks, polish the brass fittings and do whatever was required.

Barend was obsessive about the maintenance of his ships and whenever they returned to Genoa he would carry out a full inspection. He carried with him a tiny bronze hammer which he tapped along the length of the brass propeller shafts to check for any developing defects. The shafts were always covered with heavy coir matting so that they underwent constant polishing as they turned.

As a businessman, he also made sure that he extracted the maximum profit out of every consignment. He did his best to ensure that he remained on the friendliest terms with the port authorities and had no scruples about plying these authorities with as much alcohol as they could consume when he needed them to sign papers permitting his ships to sail when the cargo exceeded the Plimsoll mark or load water line. Being Italians with whom he was dealing, it wasn't difficult to fudge the regulations. He was never going to jeopardize the safety of his ships but neither was he going to risk his profit margin: a couple of tons over the limit represented pure profit.

There were few luxuries aboard and all bath water was salt water with only a little fresh water being carried for drinking. What was a memorable treat was the freshly-baked bread which the cook provided at every meal. The sailors also rigged up a swing on deck for the children, which they loved and on which they spent many hours. Near Gibraltar they encountered very rough seas but this didn't deter the children at all and their swinging continued unabated through the turbulence.

They carried alternating cargoes of wheat and coal and Elena remembers the horror she felt at seeing what came out of the holds when they were being cleaned after a load of wheat. The abundance of dead rodents was repellent but what was even worse was watching the men in the holds. Their task was to smooth and guide the wheat towards the suction pipes and when they encountered a nest of rodent babies, they would scoop them up on their spades and hold this offering up to the mouth of the pipe to be sucked away.

Of course, the ship had its resident cats and Elena has a particularly painful memory relating to one of these cats. She was alone with Captain Balla one day and he asked if she wanted to see a cat eat coal. Unsuspectingly, she said yes. He grabbed a cat and twisted its tail so viciously that in its pain and desperation, it began scrabbling, open-mouthed, at the chunks of coal on the deck and actually crunching the coal. He thought this highly entertaining but she was so appalled she couldn't even bring herself to tell anybody about it.

They had sailed from Genoa, called in at Algiers and then headed for London. In the mouth of the Thames they were struck by an almighty storm. Lucia and the children were all on deck and nobody thought, or had the time, to send them below decks. Consequently, they were able to witness all the proceedings. The pilot was already on board and ordered the captain to get as close to the bank as possible and cast anchor. The children were clustered around Lucia as they sheltered from the worst of the spray, battling to keep their balance on the heaving deck and trying to stay out of the way of the running deckhands. With some relief they heard the clattering of the anchor chain but this respite was short-lived. The anchor pulled out so fast that the friction started a small fire and then a giant hand seemed to wrench the whole ship as the anchor was torn out of its housing and was lost. Fortunately the second anchor held. It was pitch-dark and a very frightening experience.

From England they sailed to Holland and then made their way home. They never managed another cruise together as a family but Toly took a trip after she had matriculated in 1937. Her trip included the Dardanelles and the Black Sea. She was utterly astounded that the chandlers at every port in Romania worked stark naked. This habit included the officers. When Lucia wanted to know how she knew that they were officers, she said she could tell because they were wearing their caps! When a chandler escorted her on a swim, and she was changing into her costume, she was suddenly alarmed at the thought that he might not be wearing a bathing-suit. To her great relief he had donned a pair of swimming-trunks.

In typically Toly fashion, she put her time aboard to good use and learnt all the intricacies of navigation, a skill which would have unforeseen consequences for her life.

Barend's shipping interests seem to have flourished during the twenties and then again in the latter years of the nineteen-thirties. Family pictures show jaunts into the Dolomites and seaside escapades. One picture taken in the Dolomites shows the children scaling a vertical mountain rock-face. The picture is taken from below and presents an alarming scene for the safety conscious! Lucia nearly had a fit when she saw the photo'. Typically, the picture had been stage-managed: it was a very ordinary rock at ground level and no mountain at all.

CHAPTER 4

After Mussolini came to power in 1928, there was no escaping his dictates and the growing influence and iron grip of Fascism. He had come to power on a groundswell of popularity with all facets of society. The industrialists and business sector were bouyed by his promises to revitalize the economy, the peasants saw him as a socialist saviour and the Catholics saw him as a saviour of the faith against the atheistic communist threat.

Access to all educational, employment, sporting and cultural opportunities was channelled through the Fascist movement. Consequently, there was little practical choice but to go along with government dictates and the children entered state schools after leaving their little Swiss school.

An insight of how impossible it was to avoid the control of the Fascists and still lead a normal life, lies in the story of a young man who knocked on their door one day. Lucia happened to answer the door and when she asked what she could do for him, he asked for a piece of bread as he was desperately hungry. On being questioned, he told Lucia that he was unemployed and it was very difficult for him to get a job because he didn't have a Fascist Party membership card as his principles wouldn't allow him to join the party. Lucia invited him in for lunch and then told him to come back every day to share their midday meal until his fortunes changed. This he did for almost two years and then arrived one day with the glad tidings that he had finally found a job.

In addition to these strictures, it was compulsory for all state school pupils to join the Fascist Youth Movement. Barend told his children that if they were going to have to take part, then they had better get themselves into positions of authority because it was unacceptable to allow themselves to be bossed about by the 'Eyetes'. This was Barend's derogatory term for Italians who were committed to Fascism. Consequently, they all took the exams which qualified them as sergeants in the school cadet system, in which, of course, participation was also compulsory. Elena was appointed as the head of a squadron because of her extremely powerful (and unmusical) voice which gave her great command. On one occasion when they had to take part in a parade for Mussolini they had to sing 'Va pensiero sulle aliduarte' (*'Go my Thought on the Golden Wings'*) as members of a 5000-strong choir. Because of the falseness of her voice Elena wasn't even allowed to sing in this throng and was ordered to mouth the words!

Elena's burning desires in life were to be a great singer, painter and ice-skater but her singing was certainly not to be. She knows the words to many operas and didn't relinquish her dream without a fight. Lucia eventually sent her to an opera singer for lessons but after the second lesson the singer asked her mother to take her away and not bring her back as she was so bad she was making the teacher sing off-key. George told her never to sing before twelve o'clock because no human being could be expected to tolerate such torture early in the day. When she sang her opera in the bathtub, Suzy, the Great Dane, used to howl.

Her desperation to be an ice-skater had to be satisfied by learning to roller-skate. Barend was most concerned that she shouldn't injure herself. No-one can be forbidden to get hurt and perhaps his strange insistence arose from knowing how impulsive and devil-may-care his daughter was. It didn't take long for her to start bragging about her prowess on her skates. To demonstrate her 'expertise' she had Barend sit at the head of the dining-room table, which was a long one. From his seat he couldn't see the floor between the end of the table and the door. She had Orso sit on the floor, out of sight beneath the table, and she glided through the door performing all her newly-learnt balletic moves and looking very impressive. Barend was suitably awed. What he didn't know was that she wasn't wearing her skates – Orso had them under the table where he was running them across the floorboards to create appropriate sound effects.

In compensation for her lack of singing skills, Elena was very athletic and agile and excelled at gymnastics, an activity held dear by the Fascists. Gym at school was very important and balancing on bars and leaping over the horse presented her with no difficulties. Not so for the less agile and timid, who were severely castigated by the teachers. One particularly fat and clumsy girl evoked great pity in Elena because she was so abused by the teachers.

When Elena was sixteen, a gymnastics extravaganza was organised in Rome at the enormous athletics stadium built by Mussolini as one of the structures which celebrated his Fascist renaissance of Italy. Part of this statement of power consisted of sixty enormous male statues, carved out of marble, each representing a particular sport. Probably inspired by the wonderful ancient Greek statues of athletes, these statues were far bigger and bolder but had a coarse, angular brutality about them which, to Elena, lacked much aesthetic appeal. Many of the statues were resplendent with male genitalia and this was the cause of great controversy which amused the Van Praags greatly. In Elena's case, such prudery was pointless anyway. As a child she had developed a great love of sculpture and was fascinated by the statues she encountered. She was captivated by the detail but failed to make a connection between the male genitalia on the statues and the real thing. It would be years before her appreciation was fully awakened.

Each of the larger Italian centres sent a team of twelve girls to participate in the display which involved a number of activities. One was a co-ordinated dance movement, or exercise, to music for which the girls wore black skirts, all with hems which measured exactly ten centimetres above the ground, white shirts and black ties. Any form of jewellery was forbidden. Elena's group used fencing foils for their sequence and her team was placed third. She also performed on the balancing beam (something at which she excelled) and took part in the archery competition. Toly had also been included in the group to play basketball. The festivities culminated in a mass gymnastic dance in which every participant at the games took part. Lucia accompanied her girls at her own expense and Elena and Toly thoroughly enjoyed their week in a hotel in Rome at the Facists' expense.

Topping all these activities was Elena's passion for horses and riding. The equestrian unit (Opera Balilla) was one of the military branches of the Youth Movement and it only had male members. An appeal went out for girls to join the unit and Elena was one of the three girls who were selected – all blonde!

The uniform of brown breeches, navy blue woollen top with a diagonal zippered front opening and collar, and asymmetrically placed white lettering 'O' and 'B' for 'Opera Balilla', brown beret and boots, was stylish and becoming.

The girls were told that they would receive exactly the same training as the boys and could not expect any special treatment. Their coach was strict and demanding but a very likeable and kind man.

Training took place almost every day of the week. It was arduous and unrelenting from the very first lesson. However, Elena was hooked from the moment she was tossed into the saddle. Her view from the saddle of the drifting mane, sinuous, muscular neck and jauntily-pricked ears of her mount, created a sight which never failed to stir her.

There was no gentle introduction to the pleasures of Sunday outrides, with time given to the initiate to recover from sore muscles before the next lesson. Her natural sense of balance no doubt helped, but the first few weeks were a blur of intensely sore thigh muscles, so stiff that walking became a painful, hobbling affair and her skin was at times rubbed raw. At some point in every lesson the stirrups had to be surrendered. To start with, every time the stirrups were taken away, Elena felt as though she had had a lifeline ripped from her.

But there was also the immense satisfaction of achieving a succession of goals in her mastery of the tasks set, her own strengthening body, and her horse. All this fed her competitive spirit and stimulated a joyous ambition which school had never done for her.

The horses and instructors were based at Marassi, a sports centre and racecourse in Genoa where all sorts of sports took place. There was an indoor training arena with sawdust-covered floor, and an outdoor sand racetrack, around the soccer fields. The track was used for flat-racing, jumping over the usual variety of jumps, steeple-chasing, and half-section jumping.

It wasn't long before Elena decided that she wanted to take this sport even more seriously and started having private lessons, in addition to the coaching provided by the government. Her private trainer was called Graziani, one of the older students. He was not nearly as tolerant as their Fascist coach. One of his methods was to supervise jumping sessions with a hunting whip in his hand and when Elena didn't meet his standards she was subjected to a sharp lash between the shoulder-blades.

When she declared her desire to ride privately, Barend took his usual generous and particular approach and made sure that Elena was properly and elegantly kitted. He escorted her to his own tailor where she was measured for breeches and jacket and shod in an exquisite pair of leather boots. Barend's tailor was gay and made her take her own crotch measurement. (The same tailor had no such qualms when George visited him some years later: George was alarmed and indignant when the tailor commented on his fine, manly chest.) Of course, no thought was given to protective head gear – nobody seems to have bothered with that then.

Competition, naturally, was an inevitable part of this training – a means of proving that Italian Fascists were bolder and better for their allegiance to Il Duce and the Motherland. Such thoughts never entered Elena's head. For her it was the fun and exhilaration of competing, no doubt aided by Barend's belief in his children that they could succeed at whatever they wanted – and a good chunk of his indoctrination that they were better than any 'Eyete'.

Both jumping and flat-racing excited Elena enormously. Her first jumping competitions filled her with nervous energy and a tingling in all her extremities. Her forearms and hands, particularly, felt to her to have an explosive lightness of their own. Forced to focus and breathe to calm these sensations, as soon as the bell sounded, she moved into another zone where nothing mattered but the obstacle and her body welded to her mount, a symbiosis beyond anything she'd ever experienced.

And then there was the glowing satisfaction of an efficiently executed round in which no poles fell and she'd clipped the time to the bare minimum by taking every chance she could without jeopardizing her performance. A lot of Barend showed in his daughter at these moments – taking just enough chance to succeed through calculation and not bring about her own ruin through foolhardiness. Even the moments after the event, as she exited the arena at a trot, filled her with pleasure and gentle gratitude towards the horse which had joined her so willingly in the venture: the patting hand on the sweating neck and the quiet words of praise acknowledged in the flicking ears, even in the midst of excitement and noisy applause – moments Elena has never forgotten.

Flat-racing held its own excitement, different to jumping, but just as compelling. To line up, knee-to-knee and neck-to-neck, jostling for the smallest advantage, waiting for the second the bell clanged to press in her heels and throw herself and her horse forward, satisfied every childhood restraint ever placed on her impetuous nature. Thundering round the track with so many other horses and riders wasn't so much about individual competition and winning, as about being part of a much bigger, glorious creation of power and single-minded focus.

She certainly wasn't above the immense satisfaction of winning either, and the Italian spectators loved nothing so much as a winner – especially when that winner was a very pretty girl with strawberry-blonde hair, and usually the only girl in the competition.

In one memorable jumping incident, Elena lost her seat but managed to stay on. She discovered, however, that she had split her breeches spectacularly.

In addition to jumping and flat-racing, the students also had to do dressage and half-section jumping, in keeping with the military nature of their training.

Half-section jumping entails being partnered with another rider and horse to complete a jumping course together. It is imperative that both horses stay together over the course and neither horse-and-rider unit lag behind. Therein lies the challenge. Elena was usually paired with Giancarlo Coldarini and the two formed a formidable partnership – and a great friendship.

Giancarlo was a very good-looking, tall, athletic Italian with an admirable pedigree. He came from a wealthy family who owned a beautiful villa and estate to the north of Genoa which they used as a summer holiday residence – La Villa Novi Ligure. The villa boasted its own chapel and full-sized billiard room. The dining-room table could seat thirty-six people and there was a magnificent thirty-six place-setting dinner service to go with it. The road that swept up to the pillared portico was wide and covered in gravel chips, which were always kept pristinely raked. The walls of the villa were pink stucco.

The Villa is now a hotel known as 'Relais Villa Pomela – Novi Ligure'. It is still pink and the gravel driveway, which so impressed Elena, is still there. According to the review of the hotel on the Trip-Europe Hotel and Travel Corporation website, the establishment is "*one of the most magnificent villas in Northern Italy. With the classic 17[h] Century architecture, reach* (sic) *of windows and terraces, the sharpen* (sic) *roof lopping* (sic) *to the sky, Relais Villa Pomela is set on the top of a hill, amidst the private gardens, dominating the Novi Valley. Elegance and charm characterize the interiors. ...*" The hotel provides forty-seven bedrooms.

Elena and Giancarlo were keen on each other and Giancarlo's parents loved her. She had a very relaxed and happy relationship with them. They spoilt her dreadfully: his father even kept her supplied with gold-foil-tipped cigarettes. His mother was a plump little lady who was always impeccably dressed. Despite her smartness she had an easy-going, jovial manner. To Giancarlo she would say "Janca!" and waggle her finger at him to indicate that his flies were open.

For all her sporting ability, Elena couldn't ride a bicycle. Giancarlo undertook to teach her, which he seems to have enjoyed greatly. To her squeals he would shout: "Mama mia!" – "I've got you!" His teaching methods must have been novel as he was sitting on the bicycle with her. When he peddled too fast downhill and she screamed, his threatened punishment was a kiss. As speed held no fear for her, there is little doubt as to her motivation for yelling.

Giancarlo was conscripted into the Fascist army while he was still at university. Tragically, this only son was killed in Yugoslavia in 1942 or '43 in a senseless accident. He was travelling on a troop truck when it was passed by an oncoming timber lorry. A branch, which was jutting out from the lorry, struck him on the head and he died instantaneously. He was buried in an unmarked grave on the side of the road.

Elena discovered all this later when she was at a dance with George and bumped into Giancarlo's sister, Puppa. Elena also met his mother again later in Genoa. Giancarlo's family and Elena's family had taken the romance seriously and it is not inconceivable that marriage would have been considered. In any event, a marriage would have been doomed as Elena was unable to have children and this would have meant divorce or annulment as childbearing was a given, especially in a family such as Giancarlo's.

The arrival of any new rider provided Elena and her team-mates with much amusement. On one of the side walls of the indoor arena was a disused, but live, electrical plug socket. The newcomer would be challenged to a gallop around the arena in which he had to attempt to stick his finger into the socket. Of course, all the regulars made sure they missed the socket, and the newcomer, desperate to impress, would often manage to get a finger into the socket, with shocking consequences!

There always seems to have been someone on hand to chaperone her and her competitions were well supported by the whole family. Her favourite horse, the one she managed to ride most often and which features in most of her photographs, was Racci, a big dark bay gelding. He always seemed to know when he had jumped well and would turn his head in anticipation of the sugar lumps Elena kept in her pocket. He did have the unfortunate habit of farting loudly every time he landed after a big jump, which never ceased to embarrass Elena. He was also no armchair ride and quickly taught Elena not to take his co-operation for granted. She was jumping him one day when, out of the blue, he suddenly stopped in front of a jump and Elena went sailing over his head. She looked up to see him peering over the obstacle at her as if to say, "You're getting too cocky, Miss. Don't make too many presumptions about me!"

The event that crowned her riding career was a showjumping competition at Marassi on the 5ᵗʰ of April 1938. The trophy was sponsored by the Institute of Andrea Dori. There were 25 competitors and Elena was the only woman. She completed the course with no penalties in 1 minute 33.5 seconds. Giancarlo came fourth, also with no penalties but a slower time. The newspaper photograph shows a triumphant Elena surrounded by other competitors and being interviewed by the press. Not only did she win the trophy but she was also presented with a lovely bouquet of white tulips for being the only female competitor. Giancarlo is in the background with his back to the camera. The other competitors seem to be joshing him and he certainly looks as though his patrician nose is out of joint.

Not all the boys took defeat at the hands of a girl quite so graciously. During one event Elena had to retire because her stirrup-leather broke. When she got back to the stable, her coach took a look at the leather and discovered that someone had cut through it.

*   *   *

Elena and school continued to be incompatible but Toly, who was extremely conscientious and competitive and regularly won academic prizes, continued to excel. Her competiveness applied to all subjects. For Catholic Religious Studies she won a replica of a nail from the Cross. This nail had been blessed by the Pope and she always carried it for luck, although she had not yet adopted the Catholic faith. Her Catholic education must have had a profound influence on her because before she wrote her final school exams, she went on a month-long retreat in a convent. In her latter years she donated the nail to a Catholic church in Cape Town where it was received with rapture.

The children were told that they could ask for anything they wanted if they did well in their final school exams, which, of course, Toly did. Her request was a refurbishing of her bedroom. This was done in shades of grey and touches of pink. It was most luxurious and elegant and became a haven in which Toly increasingly secluded herself as she pursued her university studies, ultimately qualifying as a chartered accountant.

Mussolini had introduced a system of funding university education in which families had to pay for the first year of their children's university education. If they passed the first year, the rest of their education was free. Toly's great competition at school was a boy. When Barend asked him what he would be studying he said that he wouldn't be able to go to university as his family couldn't afford the fees. Barend couldn't bear this waste and paid for his first year of tuition.

Orso also made it to university, for which he was given a car. He was never as dedicated as Toly and he frustrated her enormously. Whether he liked it or not, Toly tutored him and supervised his progress and he, too, qualified as a chartered accountant.

Elena continued to do battle with the system. Exams were a torture and she would chew her nails so badly in the exam room that she often bloodied two handkerchiefs. Her nails were often gnawed down to the bed. In desperation Lucia took her to a manicurist who asked what on earth they expected her to do as there were practically no nails for her to work on. They hit on the idea of painting what little there was, so that she could chew off the paint. This solved the problem and even now Elena's nails are always well-manicured and enamelled.

In maths she was quite capable of working out the answers but writing down the process of arriving at the answer floored her. Remembering a formula was also beyond her. To overcome this obstacle she took to cheating by writing the formulae on scraps of paper which she placed under her stockings, beneath her skirt. She would pull the hem of her skirt down over her knees as the invigilator approached, knowing that the man couldn't very well ask her to reveal her thighs.

The family showed little concern about Elena's lack of performance but she did surprise them on occasion: in a maths discussion between Toly and Barend, Elena chipped in with the answer, startling them both!

Six months before she was supposed to matriculate she went to Barend and told him that there was little point in her continuing as there was no chance of her passing. She wanted to attend the Artistic and Commercial College. Barend readily agreed.

Elena finally found her niche here after years of struggling to adapt to a system which suited neither her academic needs nor her personality. The college seems to have been remarkable in the scope and standard of the training it provided. If this was the calibre of practical education, it is no wonder that Italy, especially Northern Italy, has been able to provide the world with the quality of goods for which it is renowned.

The college also provided Elena with many skills she would need to survive and flourish during the war and after. She was particularly partial to the filigree silverwork they taught. Amongst the skills that were taught, the students learnt to make shoes, carpets in the Persian tradition, silk flowers and how to do filet crocheting. Many years later Elena won 'Best Work on Show' at the Royal Agricultural Show in Pietermaritzburg for a tablecloth of filet crochet work which took 630 hours to make, 50 balls of number 60 crochet thread and six crochet hooks. It measured 2.2 metres by 2 metres and featured a wide range of flowers indigenous to South Africa including the king, pincushion and wooly-bearded proteas, ericas, strelitzias, ground orchids and red hot pokers. Anyone who has ever stood admiring the prize-winning, hand-crafted articles at the Royal Show will appreciate the quality of the work and the enormity of Elena's achievement! Sadly, George never saw her Royal Show win.

Elena has a photograph of a special occasion at the college when the Bishop of Genoa visited the school and was served by the girls. The photograph shows the Bishop in the centre, seated at a table, with Elena standing behind him to the right. On the wall directly behind him is the Crucifix. To the left of the Crucifix is a portrait of Victor Emmanuel II and to its right is a portrait of Mussolini. To the Bishop's right sits a well-known Fascist and Lucia is seated at another table to the left of His Eminence. Such are the ironic confusions of a socially-engineered society.

It was around this time that Agnese was selected to be photographed at school as the perfect example of an Arian child. This was intended for some propagandist state publication. She was ordered to come to school on the said day in her Fascist uniform. She arrived looking spick and span for the occasion and her picture was duly taken.

Two weeks later it was discovered that she had Jewish blood. She was summoned by the headmistress, Direttrice Gisella, an extremely thin, austere woman who wore a tight bun. She informed Agnese that she was no longer welcome at the school and had to vacate the premises immediately: "You are an undesirable in this Fascist school!" The fourteen-year-old was confused and devastated. Even when she tells the story today the hurt of this rejection lingers. Her Latin teacher found her weeping and asked, "What happened, Van Praag?" The teacher comforted her as best she could by telling her that "all would be well". Agnese transferred to a Catholic school. To this day she receives a pension from the Italian government as reparation for this discrimination.

Mussolini's dictates infiltrated every aspect of their school lives and his political affiliations were imposed on them at every turn. During the Spanish Revolution he decided that it would be a nice gesture for school children to give some emotional support to Franco's soldiers and so every pupil had to send letters of encouragement to these soldiers and become their pen-pals. Toly's pen-pal, a lad with the surname Caldillo, paid the family a visit after things had settled a little in Spain. At the dinner table he told the family about the dreadfully hard time he had had during the Revolution. Oh, how he had suffered. There was never a moment when he was free of pain and discomfort. Sympathetic and intrigued, they asked him why he had suffered so greatly. His answer was, "My shoes were too tight!"

Through the thirties all children over a certain age had to take part in Mussolini's endless parades. They would have to stand on parade or march for hours, becoming very thirsty and tired. Elena's biggest concern was always the unavailability of a toilet. She remembers, still with fascination, standing next to a rather plump girl who had a pouch for sweets stitched inside her skirt waistband, into which she dipped regularly.

She also remembers how mesmerizing Mussolini's eyes were, seeming to look directly into her own even in such vast crowds. When she was older, she and the two other girls in the equestrian unit were required to ride in one of Mussolini's parades in Victory Square. In a photograph, Elena, on a grey, is flanked by the other two girls on bays. On this occasion she spent five hours in the saddle and ended up with very sore legs.

The Fascists always seemed to be arranging protests against someone or something and they had no compunctions about boosting the numbers in the protest by using school children. It was often compulsory for all schools to attend their demonstrations. The most common demonstrations were anti-Semitic. Anti-British demonstrations were also popular pastimes.

Barend and Giancarlo were both involved in a particular demonstration outside the British Embassy but from two completely different vantage points.

Barend happened to be in the Embassy at the time, in a meeting with the Ambassador. Hordes of Italian youngsters were gathered beneath the Ambassador's window and he was in something of a panic. Barend's unfailing sense of humour led him to collecting as many sweets as he could find. He opened the window and stood surveying the crowd until he had the attention of the children, and then broadcast the sweets into the horde. This destroyed the focus of the demonstration as the children scrabbled about trying to retrieve the sweets before they were trampled.

Giancarlo, a good Catholic lad, was attending the same demonstration, but with great reluctance, and decided to make his escape. Unfortunately for him, he was spotted by a teacher who ordered him to stay. When he told her that he was Jewish she chased him away yelling, "Go away, you dirty Jew!"

Later, Elena happened to be standing in Victory Square when she heard the public announcement that Mussolini had thrown in his lot with Hitler. Barend had made sure that his children were politically aware from an early age. He was in the habit of following all political developments and discussing them with his family. They knew what Fascism had done to Spain and what Nazism was doing to Germany. In fact, they were intimately involved in the catastrophic consequences of Nazism for many German Jews. Elena knew how this announcement would affect Italy and how families and friends would be torn asunder. She thought of her riding companions and what probably lay ahead for these young men. In the midst of the excitement and cheering, she wept.

Nothing was quite the same again and the changes were to come very rapidly from this point.

*   *   *

Despite the political upheavals, growing up could not be put on hold. Experiencing the changes of adolescence, and gaining the privileges and independence that went with increasing maturity, still took place.

When she turned eighteen, Elena decided that she needed a driver's licence. This was only one facet of her rite of passage but one which could be expected to take a little more planning than the buying of a fur coat.

Not for Elena, though. By the time the day of her test arrived she had never even sat behind the steering-wheel. The only preparations she made were to wear her French perfume and a skirt which was short enough to ride above her knees with ease.

For the test she was required to move the car forward a metre or two and then reverse it a ridiculously short distance. After that she would have to answer three compulsory questions. Whether the rest of the family decided to stay out of the way for their own safety or sheer potential embarrassment, we don't know, but it fell to the chauffeur to accompany her. He had to sit next to her to change the gear lever into reverse because she couldn't even manage that. The inspector was relegated to the back seat. She didn't manage to move forward or backwards without jerking and was only able to answer two of the three questions correctly. However, she passed the test – charm, good looks or Italian disregard for the finer points of the law – who knows?

The car Elena had at her service once she'd got her licence was a tiny, red, four-seater, open-roofed Fiat Toppolini (*mouse*). Despite its miniscule size, she regularly managed to squeeze six or seven young men from the riding-school into the back seat, piled on top of one another, while the chauffeur continued to occupy the front passenger seat. The so-called reason for this happy communion was so that the boys wouldn't have to climb all those Genoese street stairs.

After the war Elena visited their trainer in Genoa who, by then, owned a haberdashery shop. She had assumed that he was a Fascist but he had later joined the partisans. It was he who told her that virtually every one of those young men had been killed during the war. The two of them shed tears together.

The horses, too, were all gone. Those carefully selected, beautiful creatures, which had been so finely schooled, and which had been such an important part of the formative years of so many young people, were no longer. They had all gone to the knacker's yard to feed a starving population, Elena's precious Racci included.

Through her driving experiences in Genoa, she made the acquaintance of a number of policemen. Her driving skills being what they were, she didn't always manage to stop in time for red traffic-lights and pointsmen and this earned her several reprimands. Vociferous Italian policemen waving enraged fingers at her and shouting all manner of curses, insults and reprimands, didn't disturb her much. If she had time to remove a hand from the steering-wheel, they got a cheery wave as she careered past. Eventually they gave up trying to correct her and would simply wag a finger as she sailed merrily through the intersections. She and Lucia were on foot in the city one day when Elena was greeted warmly by a man Lucia didn't know. She asked Elena who he was – one of her policemen, of course.

Elena drove in Port Edward for years without bothering to get a South African licence. Only when she committed some outlandish misdemeanour outside the post office, and was asked to produce her licence, did she realize that she would have to conform. She told the traffic officer that she only had an Italian licence. He let her off the hook on the proviso that she obtain a South African licence. This was easier said than done and she failed the test six times. When, eventually, she passed, George's comment was that she'd only got it for good attendance.

She continued to drive without further brushes with the law until very recently, and renewed her last licence at the age of 87. As she walked into the office where the eye testing takes place, she was reading the form. The examiner told her to take out her contact lenses which, of course, she doesn't possess. Her eyesight is remarkable: when we read a document together, I have to fumble for my glasses and Elena doesn't even have to extend her arms to view the paper.

Her decision to give up driving and retire her little yellow Citi Golf, which was eighteen years old and had only done 28 000 kilometres, came when she pulled out in front of a local taxi at Strawberry Lane, not having seen the car because of the vegetation on the island which blocked her view. The Zulu driver followed her down the road and informed her that 'Miesies' was too old to be driving and in future he would collect her for her weekly shopping trip. He also wanted to charge her an exorbitant fee for the service. Instead, Rina van Schoor, the manageress from Spar, fetched her every Monday. This arrangement continued until George's niece, Lynette, and her husband, Pierre, moved to Port Edward to give her a hand. An old friend, mechanic Dick Hooper, bought her little car which was in immaculate condition.

Another rite of passage at eighteen was to be kitted out in ballgowns and the ubiquitous and unquestionable fur coat. The trip to the furrier was a momentous occasion and the selection of a coat was a weighty process. It was a serious, long-term investment in a young woman's wardrobe and her social standing. The choice was carefully supervised by Lucia with both Toly and Agnese having their say too. When it was brought home and Elena paraded it in front of Barend, he told her to take it off immediately and return it to the furrier as he hadn't given permission for the purchase. Elena fell for his story and was quite devastated. Of course, he was having her on. Times have changed, and with Elena's love of animals she would no more own a fur coat today than fly to the moon.

Her first real ballgown was a very pale lilac taffeta with a train. White was traditional for a first evening-gown but with her strawberry-blonde hair and pale complexion, white didn't do very much for her.

Several ballgowns were made for her by Lucia's dressmaker. Elena was flat-chested and much attention was given to designing dresses which would flatter her bosom and create the illusion of a good bust. In contrast, Toly was able to flaunt her generous assets in low-cut, revealing gowns.

Naturally the gown wasn't the only consideration in preparing for a ball. Every aspect of dress was given careful attention. Each dress had matching shoes and often the shoes were covered in the same fabric as the dress. The manicurist and the hairdresser were also visited, with time spent with the latter discussing the style and planning the inclusion of embellishments such as sprays of flowers.

At this stage in her life there was a great surge in formal social occasions and, in addition to the dances the family attended together, Elena had a number of formal balls to attend as a result of her riding activities. At these balls she was expected to mix with the hierarchy of the Italian cavalry units – some fearsome-looking men in their dark military uniforms and chests full of medals. This was a little unnerving for a father because Italian men never seemed to lose their faith in their own desirability, no matter what their age or rotundity. These events were carefully chaperoned, however, and the girls' own social standing and naïvety provided a measure of protection. Usually Lucia provided the chaperonage, especially for Elena's official functions. Orso was also extremely useful as a chaperone and this made it possible for the girls to get about far more than Lucia's time and energy would have allowed. It also meant that when they went out as a family, Barend and Lucia could enjoy their own socializing whilst their offspring mixed with their own, more youthful circle.

Elena only ever experienced one really unpleasant incident. She was only seventeen at the time and, despite her merry manner, was actually quite reserved. A Dutch naval ship had arrived in Genoa and the Dutch Consul had organized a very grand reception to which the Van Praags had been invited. There was much excitement and preparation for this very splendid occasion.

The girls had been taught that it was impolite to turn down an invitation to dance and that it was completely inexcusable to reject a request on the grounds that the man who was asking was unattractive or old. At their table was seated an elderly Dutch officer who had got himself more and more inebriated as the evening progressed. Barend and Lucia didn't notice this but Elena was well aware of his state. When he asked her to dance, her reluctance was very clear. Barend gave her a stern look and so she had no choice but to accept the invitation.

The man was far from steady on his feet and her embarrassment grew rapidly as he bumped into other couples. The dance seemed endless but it was probably her humiliation that stretched the duration. His steps degenerated into stumbling and the final indignity came when he actually fell over, knocking Elena to the floor, and landing on top of her. She was mortified. When she managed to extricate herself, she left him on the floor for his fellow officers to sort out and she returned to the table in tears. Lucia and Barend had been aware of some disturbance on the dance floor but hadn't been able to see exactly what was happening, or that their poor daughter was at the centre of the fiasco. Barend was filled with remorse for not having realised the state the man was in, and for having pressed Elena into accepting the invitation. He couldn't have apologized more for having let her down.

CHAPTER 5

In the midst of normal teenage fun and family life, the Van Praags became increasingly involved in assisting Jewish refugees from Germany, escape Nazi persecution.

Things had become a great deal more difficult for Jewish refugees in Italy with the introduction of discriminating racial laws in 1938 and the pressures on them continued to escalate at an alarming rate.

Barend was a member of an organization called 'Delegarzione per l' Assistenza Emigranti Ebrei (Delegation for the Assistance of Jewish Emigrants, better known as DELASEM). This organization was only officially organized on the 1st of December 1939. However, it would seem that a similar movement, and probably the forerunner of DELASEM, had been operating for some time prior to this and it was in this group that Barend was most active.

At the same time as DELASEM was constituted, it was authorized by the Italian government. Officially, it was meant to help refugees and foreign internees with charitable aid and, in particular, to organize emigration for the refugees. These refugees found themselves in desperate straits with the introduction of the racial laws of 1938 which stripped them of their rights to residency. This was exacerbated from mid-1940 when they could be arrested and imprisoned in concentration camps.

DELASEM continued to operate until 1947. However, it was forced underground on the 8th of September 1943 when the Germans took occupation of Italy. In November of 1943 all Jews in Italy were labelled 'foreign enemies' who could be deported from Italy and sent to concentration camps. Six thousand such Jews died in Auschwitz alone, as a result of this legislation.

After going underground, DELASEM provided secret sanctuary and compiled and distributed false documents.

The headquarters of DELASEM was in Genoa under the leadership of Dante Almansi and Lelio Vittorio Valobra but it had a network of branches in all the major centres in Italy.

Because of Barend's shipping interests, he was well placed to help refugees find berths on ships bound for America but the family's involvement was more hands-on than simply making these arrangements. Refugees often arrived en masse with little to their names. Lucia, Toly and Elena helped run soup-kitchens and arrange accommodation.

Amongst these people, and probably their most famously-connected 'client' was Albert Einstein's sister, Maja. She was two years younger than Einstein and evidently his only childhood friend, so they were very close.

In 1910, Maja had married Paul Winteler who was the brother of Albert's first wife, Maric. Maja and Paul lived in Colonnata near Florence. In 1939 Albert invited Maja to the USA to live with him in Princeton, New Jersey. By then he was a widower. Paul was not granted permission to immigrate by the US authorities because of his ill health and he was forced to remain in Europe. He lived with his brother-in-law in Geneva where he died in 1952.

It was prudent to keep Maja's departure as quiet as possible for fear of reprisal and this was where Barend's skills were put into operation. Every stage of her removal from Italy was meticulously planned and kept secret.

Albert and Maja shared some happy years together but in 1946 she suffered a stroke and became bedridden, her condition being aggravated by progressive arteriosclerosis.

Albert sent the following letter of gratitude to the Van Praags for their involvement in helping Maja escape.

Much loved Van Praag!

I feel the urge to express my heartfelt thanks to you and your family for the trouble and care which you took regarding the affairs of my sister. I also know with how much energy and courage you have helped endangered 'fellow tribesmen' in these difficult times.

All my admiration
Friendly regards and wishes

Yours

Albert Einstein
February 1946

Agnese also has an autographed photograph and letter sent to the family by Einstein's step-daughter, Margot, after his death. The note on the back of the photograph reads: "To the good Van Praags - In heartfelt gratitude and thanks. Always yours. Margot Einstein.

As part of his work in assisting escaping Jews, Barend bought and fitted out a scrapped ship which he used to smuggle Jews to Palestine. Helping them board the ship was fraught with risk and had to be done in secret at night. Only Barend and Orso were involved in this. Often they had to improvise as in the case of the young mother carrying a tiny baby. She was expected to climb a rope ladder whilst holding the baby. Barend was concerned about how she was going to accomplish this perilous manoeuvre and Lucia, who knew more about the realities of carrying babies, realized that it was far too risky to expect her to manage. She had visions of this tiny baby falling into the murky harbour waters in the middle of the night and being lost beneath the greasy surface, or dashed against the ship. Lucia set about making a very effective rucksack-papoose which carried the babe safely aboard.

An incident which delighted Barend involved an elderly Jewish couple he met one evening. They were standing in a doorway counting their money and asked Barend if he could recommend a restaurant. They told him what they could afford to pay, which was very little. He took them to his favourite restaurant and arranged with the maitre d' to feed them well at his expense and not to let them know that he was sponsoring their meal.

Towards the end of their meal he overheard some German officers asking the waiter for strawberries and cream. The waiter said they were out of season and unavailable. Barend knew better and sent a waiter to a nearby delicatessen. He returned with the strawberries and served them to the couple with a flourish, to the astonishment and irritation of the Germans and to Barend's mischievous glee. The couple thoroughly enjoyed the meal and they were amazed at how reasonable the cost was!

Lucia and the girls devoted many hours to helping out at the soup-kitchen in a synagogue which had been set up to feed the refugees while they awaited transportation. In addition to being hard physical work, it was a harrowing experience to witness the suffering of these people. They possessed little more than the clothing on their backs and as much hand luggage as they could manage. Many showed the signs of poverty and starvation. They were leaving behind the homes and accumulated possessions and memories of generations of European citizenship. Many were also leaving behind loved ones who couldn't go with them and whom they knew they would probably never see again. Most had already suffered great hardship and anguish and now faced a completely unknown and insecure future. There was quiet despair, but no complaining, and only gentle gratitude.

Elena remembers an elderly woman who had escaped Germany with her much loved German shepherd. At the soup-kitchen, when she was handed her soup and bread roll, she gave half her roll to her dog. Elena, in her adolescent thoughtlessness, was incensed at what she saw as the woman's profligacy in giving her dog what she, and others, needed so desperately. She expressed her teenage disapproval loudly. It was only when Elena herself was much older that she understood what the companionship of that dog meant to the woman.

At some point the Italian government agreed to provide a refugee ship to carry the émigrés to America. The ship was no more than a worn-out tub. It set sail from Genoa, jam-packed with refugees. Just outside the harbour there was an almighty explosion on board. It was strongly suspected that this was sabotage perpetrated by the Italian government itself. Miraculously no one was killed in the explosion or drowned. The boat burnt ferociously and sank very quickly. The weather conditions were icy and the water was freezing: one woman had both frostbite on her hands and feet and burns on her bottom from the heat of the deck on which she had sat.

Because the explosion had taken place so close to the harbour, and was witnessed by so many people seeing off the refugees, rescue boats were quickly on the scene.

One passenger was a young violinist, hoping to use her violin to survive in her new country. She lost all that she possessed, including her violin. The Genoese replaced her clothing and friends of the Van Praags gave her a violin. They were a Dutch family, called Van Straaten, who were all very musical. Their son played the violin and he gave his spare violin to his father, Oom George, to pass on to Barend for the girl.

Barend then arranged for another ship to transport them to America.

After the war, from 1945 to 1947, DELASEM continued its work in helping refugee families by reuniting scattered relatives. It also organized emigration groups, especially to Palestine.

To what extent Barend remained involved with DELASEM after the family was forcibly moved to Florence, is a mystery. He was, though, very involved in forging documents. He was skilled at using German script and very innovative at creating official-looking stamps. However, how and where he sourced examples of documents and all the other information and paraphernalia he would have needed for successful forgery, is also a mystery. It would seem that he was part of a larger organization. His steady stream of clients also suggests that people were being directed to him from sources other than word-of-mouth.

When the war was over Barend continued his philanthropic efforts by working with the International Refugee Organisation (IRO) which was officially founded in April 1946 but had begun preparatory work at the end of 1944. Barend began his work for the IRO at about this time.

*   *   *

In the late 1930's pressure was mounting on the family as Barend openly and defiantly acknowledged his Jewish heritage.

The Van Praags were friendly with a Russian couple called Cobilinski. The husband, Misha, a psychiatrist, was an adviser to Mussolini and was laughingly called the 'The Grey Eminence of the Government' by the Van Praags for his very formal and pompous manner. His wife, Sasha, was also a doctor. Early in 1938 Sasha travelled to Genoa from Rome, where 'The Grey Eminence' had retired and was awaiting an appointment as an ambassador. She visited specifically to warn Barend to flee to America. Barend looked into the possibility but discovered he would have to forfeit two-thirds of his property to the Fascists. This he wasn't prepared to do and set about finding other means of surviving.

The Cobilinskis, too, experienced their share of grief later in the war. They had an only child, a son, Alessandro, who was sent to Russia as a member of a tank unit. In about 1943, after hearing nothing from him for a long time, they were told that he had been seriously injured. Then his mother received word that he had returned to Italy and was in a military hospital somewhere in Italy and that he was suffering from gangrene.

Sasha visited every military hospital throughout the country and questioned every gangrene patient she came across. By then the Van Praags were living in Florence. When Sasha eventually reached Florence, she was exhausted and despairing. As she had put herself at risk by revealing her true loyalties when she had tried to persuade the Van Praags to emigrate, Elena offered to accompany her in her search through Florence's gangrene wards, an offer which was gratefully accepted.

Innumerable young men were suffering from this appalling condition. Some had it as a result of wounds but for most it had been caused by frostbite inflicted by the weather conditions on the Russian front and the fact that their footwear was so poor. The soles of their shoes were nothing more than cardboard, the result of Italian duplicity and Fascist incompetence in the awarding of tenders for the manufacture of shoes for the military. Of course, the high-ranking officers' footwear was nothing like this. Another problem arose from the ancient Italian tradition of wrapping strips of cloth around the feet and legs instead of wearing woollen socks, a tradition, one would have thought, any self-respecting modern army would have scrapped.

Sasha and Elena couldn't find Alessandro but they did find one of his comrades. This man told them that the last he had seen of Alessandro was in the thick of battle when Alessandro had been standing up in the turret of his tank, shouting and waving to the vehicles and foot-soldiers behind him to retreat. As this soldier had watched, Alessandro's tank was hit and everyone inside was obliterated.

Elena says she will never forget the smell of those gangrene wards.

The details of what steps Barend took to ensure his family's survival, Elena doesn't know, but she does remember a trip he took to Holland in 1939 from which he returned with a large number of Kruger pounds. These he used to keep the family going through the war years. Later in the war, every member of the family wore a pouch around his/her waist, under clothing. The pouches were worn day and night and contained their passports, other important documents and a Kruger coin. Elena still has her gold coin.

When Agnese last visited South Africa, she took out the little card which she carried then, and still carries now. On one side is a picture of the Virgin Mary and on the other is a note written for her by Toly. If Agnese had got lost and was found by the Allies, the message was to tell them that she was 'a little Dutch girl'. Unfortunately Toly got it wrong and wrote "I am a little Deutsche girl". In sixty years of carrying the card Agnese had never noticed the mistake and it was only when she and Elena went out to lunch with friends, and showed the card to the friends, that they spotted the mistake. They were still chuckling when I saw them the following day.

One evening, early in 1939, Lucia and Barend announced to their assembled offspring that they would be getting married shortly. After the ensuing bewilderment and suggestive joshing, their parents explained that they were going to be married in the Catholic Church, having originally been married in a civil ceremony. This was to give some documentary legitimacy to their claim of being Catholics in their papers. Some of their Jewish acquaintances converted to Catholicism and then, a short time later, became Protestants. The reason for this was that the Germans often asked suspected Jews, who claimed they were Protestants, what they had been before becoming Protestants. In all honesty, they could say that they had been Catholics.

Everyone joined in to turn the event into an occasion. Toly and Elena designed an invitation announcing the marriage which read:

> *Mrs Hulsker*
> > *announces the marriage of her daughter, Lucia,*
> > *to Mr B. van Praag*
>
> *Toly van Praag*
> > *announces the marriage of the father of the Van Praag children,*
> > *Mr Barend van Praag, to their mother, Mrs Lucia van Praag.*

Agnese asked her teacher, a nun, to excuse her from school for the day and when asked why, she delighted in telling her that it was to attend her parents' wedding ceremony.

Before the day, all the children, and Barend, were baptised into the Catholic faith. Elena's godmother, who was also the head of the art school, gave Elena a medallion with the tiny figure of an angel. This momento Elena recently gave to Agnese because Agnese had remarked that it looked like her son as an infant.

They were married on the 25th of February 1939. Orso escorted his mother to the altar. The ceremony was followed by a champagne reception at which they were given an assortment of witty and whimsical gifts including a rather lovely Mirano glass stork, prompting Orso to ask when the baby was due.

For Christmas of 1939, Barend took his family on a special holiday to the coastal resort town of Sanremo, near Nice, regarded as the Monte Carlo of

Italy. Here he booked them into a very luxurious suite which, it was claimed, Hitler, Goering and many of their inner circle had occupied.

The hotel was large and sumptuous and the service was magnificent. On the morning after their arrival, Elena awoke to find a strange man in their room. He was clad in full evening dress, including tails and gloves, and her first alarmed reaction was that Toly had got carried away the previous evening and brought him back to their room. She kept trying to catch Toly's eye as he served Toly her coffee. Toly had done no such thing and reacted with mock outrage when Elena got the chance to make her accusation – he was just the waiter!

Dining every evening was an occasion. Elena remembers the food and table settings being magnificent. Dressing up for dinner also gave the girls great pleasure. Toly often clad her splendid figure in her favourite gown of royal blue taffeta with a plunging neckline. A young waiter, bedecked in his smart tails, was putting cheese in her soup and was so engrossed in admiring her décolletage that Barend had to say to him, "Young man, that's enough cheese!"

After dinner, while Lucia and Barend went gambling, Elena and Toly went dancing, chaperoned by Orso. The hotel management went to a great deal of effort to ensure the success of the evening entertainment. As the guests arrived in the ballroom each lady was given a corsage and the men a single flower in the form of a button-hole. These flowers had to be matched up during the course of the evening when changing dance partners during the many cotillions. On Christmas Eve, instead of the corsages, they were given miniature, hand-held Christmas trees. At the centre of each was a candle. When these were lit and the lights were put out, a holy hush descended on the room – not inappropriate for what was going on in the world outside.

Barend's maxim for the holiday was that the more they spent the better, because it meant less for the Fascists to grab.

On their return to Genoa, Barend was forced to sell his share of the four ships to his partner who was a gentile. In addition to the great pride Barend had always taken in the maintenance of his ships, he also had a very hands-on approach to running the business. He had come close to sacrificing his sanity and the welfare of his family in his struggle to save the firm during the Depression. This enforced sale, therefore, represented much more to him than simply selling a business – this was a big chunk of his life.

Before the sale was concluded, one of the ships ran on to rocks in Portugal. Fortunately, everyone was saved, but Barend had to spend a month in Portugal dealing with all the ramifications. Also fortunately, insurance paid out. It doesn't seem that his partner was very involved. Eventually the remaining ships were torpedoed and sank.

Barend invested the proceeds of his share in more property. One of his investments was a new block of four flats. He had an arrangement with his young tenants that when they produced their first child, they would not have to pay rent for a month. When one couple produced twins, he told them that they were "trying to do him" but he allowed them two months' rent-free accommodation any way. Only one of these flats was slightly damaged during the war.

Most of these properties were commandeered by the Italian government for the duration of the war. Barend received no rent but still had to pay the rates. Before the war the lire was valued at 70 lire to the British pound. After the war the pound was worth 2000 lire. However, compensation for damage inflicted by the Italian government to the properties was only paid out at the pre-war 70 lire to the pound. The 'Eyetes' also had to compensate Barend for having been compelled to sell his shipping business for very little.

As 'hostile aliens' i.e. Dutch citizens, the family was forced into civilian internship and was not allowed to remain in a coastal city. They could choose their destination anywhere inland. Florence was chosen by Barend as it was a large city and he thought they would be less conspicuous.

Being branded as hostile aliens because of their Dutch citizenship, was probably crucial to their survival. The irony of this situation was that this 'status' overshadowed their Judaism. Had they been identified by the state as Jews, it would have been very difficult for them to escape the notice of the authorities after the Armistice of Cassibile, signed on the 8th of September

1943. This agreement marked the beginning of the German occupation. It also led to the Manifesto of Verona, finalized in November of 1943, according to which all Jews in Italy were labelled 'foreign enemies'. As a result of this, thousands of Jewish men, women and children were deported from Italy and exterminated in gas chambers or worked to death. One of the safety measures on which Barend always insisted, was that they all carry their Dutch passports with them at all times.

Orso remained in Genoa and lived with his aunt in order to complete his degree as he was only in his second year and non-Aryans were not allowed to transfer between universities. However, Toly was allowed to finish her degree in Florence, possibly because she was close to completion.

CHAPTER 6

The Van Praags moved lock, stock and wine barrels. Toly even managed to transfer her beautiful new pink and grey bedroom in its entirety. They moved into a two-storey apartment with a cellar on the Viale Giacomo Matteoti.

The building in which their apartment was located, dated back to the 1400's. It was close to the railway-yard and formed one side of the boundary which surrounded a large park-like private garden. This garden is one the largest, if not the largest, of the gardens within the confines of the old city. More apartment blocks and a closed-order convent formed the other three sides of the park boundary. Most of this complex was owned by one family and was known as the Palazzo della Gherardesca.

During our discussions Elena had told me that these buildings were being transformed into a very posh hotel. I had forgotten this piece of information when, absent-mindedly paging through a 'Time' magazine, I came across a photograph of a very sumptuous, ornate, Baroque-style hotel bedroom. For some reason I jumped to the erroneous conclusion that it had been photographed in a Hollywood hotel and thought the décor ridiculous for an American hotel. As I read the article, bits of information filtered through my prejudice and when I read that the hotel was a fifteen-minute walk east of the city centre of Florence, the penny began to drop that this could have been Elena's old home. The description of the garden fueled this impression.

Elena was interested but a little sceptical and 'phoned Agnese who had continued to live in their old apartment (the second apartment they occupied in the complex), until relatively recently and had maintained contact with the owners. Agnese confirmed that this was the very place and, astoundingly, the room in the photograph had been their old dining-room and is now the best suite in the hotel! It is also the same room in which Elena clapped eyes on her George for the first time.

This hotel is the glorious new Four Seasons Hotel in Florence. The 'Time' article (20 April 2009) provided some interesting historical snippets: *"With a choice of accommodation in two Renaissance buildings overlooking a historic garden, guests at Florence's latest luxury hotel – the late 15th century Palazzo della Gherardesca – might as well be living in a museum. Previous owners have included an order of nuns, a pope, several generations of Florentine nobility and – from 1883 to 1885 – a viceroy of Egypt who sold it when he was refused permission to house his harem there. Thanks to its rebirth as a Four Seasons hotel, you have a chance to see what the ladies were missing."*

From 1940 something of a community began to develop amongst the residents, many of whom came from the flotsam of war experiences.

In the garden was a hillock covered in trees. Burrowed into this little hill was a storage area built long ago and which now served as a very good bomb shelter. It had entrances at both ends, a domed roof and benches which ran the length of the shelter.

Elena found a particular friend in a woman who lived in the block opposite theirs. They had met at the entrance during a bombing raid and this woman announced that she had a bottle of brandy which Elena could sample if she shared her cushions. Elena always took two cushions – one to sit on and the other to clasp over her head to block out the sounds of the bombing. This became a familiar ritual to which was added Elena's contribution of glasses.

The apartment was large and in the kitchen was an enormous old brick, wood-burning stove, or range cooker, dating back a couple of hundred years. It proved very useful later, when the Germans blew up all the gas mains and left the citizens without fuel.

One of the staircases in the apartment was wide and free-floating on one side. Barend had this side bricked up and left a cavity in the wall, into which were stowed the family's valuables. These included the canteen of cutlery which Barend had commissioned some years before. It was made from four kilograms of silver and each piece was embossed with the letters 'VP'. The canteen was a little cabinet with drawers.

Lucia's great pride and pleasure, her hand-painted Cantagalli dinner service, also went into the space. 'Galli' means 'roosters' which, in turn, are symbols of prosperity, good health and good wishes. This was a traditional Italian design dating back to the Renaissance and the Umbrian town of Orvietto. The traditional colour used on the white base was green, but blue and red were also popular. Lucia's service, though, did not have the rooster motif. It was a floral design in green but was made by the well-known studio called 'Cantagalli'. The founder of the studio, having the name 'Galli', used the rooster as his emblem. Incidentally, when they were still living in Genoa, and Elena was attending the Artistic and Commercial College, a maid had broken a serving platter which upset Lucia no end. Elena found an unglazed platter of the same shape, copied the floral design and had it fired at the college. The result was indistinguishable from the rest of the set, apart from her signature on the reverse side of the plate. She was immensely proud of her accomplishment.

Also included were Lucia's jewellery and two Chinese vases, believed to be very old and valuable. Years later Toly, as the eldest, laid claim to these vases and brought them back to South Africa where she took them to the Chinese Embassy in Cape Town to be valued. She was none too pleased to be told that they were practically valueless.

The wall was bricked up and plastered and the new paintwork grubbied to disguise the alteration.

Elena's formal education had come to an end and she obtained an internship with an interior-design business. The business had been owned by a Dutch artist, Buselli (brother to Barend's vintner friend from Radda in Chianti who supplied Barend with barrels of wine), and his wife. By the time Elena began work the artist had died but his wife continued the business using his designs. This wife had found herself a live-in boyfriend, a man Elena describes as being big, fat and bone idle. He spent most of his day sleeping and complained to Barend that he slept well during the day but battled to sleep at night. He asked Barend what he could suggest to solve his problem. Barend told him to migrate to the other side of the earth where it would be night-time.

Elena's job was classified as manual labour which qualified her for an extra bread allowance. She made lampshades and desk sets and earned 2/6 per hour. She painted the shades in designs and colours which matched curtain designs, then sealed the paper with oil and varnish, attached this to a frame and finished off the shade with ribbon. She particularly loved doing Beatrix Potter designs on children's lampshades.

Elena found a friend in a girl who was later to become her sister-in-law. Gabriella (called Gea) and Elena would often walk home together and Orso, when he had completed his degree and come home to Florence, regularly accompanied them. A romance blossomed between Gea and Orso and their marriage came about sooner rather than later so that Orso could avoid being drafted into the Dutch army because his health had never been robust. Elena suspects that he might have entered the priesthood had he not married but instead he went into banking. He and Gea had three daughters, which impressed Elena but George's comment was that Orso only produced daughters because his foot kept slipping.

Gea was quite a character. In her old age she continued to ride a bicycle well into her eighties. When she was eighty-four she developed a brain aneurism which was discovered in time. She underwent successful surgery and was soon back on her bicycle. On Elena's last visit to Italy, she and Agnese visited Gea where she lived, near Genoa. Gea was still very much in charge of her family and Agnese and Elena were included in a big family gathering for the celebration of a grandchild's first communion. Matriarch Gea was organizing the whole affair.

Unfortunately her organizational skills were somewhat lacking and she wouldn't take any help, or criticism, from anybody. As an occasion, it was a bit of a disaster. The food was extremely late in arriving and was ice-cold by the time it was delivered. Nobody seemed to know what was happening, or when it should happen, and eventually the tumult and chaos became too much for Elena.

Gea had also dictated that Elena and Agnese should stay with her but when they had arrived earlier in the week she had forgotten to do the shopping so they went hungry. She also couldn't find the bedlinen and their towels were not much bigger than facecloths. Elena decided that she had to make her escape and Agnese was in full support. She announced that she had left her blood-pressure pills in Florence and urgently needed to return. This elicited a noisy debate about the relative importance of the pills with someone declaring that it wouldn't matter if she went without for a couple of days and someone else telling a gruesome story about an acquaintance's relative who had had a massive and debilitating stroke. Eventually one of the throng, probably also wanting to run away, offered them a lift back to Florence.

Gea continued to ride her bicycle until a car knocked her off it and killed her.

It was Gea's father, Alberto Lunetti, who made the frames for Elena's lampshades in his spare time and what an enterprising man he turned out to be! He was in charge of the telephone exchange in Florence. This unassuming and unobtrusive, but remarkable, little man managed to replicate the entire telephone exchange in the basement of the building – and he did it all in secret. When the Germans bombed the building as they were leaving Florence, they completely destroyed the old exchange. However, it took our hero under two hours after the bombing had ceased to have his exchange connected and running.

The desk sets were made of cardboard and the wood for the blotters had to be French polished. Elena also made tea trays and cocktail trays, decorating these to match whatever the client required. The trays had a chalk base which was then painted. She made a tea trolley for Toly with a lily design which matched a porcelain receptacle which Toly cherished.

Later in the war she turned her skills to a much more nefarious activity. An Italian printer suggested that he provide her with copies of English country scenes which she could colour by hand. These works were to be sold to American soldiers as antique English prints.

Elena thought this a very clever idea and quickly developed her own 'production line'. Barend was scandalised but this didn't stop her.

To save time, she would lay out a large batch of the prints on the floor and then paint in the same colour on each of them before moving on to the next colour. Eventually she was churning out so many of these that she didn't stop to wash her brush between colours and would simply put the brush in her mouth and then wipe it off on the sleeve under her armpit. This habit eventually made her ill - she was probably poisoning herself, especially on the green paint.

Elena also occupied her time by attending a theatre school. All the performances put on by the school took place at the Teatro della Pergola. This opera-house was built by a Medici in 1656 and is the oldest theatre in Italy, having occupied the same site for more than 350 years. The school's most famous graduate was heart-throb Rosanno Brazzi, one of the stars of 'South Pacific'.

Elena was involved in a number of productions but she was never allowed a speaking part because her bray (the trait of pronouncing the 'r' sound as a glottal fricative or scraping sound at the back of her throat) was too distinctive. She became adept at crowd scenes and counting in Italian in pretended conversations in these scenes. The comedies were largely burlesque and done in mime which suited her talents. Attendance at the school continued until the intensity of bombing made it too dangerous to go out regularly.

Toly's and Elena's romantic lives in Genoa had, for a time, centred on two young Italian submarine officers. Much of their training took place on the coast of France and whenever they returned to Italy on leave they brought with them gifts of glorious French perfume which was greatly prized by both girls.

Barend wasn't too enchanted with these romances as he was very suspicious of Italian men and was doubly suspicious of anyone serving in the Italian armed forces. Elena was quite taken with her boyfriend, Pierre-Giorgio Pina, nicknamed 'Il Gatto' or 'The Cat'. Whilst these romances were blossoming the sisters went to see a fortune-teller. The old lady told Elena that she would not marry Il Gatto. It would also be a number of years before she did find the man she would truly love and that she wouldn't marry him until she had crossed great oceans three times. This seemed like a highly unlikely scenario. Elena was unimpressed and decided never to go near another fortune-teller – a decision which was reinforced when the old lady's prediction proved true.

Il Gatto was killed off the English Coast in the Channel, during his first mission, when his submarine was torpedoed. Elena was haunted by images of the horror of dying in this way. Barend, however, wasn't the least sympathetic and declared that it was one less submarine to worry about.

Toly's romance with her boyfriend, Rafael Pollidori, nicknamed 'The Little Count', continued until the latter months of 1943 when Mussolini was rescued by the Germans from his mountain-top prison. Rafael made his loyalties to Mussolini very clear at this point. Up until then the family had given him the benefit of the doubt that he wasn't a Fascist but now there was no avoiding the truth and Barend put his foot down: Toly was, under no circumstances, to see him again. Barend didn't often place such embargoes on his family's activities and she knew this ban wasn't negotiable. She didn't find this order easy to accept.

*   *   *

In Genoa all three girls had played basketball. In Florence Elena and Agnese continued to play. The games were pretty dirty and Toly's coach in Genoa was a little man who taught his team every underhanded trick in the book. On one occasion he was showing a very large girl how to use her elbow. When she practised the manoeuvre on him, she knocked him out cold. For important matches the match referee would cut the girls' nails as they came on to the court. Elena was a wing and was very proud of her ability to basket a ball from the centre of the court.

In Florence, Elena and Agnese played for a Fascist-sponsored team. It was through basketball that they got to know the Einstein family. The father of the family was Albert Einstein's cousin. Roberto and his wife, Nina, had two daughters. The elder daughter was Luce (who was born in 1917, making her three years older than Elena). The younger daughter, Cici, was born in

1926. In 1942 Cici was in her final year at school and Luce was in the final year of her medical studies.

The family also included two cousins, Lorenza and Paula Mazzetti, who were younger. Lorenza was born in 1928 and Paula was slightly younger. Their father was Mrs Einstein's brother. Their mother had died some years previously and they were being raised by the Einsteins while their father continued to live in Rome. Elena remembers them as happy girls. In a photograph that Elena has of their basketball team, of the eight girls in the team (which included the Mazzetti and Einstein girls) six were of Jewish descent. Their coach and the manager, proud in their Fascist uniforms, are clearly oblivious of this fact.

The Einsteins lived in Florence but also had a country estate, 'Il Focardo' in the region of Le Corti in Tuscany. It was here that they took refuge, thinking that they would be safer from the Germans. Roberto suggested that Agnese also live with them to avoid the danger of the bombing in Florence. Barend turned down the offer because of his firmly-held belief that his family should not be split up.

How wrong the Einsteins were to believe that they would be safe at Il Focardo.

Lorenza recorded the horrific events that befell the family on the 3rd of August 1944 in a prizewinning children's story, 'Il Cielo Cade' ('*The Sky Falls*') which she wrote in 1961. The book tells the story through the childhood eyes of Lorenza and Paula. She has taken some literary licence, such as changing the names and making Paula much younger, but essentially the details of the story, translated from the Italian for me by Elena, remain the same as the reports of the tragic events Elena remembers.

Roberto was born in Munich but studied in Italy before the First World War. Nina was a fellow student of Italian-Jewish descent and when they married they remained in Florence where Roberto worked as an engineer.

A number of friends had tried to persuade Roberto to flee to Switzerland with his family but he refused to go. As the war progressed, a Catholic priest persistently told him to leave but even this didn't change his mind.

Lorenza begins her story by describing a walk amongst the trees in the grounds of the villa where she encountered an elderly, bearded man. When she asked who he was he said that he was San Guiseppe and that he'd come to help her uncle because the Germans were coming. He told her to tell her uncle about him but not to tell anybody else.

A group of German soldiers had already billeted themselves in the outbuildings and stables of the villa and there were officers living in the villa. Guiseppe asked how many Germans were living there and wanted to know the name of the commanding officer. The Germans don't seem to have bothered the family much and the relationships were fairly cordial. The only thing that had really distressed the children was hearing the squealing of the pigs and cries of the calves from the stables when the Germans slaughtered them. The soldiers also tended to be very noisy and Lorenza comments that a few days earlier their noise in the villa had drowned out the sound of the birds as the family walked in the woodland surrounding their home.

At dinner time on the day she met Guiseppe she asked one of the peasants working for them for food for San Guiseppe. The peasant took off his belt and said he'd give her a hiding for San Guiseppe. At dinner she told Roberto that San Guiseppe was waiting for him. This seems to have been the name used for the local partisan chief. Roberto said he would deal with San Guiseppe and would take him some food but they were not to talk about it.

The following day Roberto said he'd seen San Guiseppe and when the girls asked what he'd said, Roberto replied that nobody was to know about him and that they were to forget about the whole incident. He hugged Lorenza but seemed distracted as he gazed at the particular tree where Lorenza had spoken to San Guiseppe. At that moment there was a huge explosion and Lorenza's concern was that it would frighten San Guiseppe. Roberto's response was that saints were never frightened. The rumble of guns drew nearer and the billeted Germans began to leave. Finally the last truck of

Ruth Fifield

soldiers left the villa and to Lorenza the air seemed to be alive with whistling bullets and shells. Roberto forbade the children from playing outside and included the peasant children in his command. The main road was deserted and for three days there was no sign of any Germans.

Then there was a sudden rumble of guns and a chatter of submachine-guns followed by silence and an eerie calm. After some time the peasants emerged, shouting jubilantly that the war was over and that the partisans were coming. At the end of the road a group of bearded, armed men appeared. Roberto left the villa and ran towards them. The girls and Nina were watching from a window and they asked their aunt where he was going as he disappeared into the bush with the partisans. Nina hugged them and started to cry because she was happy. The five of them danced and sang and Nina shouted, "The English are here!" With that, they heard a car, followed by a truck from which twenty soldiers alighted. Paula ran towards someone she thought was Heinz, a German soldier who had been particularly pleasant to the children. Suddenly she realized that he was dressed differently and then she knew that it was not Heinz at all. These men were in SS uniforms.

Lorenza and Paula watched in horror as Nina and their cousins were herded up the stairs into the villa with machine-guns aimed at them. Then they, too, were pushed into the villa. All the girls were locked into a room with a guard. Paula was particularly upset and her aunt held her and told her to be good.

An officer came in and asked Nina where her husband was. He left but later returned and questioned them in various languages. Paula reportedly said he'd gone with San Guiseppe and then told one of her cousins that she wanted to go to the toilet. Her cousin asked the German and he took her from the room with a gun aimed at her.

When she returned, they could hear banging, shouting and laughter, followed by shattering crystal and glass which they deduced was coming from the sitting-room which was decorated with a number of chandeliers and mirrors. There was the sound of roller-skating in the passages. The noise was such that the whole house seemed to be reverberating.

Their dog, Ali, cried out as it was kicked. They could hear distinctly what was being broken and where. The breaking of crystal and glass was followed by great merriment. Paula was particularly concerned that Roberto would be very angry at the destruction of the books and glass in their sitting-room.

Eventually they were all taken to the sitting-room they referred to as the 'mirror room'. As they were pushed into the room, they stumbled over piles of books. In addition to the smashed glass, all the paintings had been slashed.

Luce told a soldier that it wasn't right to treat them like this as they had done nothing. Mockingly, he told her that they would have their court case.

The mockery continued with the roller-skating and throwing around of the children's toys. A yellow bear was stuck on the end of a broomstick and used to target the sights on their weapons. One soldier adorned himself with Luce's evening stole and then paraded himself up and down the staircase. Another put on Nina's special-occasion hat and joined the mannequin parade on the stairs. The white walls in the entrance hall had been besmirched with graffiti.

By this time it was nearly dark and the commanding officer was sitting at the piano. Soldiers brought in burning torches. The officer smiled and bowed to Nina and, still with a smile on his face, told her that he would be conducting a proper and fair hearing, all of which was a mere formality. He asked her to forgive him but it was necessary for him to interrogate them one by one. Once this had been done, he said that they would leave. Paula complained that they had been hurting Ali, and Luce told him this in German. Again he smiled, and ordered his soldiers not to touch the dog.

They were all returned to the room where they had been held under guard and were told that the interrogation process ("Just a formality") would begin. Nina, then Luce, and finally Cici, were taken back to the mirror room.

Lorenza reports that when she and Paula asked if they were to be taken to the mirror room they were told, by a soldier, that they would not be included as they were not Jews. In her story she says that they heard a shot and a scream, then another three shots. She and Paula escaped from the room and ran down the stairs, shouting for their aunt and cousins. They managed to get past soldiers who were coming up the stairs. The doorway into the mirror room was lit by the burning torches and they could see the feet of people lying on the floor. The commanding officer was standing in the doorway and pushed them away.

Elena and Agnese say that they were told that while the interrogation was going on, the officer who was orchestrating proceedings, sat at the grand piano playing beautiful classical pieces of music. The piano was then smashed and this man left a note propped on the piano. It was addressed to Roberto and read: "A gift from the Führer to Albert Einstein."

As the Germans were preparing to leave, the peasants fetched the two sisters and ran into the dark with them. When they looked back they heard an explosion from the villa and saw it go up in flames. They stood with the peasants on a hillside watching the villa burn. The overseer held Paula in his arms, preventing her from returning to the villa. They could hear what they thought were cries but they were told, by the peasants, that these were simply the noises of the Germans leaving.

A little later they heard a speeding truck and then squealing brakes as it negotiated the hill. The overseer shouted, "There is our patrone!" Running towards the villa was Roberto. The peasants chased after him to stop him going into the villa. Behind him was a group of armed men. He turned and ran screaming down the road where the German truck was disappearing. Lorenza says he was dressed in white and looked like a ghost. He fell to the ground weeping and she watched the lights of the disappearing truck. Paula had reached him and was hugging him and crying. He began shouting for a gun and beating at the armed men with his fists.

Roberto and the sisters sat together outside the villa, crying. They sat there for hours watching the villa smouldering. Roberto continually told everyone to leave him alone and eventually the peasants retreated to their homes. The partisans also left to pursue the Germans, leaving one man behind to keep an eye on Roberto. Paula tried to cover his eyes and he continued to shake.

Some time later he suddenly said, "See, I don't cry anymore." Evidently the girls fell asleep with their heads in his lap. When they awoke, he had gone. Later, they found him in the ruins of the villa but when Lorenza started to shout and cry, the peasants took the girls away.

The peasants prepared the bodies and placed them in coffins one of them had made from wooden doors retrieved from the villa. The coffins were loaded on to a cart pulled by oxen while the women prayed and lamented. When the priest arrived they took the bodies to the cemetery of Badiuzza which is situated above Florence.

Eleven months later, Roberto committed suicide on their grave.

According to Lorenza he had left the girls a note in which he told them to remember him, their aunt and Luce and Cici and to remember what they had taught them. He apologized for the times he had been boring and impatient. He also told them not to wear black.

This concludes Lorenza's story in 'The Sky Falls' but not the end of the horror experienced by the family.

In an article published on the Internet on the 3rd of August 2010, titled '3 Agosto 1944: il drama dell'Einstein italiano' the writer emphasizes that Roberto was much loved by his overseer and the peasants living and working on the estate and that there had been no persecution by the first group of ordinary German soldiers who had been billeted on the estate.

For some time the Germans had been doing their best to eradicate the problem posed by the partisans through horrific acts of retribution on the partisans and the general populace living in rural communities. As the Germans came under increasing pressure and were forced to retreat northwards by the Allies, these acts or retribution became increasingly vicious.

Fearing for Roberto's safety, the overseer and peasants told him to hide in the woodland surrounding the house. They were not concerned about the safety of Nina and his daughters. Their concern was for Roberto as he was Albert Einstein's cousin. According to this report, Nina, Luce and Cici were subjected to humiliating acts of servitude and atrocious torture for the entire night. At one point Nina was taken into the woods and forced to call for Roberto. Roberto could hear her and was desperate to get to her to put an end to her suffering but the peasants thought that this would be pointless and restrained him. Nina was taken back to the house and then the peasants heard screaming and gunfire. The writer claimed that all three women were raped before being killed. The following morning the SS burnt down the villa and then left.

Lorenza and Paula were sent to live with an unmarried aunt in Rome. There is no mention of their father.

After the war Elena and Agnese met up with Lorenza and Paula. Lorenza moved to London in the early 1950's where she studied at the Slade School of Arts. She became very involved in the experimental film movement and made the highly-rated film 'Together', a story about two deaf-mutes living in the East End of London. This film was included in the Cannes Film Festival. In 1959 she moved back to Rome where she made television programmes for RAI TV. Her book was made into a film in 2000 as 'The Sky Will Fall' and starred Isabella Rossellini and Jeroen Krabbe.

Lorenza's book,'The Sky Falls', came out as a new edition in 2000 and Lorenza wrote the following in her dedication: "*I dedicate this book to my uncle, Robert Einstein, Albert's cousin, my aunt, Nina Einstein Mazzetti, my cousin Anna (Cici) and Luce. Everybody is sleeping in the cemetery of Badiuzza above Florence. On their grave are the words: 'massacred by the Germans August 3, 1944.'*

"*My sister and I lived at the villa from an early age (because our mother had died). We were spared by the SS because our surname was 'Mazzetti' and not 'Einstein'. With our beloved family, we shared the joys of life and received their affection for years but at the moment of death, we were separated from them.*

"*This life was given to me only because I was of another race. All survivors bear the brunt of this privilege and need to testify.*

"My book describes the joy and happiness that this family gave me in my childhood, accepting me as an equal member of the family. I was part of them in joy but separate and different in death.

"They sleep there on the hill and I remember them. If you pass by, leave a flower."

CHAPTER 7

Every aspect of life was profoundly impacted by the political situation and Mussolini's machinations. From a distance of years and changed times it is difficult to understand how it was possible for someone of Il Duce's ilk to gain such over-riding power. It might, therefore, be useful to look at how he came to power and the circumstances surrounding his rise.

The political situation in Italy after World War I was chaotic and Italians were desperate for a leader who would pull them out of the mire. Unfortunately, it was the unscrupulous Mussolini who emerged as the charismatic personality promising such leadership.

In the elections of 1921 he managed to win 35 seats through various alliances. People from all sectors of Italian life saw him as the one person who could secure a resolution to their fears and problems.

Victor Emmanuel II, in his self-interest, was afraid that if he didn't support the Fascists they would depose him and so, in October 1922, he invited Mussolini to Rome to form a ministry, instead of backing his cabinet which had issued a decree banning a Blackshirt march on Rome. This so-called 'march' took place with Mussolini doing nothing more heroic than riding to Rome in a luxury train carriage while his followers did the actual marching.

Mussolini was now in a position to entrench his power through legislation. This he did through the passing of the Acerbo Law, effectively destroying Italy's democracy. In his first nationwide election he won 65% of the vote.

In 1925 Mussolini formalized his dictatorial control through legislation and in 1929 Pope Pius XI reconciled with Mussolini, thus adding to Mussolini's stature, by declaring that Mussolini was something of a saviour to Italy. This reconciliation also brought the long-standing conflict between church and state to a close, again reflecting positively on Mussolini.

Mussolini's government took the form of a so-called 'corporate state' which he claimed was a superior alternative to communism and capitalism. The enormous bureaucracy which he proceeded to create enabled him to spread his tentacles into all sectors of the economy.

His ambition was to make Italy self-sufficient but his manipulation of various sectors, such as agriculture, more often led to collapse than success. Consequently, he spent the early 1930's exploring the possibilities of empire-building as a cover-up for these failures.

Mussolini invaded Ethiopia in October 1935. The League of Nations imposed sanctions and most of Europe refused to acknowledge Italy's 'Ethiopian Empire'. In a pet over this snub, he formed an alliance with Hitler, imagining himself to be the 'elder brother' in the partnership and claiming that Hitler had filched his ideas, such as his Roman salute and appelation, 'Duce'.

In 1936 Mussolini joined Hitler in Spain in support of General Franco in the Spanish Civil War. This three-year entanglement seriously depleted Italian military resources.

In 1939, in a pique because Hitler had not found it necessary to tell him about his invasion of Czechoslovakia, Mussolini invaded Albania.

Hitler attacked Poland and the Second World War was declared in September 1939. By June 1940, Mussolini's obsession with Hitler's stature and his envy of Hitler's successes, as confessed to his son-in-law, Count Galeazzo Ciano, had grown out of control and led to his declaring war on France and Great Britain. He marched against the French (who had already been defeated by Germany) and then launched an African campaign, which was ignominiously defeated by British forces, who were greatly outnumbered by the Italians, under the command of Field Marshal Sir Archibald Wavell. The Italians had to be rescued by the Germans. Following this debacle, Mussolini invaded Greece from Albania, on the 28th of October 1940, and again he and the Italians had to be rescued by Germany in the Balkans.

Germany's growing irritation eventually resulted in Germany occupying Italy itself in early 1943. In June 1943 the Allies landed in Sicily and in July 1943 Victor Emmanuel II had Mussolini arrested and appointed Marshal Badoglio as premier.

In September 1943 Badoglio and his government signed an armistice with the Allies. German troops continued to hold Italy to the north of Naples. German paratroopers rescued Mussolini from the mountain-top where he was being held. He was established as the head of a republican-Fascist government based at Salo in northern Italy.

In October 1944 Italy declared war on Germany. In April 1945 a group of partisans caught Mussolini and his mistress, Clara Petacci, near Lake Como, executed them and hung them, upside down (in the traditional Italian manner of dealing with a fallen hero), near a petrol station in Milan. Incidentally, George, as a captain in the military police and reconnoitring for the South African Sixth Division, was one of the first South Africans to come upon the scene.

In May 1945 Germany surrendered, bringing the war in Europe to a close.

What is utterly astounding about this part of Italy's history is how a tin-pot egomaniac could gain such overwhelming power and then wield that power on a whim to satisfy nothing more than his vanity; that such a man could make completely illogical decisions which would have an inestimable impact on the lives of ordinary people, an impact which would take years, enormous sums of money, and the goodwill and energy of so many more people, to rectify. His destructiveness was akin to that wrought by an uncontrolled brat in a giant toyshop. Most of what Mussolini got up to, and the way he conducted himself, could have come straight out of a comic opera, and makes for very amusing reading, if one can put aside the consequences of his actions in terms of human suffering. Even more devastating is the realisation that Mussolini was a far from isolated case and the world has continued to be assaulted at ever-more regular intervals by such individuals.

*   *   *

Anyway, back to the Van Praags in Florence. Barend continued to take precautions for their safety and they were constantly aware of being kept under surveillance.

Their 'phone was tapped and they developed a code to communicate with friends and to confuse anyone who chose to eavesdrop. This was also a source of entertainment – concocting outlandish, but completely innocent, messages. They would delight in making an invitation to supper sound like the assignation of anarchists.

The apartment was also watched by plain-clothes policemen who were very easy to spot. There were usually two of them on duty at a time and they hung around the entrance to the apartment. Although they weren't in uniform, their hats and coats clearly marked them. This might have provided the Van Praags with satirical amusement about their buffoonish cloak-and-dagger warders but they were all aware of the very real threat that hung over their heads.

Barend was a master in the Freemasons and he knew that he was playing a lethal game. In an article, 'The Annihilation of Freemasonry' by Sven G. Lunden (web.mit.edu) the writer says *"Hitler and Mussolini inaugurated their respective reigns with outrages against Masons and Masonic institutions, and they never relaxed their systematic persecutions."*

Their hatred and obsession stemmed from the belief that Freemasonry was the pawn of an international Jewish conspiracy. In addition to this, although Masonic philosophy was opposed to political involvement, its basic tenets supported freedom of thought and respect for human rights, everything that Fascism sought to undermine. Mussolini banned Freemasonry in Italy in 1925 and followed this up by exiling hundreds of eminent Masons to the Lipari Islands where they endured bitter conditions. Not satisfied with this, he continued his persecutions by having his Blackshirts loot the homes of Masons in various Italian cities, including Florence. At least a hundred of these men were murdered. Juan Gómez-Jurado, in 'The Traitor's Emblem', says the Masons were dragged out of bed in the middle of the night and beaten to death in the streets.

Consequently, Barend knew that if his Masonic paraphernalia were found, he and the family would be in deep trouble. Before leaving Genoa, Barend had decided to get rid of his Masonic medals but he had to do it in such a way that the medals could not be traced back to him. Toly was about to take a train journey and she undertook the disposal of the medals. Whilst on the train, she waited for moments when she was sure nobody was watching her inside the train. She also had to make sure that the area through which the train was travelling was thinly populated. As the train rounded a sharp bend she surreptitiously dropped the medals, one at a time, out of a window on the outward curve of the train. It all seems rather paranoid but such was the suspicious atmosphere that the Fascists had engendered.

The wearing of their pouches, at all times, each containing their Dutch passport, Italian identity document, and a gold coin from the stash he had collected from Holland in 1939, was another of Barend's precautions and one on which he never let up.

Lucia paid a visit to the convent, which was part of the buildings surrounding their garden, to ask the Mother Superior if they could hide in the convent in an emergency. Although the convent was a closed and silent order, the Mother Superior agreed to this arrangement.

Despite these precautions, however, Barend could be reckless and there were certain activities he couldn't resist. He had a collection of transistor radios on which he listened to French and English channels, amongst others, from 7p.m. to 10p.m. every night. He also had a large map on which he plotted the movements of the Allied and Axis forces from his radio gleanings. All this was done in a small room which he used as a study. This was a very dangerous activity which nearly got him into serious trouble, but more of that little debacle later.

Food supply had been under pressure for some time, even before the war, as a result of Mussolini's blundering economic policies. He had gone all-out to make Italy self-sufficient, especially in wheat production. He awarded medals to farmers who increased their wheat production despite the fact that before the war wheat could be imported from America far more cheaply than the

Italians could produce it. Consequently, Italian farmers produced less fruit, vegetables, wine and olive oil.

Italy had traditionally suffered from over-population and this was exacerbated by the US law passed in 1921 which severely limited the number of Italians who could immigrate to America. Mussolini added to the problem by subsidising marriage and encouraging people to have large families.

Rationing came into being. The meat ration was 500g per person per week. Queuing for meat took place on a Saturday and it wasn't unusual to have to stand in a queue for four hours.

Orso and Elena developed a system whereby Orso would keep their place in the queue while Elena flirted outrageously with the butcher in the hope of gaining a little extra. The big prize was lung, for which one did not need ration coupons.

To say that one could not always be sure of what meat one was actually eating, is an understatement. What really bothered them, though, was the increasingly common practice of passing off cat as rabbit. Lucia always made sure that when she bought rabbit it came with head and feet intact. Elena's love of cats made her a prime target for Orso's tormenting miaowing at her if they had rabbit for dinner.

Things became particularly difficult when Barend and Orso were on the run with the partisans and so lost their ration allocation. When they returned to the apartment they did so in secret. Because they were in hiding, they could not reinstate their rations. This meant that the family ration for six was cut to four. In addition, they were hiding a young doctor so the rations had to stretch even further.

Lucia was adept at turning anything into a meal. When split peas were served they were inevitably full of weevils. Barend's glasses would be 'mislaid' for him so that he couldn't see the weevils and consequently complain. Anyone who did complain was met with Orso's stock response that they were lucky to be receiving an extra protein ration for nothing.

They were allowed 200g of bread per person a day. Elena's problem was preventing Orso from stealing her share. She even took to licking her slice to put him off. This had not the slightest effect on him. The only way she could stop him was to clamp her slice of bread between her knees until she was ready to eat it. Barend was also a problem with his bread ration because he insisted on sharing it with the pigeons which got to know him and would arrive on the windowsill of the dining-room to peck at the crumbs he sprinkled there for them.

Barend, too, had few qualms about making use of the black market. He knew where various foodstuffs were available and when and where a good meal could be obtained. Of course, cost was a very limiting factor in making use of these services. He also had a number of farming friends who could supply him with wine and various other goods from time to time.

Once, when the Germans were encamped in their garden, they had 'relieved' some peasants of a number of chickens. Lucia, in strong contrast with her usual attitude towards the Germans, volunteered to slaughter, pluck and dress the chickens. When her daughters overheard her conversation with the Germans they were horrified - and mystified. What they didn't appreciate was what Lucia could do with the giblets, heads and feet. Somewhere she had learnt that if the feet were singed, the hard yellow scaliness just peeled off and there was tasty, fatty tissue beneath. Similarly, she showed the girls how to cut off the beaks and combs so the remainder of the head could be used. The whole conglomeration of left-over bits of chicken created a memorable and delicious chicken soup.

Initially cooking was done on a gas stove with the whole of Florence being supplied with piped gas. However, when the Germans blew up the gas supply system, the Van Praags resorted to the ancient stove in their kitchen. This structure was tiled on the sides and front. The top had three holes over which cooking pots were placed. There were three more openings in the front through which the fires were laid. Coal or wood was laid on a grid through which the ash fell. As coal wasn't available, the girls collected twigs from the Viale Giacomo Matteoti or the park. To start a fire they used an upside-down funnel made of metal called a 'devil'. It was like a mini-chimney with a handle.

This arrangement was very helpful but the problem was that when the air-raid sirens sounded, the fire had to be put out. On one particular day, the fire had to be restarted six times because of the air-raid sirens. No sooner had they got the fire going than the siren would wail and they would have to dash off to the bomb shelter in the garden. The all-clear would go, and back up to the apartment they would tramp, relight the fire, and then the siren would start blaring again, and so the process continued. By the time they were able to eat their meal that day it was ten o'clock in the evening and their nice piece of fish had been thoroughly spoilt.

Their kitchen window was positioned in the interior corner of the block and abutted the window of somebody else's kitchen. The windows were so close it was possible to shake hands with their neighbours. Elena and Toly were making soup one day when they heard two voices commenting on the delicious smell. The voices had the distinctive Genoese inflection and belonged to two young women of about Elena's and Toly's ages who were living in a neighbouring apartment. Their family name was Forti.

When they made proper acquaintance these lasses strongly denied having come from Genoa. Elena and Toly couldn't understand their denial. Only later did their father tell Barend that they were Jewish and had fled Genoa to go into hiding in Florence. Their flight had largely been precipitated by an Italian woman in Genoa who was paid by the Germans to identify Jews. Their father had owned a large and well-known jewellery shop in Genoa which they had had to abandon.

When Agnese last visited Elena she shed some light on the experiences of Jews in Genoa after the Van Praags had left the city. Immediately below their apartment in Genoa was a large synagogue situated in a cul-de-sac. This was the site of the first 'retata' or 'netting' to take place in Genoa.

The SS paid a visit to the chief Rabbi and demanded the register of all Jews living in Genoa. When he tried to resist their demand they stripped his wife naked and beat her in front of him. They also threatened to kill all the children in the infant class. The congregants were 'phoned and told to come to a meeting the following day to hear a communication from their Rabbi. The meeting was scheduled for the following afternoon, the 2nd of November 1943 at 5 o'clock. A caretaker of a building at the entrance to the lane leading to the synagogue valiantly tried to warn these people as they flocked towards the building. He had little success in turning them away but drew enough attention to himself to be rounded up with the people he was trying to save.

Two hundred and thirty eight people were rounded up that afternoon and sent to a concentration camp. Only ten returned after the war.

The concentration camp to which they were sent was at Fossoli, near Bologna. From there the prisoners were dispatched to Poland. As prisoners were being loaded on to a train destined for Fossoli, one couple managed to pass their baby out through a window to an Italian woman on the platform. They begged her to take the infant to its grandmother, Letizia Servadio. They never returned.

Letizia's daughter-in-law, the mother of the baby, had a brother who was a renowned psychologist and a friend of Agnese's husband. He and Agnese's husband had escaped from Hungary in the 1920's when the persecution of Jews in Hungary had already begun. They had been lured to Italy by Mussolini's promises of free medical training. Agnese's mother-in-law, Ella Krausz, had remained in Hungary.

Ella was a widow and owned a general dealer store which she ran with her daughter and son-in-law. This couple managed to go into hiding in Budapest and entrusted their two little children to the care of the children's other grandmother who lived in a tiny Hungarian village.

Ella and her sister, Rosa, were rounded up and sent to Auschwitz where they were both gassed.

To add to the horror, after the war, Agnese and her husband received a detailed list, kept by the Nazis, of every item which had been in the old lady's possession when she entered Auschwitz, including her gold teeth, shoes, underwear and jewellery. This list was sent to them by the German government in order for the family of the victims to claim compensation. The callousness of such bureaucracy is terrifying in its inhumanity. The Krauszes claimed the money and donated it to charity.

Agnese had a school friend called Lucana Sacerdote. She and her family had earlier made their way over the Alps to Switzerland where they were turned back by the Swiss authorities at the border because the quota for that period had already been filled.

Lucana's family consisted of her father, Claudio, her mother, Ernestine (née Borgetti), her sister, Laura, who later died on a forced march to Ravensbrück, the notorious women's concentration camp in northern Germany, her maternal grandmother, Faustina Artom, and her sister, Vittorina Artom. Their party also included Lucana's fiancé, Mario Fubini, who was an interpreter. Mario was also later captured and incarcerated in a concentration camp from which he managed to escape but was shot after his escape. Mario's mother, Enrietta Rimini, too, was a member of their group in their failed bid to escape Italy into Switzerland.

Lucana and her family were part of the crowd who were rounded up on that fateful afternoon at the synagogue. Lucana was one of the ten survivors who returned to Genoa. She had lost every member of her family. She might have survived Auschwitz, but she never ceased to suffer from terrible depression and would weep uncontrollably. Her comment to Agnese was, "Who must we thank for all this?"

Another school friend of Agnese's and Elena's was Dora Salmori who was also caught up in the retata at the synagogue. Dora was pregnant when she was imprisoned at Fossoli. When the Allies bombed Fossoli, she was hit in the abdomen by shrapnel. The Italians operated and she survived but lost her baby. She, too, died in Auschwitz.

The Van Praag children had three favoured relatives whom they regarded as aunts. They were, in fact, Barend's cousins, the offspring of two of Barend's father's siblings. The last time the family saw them before the war was in 1937 when they paid a visit to Holland. Tante Sally never married. She survived the war by going into hiding with a Christian family. When this family was raided, they hid Sally in a kist in their sitting-room. The German officer in charge sat on the kist for two hours while his men ransacked the house.

Tante Elena (called Lena) and Tante Rosa were sisters. Rosa had been engaged to a medical student. He nicked his finger whilst performing an autopsy, contracted blood-poisoning and died. Lena's husband died of throat cancer in 1938. Lena and her husband were very wealthy and Lena was very generous: she delighted in taking her Van Praag 'nieces' shopping.

Lena and Rosa were both captured and sent to Auschwitz. Because of their age they were of no use to the Germans and were immediately dispatched to the gas chambers. It is their deaths that still cause Elena the greatest anguish. Elena harbours little bitterness but she is haunted by the mental picture of these two gentle, gracious old ladies being stripped of their clothing, their dignity and their lives in the diabolical Auschwitz.

Lucia's family, too, did not remain unscathed by the German persecution of the Jews in Holland. One of Lucia's brothers had been born deaf. Although he could use sign language, he was also mute. He got caught up in a situation in the street one day when the Germans were stopping people and checking their identities. They were lining the Jews up against a wall. Because he didn't hear the order to stop, he carried on walking, to the intense irritation of the Germans. They grabbed him and held him captive while they continued their search. When they had ten Jews lined up, they opened fire on them. He was forced to watch as his punishment for not obeying their orders. He suffered a total mental breakdown from which he took years to recover.

*   *   *

As the friendship grew with the Jewish family in Gherardesca, the Van Praag girls became aware that these girls only ever appeared in a couple of winter dresses. They had nothing else as they had fled with no luggage. Toly and Elena each had two cotton dresses for home use. They both gave one of their dresses to the sisters which meant that on washdays they only had their petticoats to wear.

Barend also made a habit of giving away his clothing. He had a very fine, pre-war, tailor-made coat which he went out in one day and returned without. Lucia wasn't very pleased with him but he had given it to an under-dressed, shivering man in the street, on the grounds that he, Barend, had a jersey and didn't need a coat.

Shoes were a great problem to replace because they took so many coupons. Orso devised some novel footwear. He made the soles of his sandals out of bicycle tyres and the upper straps out of leather belts. These he supplied to his family and friends.

By the end of the war they had very little clothing left. Elena finished the war with only three pairs of precious knickers.

The relationship with the Genoese family wasn't all about clothing and food. There was a brother, nicknamed 'Don Antonio' (Elena can't remember his proper name) who was a comic actor and had often taken the junior lead in a well-known comedy writer's plays in Genoa. Don Antonio's gift for comedy, together with his antics and his wonderful repertoire of jokes, often kept them laughing between rounds of bombing when they were in the bomb shelter.

Don Antonio and Toly shared a brief romance which resulted in an engagement. He presented Toly with a beautiful diamond and ruby ring. It was too big for her and when it slipped off her finger she decided that was a sign of bad luck and broke the engagement. Neither party seems to have been unduly upset.

Another form of entertainment was afternoon dances. One of the residents was a young woman who had windows which opened directly on to the garden and she used to host the dances. The windows had burglar bars but one bar had been sawn through and her guests used this route for quick entries and exits, especially as the German presence began to make it more and more dangerous to be in the streets. The Van Praags gained easy access to the garden via a ladder from their balcony. The primary purpose of this ladder, though, was to provide an escape route should the apartment be raided from the street, and was particularly necessary for the safety of

Orso and the Italian doctor who was hiding with them. If the two young men had been caught, they would have been drafted into the Italian army immediately.

The girls treated these afternoons as special occasions and would titivate themselves and dress up as best they could. Then they would negotiate the ladder into the garden from where they clambered through their hostess's window. Not very dignified, but part of the clandestine fun. And then they would twirl away the afternoon to the tunes of the gramophone. The only male partners available were Orso and Don Antonio, and later the Italian doctor, but this was no obstacle to the girls who partnered each other. The dancing was a welcome relief from the stresses and intense boredom of their confined existence.

Barend had a stream of friends who called regularly and also helped to pass time cheerfully.

One of their regular visitors was Frai Jacobson. He was a small Jewish man who had also lived in Holland. He came for coffee after lunch every day. The Van Praags seem to have had a lot of fun with Frai. Elena's daily greeting for him was a 'Heil Hitler' salute. Lucia was uncomfortable with this and told her not to do it in case it offended him. On the contrary, he forebore the change for a couple of days, having his coffee as usual, but being a little subdued. Eventually he couldn't bear it any longer and demanded to know what he had done to upset them. 'Heil Hitler' was reinstated immediately.

Orso and he had identical caps but Orso had a bigger head. Orso took great delight in swapping the caps and found much entertainment in watching Frai trying to deal with the cap falling over his eyes. It took him some time to twig the joke that had been played on him.

The family legend was that his wife, who had been born in Germany, had married him for his money. The two were constantly embroiled in dreadful fights. (Perhaps that's why he had to escape for coffee every day.) Their only child, a son called Mercello, used to call their fights 'trompettere'. Evidently they only remained together for Mercello's sake. Agnese remembers accompanying Lucia to call on the Jacobsons once when they were sitting shiva. When Mr Jacobson answered the door he was wearing torn clothes, a part of the mourning process with which Agnese wasn't familiar. She was convinced that the row had become so violent that Mrs Jacobson had attacked Frai and torn his clothes.

As conditions grew worse in Italy, Frai decided it would be safer to send his son back to Holland where he would have been drafted into the Dutch army to serve largely in the Dutch East Indies. He discussed this with Barend who strongly opposed the idea because he felt that it was very important to keep one's family together at all costs.

Mercello did return to Holland where he was captured by the Germans and incarcerated in a German concentration camp. (Elena thinks Auschwitz). He survived the war but on the repatriation train after the war, he died.

Another valued and regular visitor was the artist Davidino Bueno de Mesquita. His origins were also Dutch. He had come to Italy as a young man when he received an award from the Dutch queen to study art in Italy for three years. Davidino sketched constantly and while he was visiting, he spent his time sketching the family. Elena has some charming studies in pencil of the family members going about their daily business.

Davidino was a very sensitive little man who never married. He couldn't bear to hurt anything. On one occasion he scooped up some ants in his studio and released them outside but was horrified at himself when he realized that he had put them in the snow and their feet would get frozen. When he caught a rat in a trap he kept it warm until he could release it in a park.

He was arrested by two Fascists but when he started to weep they couldn't deal with him and so let him go. He was so upset by this incident that he went into hiding and for some time the family had no contact with him. When he returned, he told Barend that he was penniless but did have some valueless share certificates. When Barend went through his papers, he discovered that the shares were very valuable and he was far from penniless.

He was equally hopeless at housekeeping and his studio was such a mess that Agnese took it upon herself to give it a thorough cleaning and tidying once a month.

In addition to keeping themselves busy with the basic business of surviving, being entertained by their visitors, and fulfilling various other obligations, there was always romance.

Toly seems to have had a string of flirtations but the great love of her youth was the Italian submariner, Rafael Pollidori, whom she'd met in Genoa. This romance survived the move to Florence but couldn't survive his fall from grace with the family when it became clear that his political loyalties were definitely Fascist. Although Toly had been forbidden to have anything more to do with him, his memory seems to have clung for some time. Perhaps this explains her rather flippant attitude to the boyfriends who succeeded Rafael.

There was certainly no shortage of male attention for Elena either. She, too, didn't take these romances seriously, but not because of romantic disillusionment or disappointment: she just didn't seem to take anything too seriously at this point in her life. She did, however, have a close friendship with Brusi Marchesi, affectionately referred to as Bruno. He seems to have had more romantic leanings towards her than she to him.

In his latter years Bruno wrote his memoirs which he called 'From the Memories of the Left Side of my Brain'. Many years later a copy of this (with a pink cover) was given to Agnese, for Elena, by his mother. He referred to Elena as "The Beautiful Prey of the War" which would suggest that his intentions were more serious than hers.

Bruno was a competent artist but was being educated as an accountant in preparation for working in his father's fabric factory. His book describes his initial meeting with Toly at university in Florence, and his subsequent meeting with Elena. Perhaps he has to be allowed a certain artistic licence in his romantic embellishments. What follows is Bruno's version of events.

CHAPTER 8

The Pink Book

Bruno begins by describing a beautiful late summer's day at the end of October 1940 when he was cycling to lectures and decided to stop off to view the Arno.

Italy had just invaded Greece from Albania and he saw people gathering at the statue of Garibaldi. The fire brigade was removing a doughnut-shaped bread roll, which resembled a chain of office, from Garibaldi's neck. The crowd was watching silently and the police were trying to disperse people. Someone told him that the message on the doughnut read: "You, who were a great Italian hero, tried to taste the bread of empire", perhaps as a warning to Mussolini that his ambitions to create an empire were doomed if even Garibaldi couldn't succeed in empire-building. This tickled Bruno and reminded him of a graffito comment he had seen written on the King's statue: "When I was King, I drank coffee. Now that I'm Emperor, only the smell is left", inspired by the invasion of Albania in 1939.

On the same day, when he got to class, he opened his desk and found a beautifully colour-illustrated magazine. On a double page was a picture of Rotterdam, completely blitzed by Luftwaffe Stukas on the infamous 14th of May 1940.

The streets had been cleared of rubble and where the houses had stood there was now only green grass. The bricks had been gathered by the citizens and piled in neat stacks. The imposing museum door which, astoundingly, had survived intact, was propped against the bricks. The caption read: "That was the place of tulips". This inspired Bruno to begin singing 'The Tulips

Talk about Love' and was flattered to notice a very attractive girl listening to him. She spoke Italian with the rising Genoese inflection and she told him that she couldn't share his song because under the bricks was the house where she had lived.

This, of course, was Toly, and Bruno goes on to describe her as having a pale and delicate face crowned by red plaits. Her white collar, according to Bruno, gave light to her face. Her dress was a dark prune colour and her lips were red and well-shaped. He says her look was austere and severe, that of a direttrice or school principal, the whole effect making her look as though she had just stepped out of a Frans Hals painting. Go, Bruno!

Elena's take on her sister's looks is slightly more prosaic. She says Toly's hair was a deep, dark red which was very striking, and although she was very pretty, she was not beautiful. She had an enviable figure with wonderful legs and an admirable bust. Her austerity was the result of not smiling much because she didn't like the appearance of her front teeth.

Bruno goes on to say that he was already aware that she was 'an enemy of the state', or a civilian internee, and had thought that she came from Genoa, of course not knowing that she had been born in Rotterdam and that her loyalties were Dutch. He apologised for his mistake to which Toly replied: "We Hollanders are very attached to our land, perhaps because we had to work so hard to claim it from the sea."

Toly and Bruno formed a steady friendship and worked together on their studies and theses. He credits Toly with teaching him how to extract the essentials from any material he had to study.

It was when he went to see a Greta Garbo film and bumped into Toly, that he met Elena, who was with her. Perhaps his artist's eye was his excuse but again he is rapturous about hair colour. He describes Elena's "golden-corn hair" which she says was strawberry-blonde.

On the 6th of December of that year, he was invited to the family's St Nicholas party and met the rest of the family for the first time.

He was struck by the differences in the style of furnishings in their apartment, being used to Italian homes in which every nook and cranny was filled. He recalled Barend and Orso having a passion for cigarettes and smoking very heavily. He was also impressed by the vast amount of food, despite rationing.

St Nicholas was dressed like a Spanish bishop and was accompanied by a blackened servant, called Black Piet, who carried chunks of coal in one bag and sweets in another. The tradition was that if one had been good during the year, one received a sweet or piece of cake, but a lump of coal if one had been bad.

In the midst of the festivities Bruno found himself sitting near a German-Jewish woman who was eating as many biscuits as she could cram into her mouth. She was also surreptitiously filling her handbag. This personage was a relative of Albert Einstein and was notorious for her eating habits. He was very relieved to be rescued by Elena who told him she would take him away to save him from being eaten by the old lady when she had finished the biscuits.

They escaped to her bedroom but propriety was maintained because the room was arranged more as a sitting-room than a bedroom. He was taken with a small, glass-paned and gabled cupboard in Dutch style which had probably been made as a prototype of a cabinet-maker's larger piece.

The cupboard had been given to Barend by an aunt and later caused much unhappiness when Toly removed it from the wall to bring it to South Africa, along with the Chinese vases. She yanked it off the wall, without having asked for permission, and damaged the plaster behind it. Agnese was furious about the whole episode and actually slapped Toly.

Agnese's reaction, in itself, was momentous because, as children, they had never indulged in fisticuffs with one another. Neither had they even squabbled. When Toly happened to come across Elena, as a twelve-year-old, in the midst of a street brawl with three boys who had knocked off her hat, she was horrified. She dragged Elena away, telling her that she was a disgrace to the family name.

George thereafter called the cupboard the 'rusiekassie' or 'quarrel cupboard'. It still hangs in Elena's sitting-room.

Bruno spotted the photograph of the submarine and its officers and was told about the French perfumes which were kept in the cupboard.

Bruno claims that by the following month he was desperate to tell Elena that he loved her but the only time he saw her was when he came to the apartment to study with Toly. Evidently Elena also side-stepped all his manoeuvres by saying that he had to concentrate on his exams.

When they graduated (Toly, cum laude), he took Toly and Elena to lunch at Fiesole. He couldn't understand why they were so tense. They hadn't told him that they weren't allowed beyond the boundaries of Florence without official permission and, had they been caught, they would have been arrested.

For him, the outing was a disappointment: he had obviously put much thought into it and had chosen Fiesole based on a romantic notion because he and Elena had often walked as far along the road to Fiesole as was permitted. Elena has a painting Bruno did of a stretch of this road with its typically Tuscan poplars and stone walls. She also has photographs of the luncheon occasion which certainly don't indicate that it was a failure. There were a number of young people present, enjoying an alfresco meal under an awning. They all look rather glamorous in their best outfits and hats and there appears to be much laughter. The party also seems to have warmed up later and the formality suggested by their clothing apparently dissolved when they opened the champagne and found a friendly donkey. Elena is at the centre of a picture engaged in an intimate conversation with the donkey.

Bruno claimed that the family approved of the relationship. (Elena says he thought this because they trusted him as he was such a gentleman and they, therefore, didn't stick as rigidly to their chaperoning rules as they might have done.) He also claimed that at his wedding Lucia whispered in his ear that the bride should have been Elena. (Elena says he definitely imagined that!)

After graduating he waited to be called up for his national service. Before leaving he wanted to take Elena out to mark the occasion but by then the only items available on restaurant menus which didn't require rationing coupons, were made of chestnuts. Their choice ranged from a slice of chestnut pudding to dried chestnuts, called patona, which were very hard.

His call-up date was the 5th of December 1941 and he was sent to Sterzing, on the road to the Brenner Pass, to do a sergeant's course. They wrote to each other but both sets of letters were so heavily censored they were usually indecipherable. Elena returned a six-page letter to him in which only the salutation, "My dear love", and the ending, "Tuo, Bruno", were readable. Even the crosses under his name had been blacked out. Thereafter he communicated in cartoons.

In May 1943 he was sent to Avellino to do an officer's training course and fell seriously ill. He was transferred to the military hospital in Naples. He didn't want to tell his mother of his condition in a letter, so sent a note to Elena who took the message to his mother. Bruno was gratified to hear that they had wept together. He doesn't say what was ailing him but does recall that he was cured by an obstetrics doctor!

He returned to Florence on the 8th of September 1943 to await posting to Vincenze. By then the Allies had landed and had begun their push northwards from Ancio Anatuno. He and Elena went for a walk and when they returned there was general family chat about the end of the war. When he got home afterwards he heard the radio broadcast announcing that Italy had surrendered to the Allies. This, however, only signalled life becoming even more complicated and difficult.

On the day that he was supposed to leave Florence to return to his regiment at Vincenze he missed his train because he had been dallying with Elena. This was extremely fortunate because the Italian soldiers on this train were rounded up by the Germans and taken to Germany.

Some time later, when he was able to return to Florence, he found that the Van Praag apartment had been bombed. Everything was boarded up and they all seemed to have been spirited away.

He discovered that Lucia and the girls had been evacuated to Dutch friends who owned a villa en route to Fiesole. Barend and Orso had also gone into hiding with their priest friend.

Bruno, too, decided to lie low for a time because the Germans and Fascists were making more determined efforts to round up able-bodied young men and send them to Germany as forced labour. They would close off the streets and surrounding buildings, trapping everybody in the vicinity. The captured men would then be forced on to trucks and taken away. This process was called '*raking*' or 'rastrellamenti' and the warning cry used by the citizenry was "Lupo!" (*Wolf*).

Initially Bruno escaped to the Appenines and remembered that winter for the fear created by the bombing and the appalling hunger he endured. Later he returned to Florence to avoid being cut off from the Allies when they arrived in Florence. He hid in the cellar of his parents' house where there was no gas supply and an ever-decreasing bread supply. For months there was also no 'phone connection to his home.

On the last day of June 1944, while the families of privileged, high-ranking Fascists were going north in German trucks full of looted goods, the 'phone suddenly rang. It was Elena, wishing Bruno a happy birthday! (Orso's ingenious father-in-law had made the connection for her – he who had had the central telephone exchange up and running a mere two hours after the Germans had blown up the exchange, along with all services, in March/April 1944 to prevent the Allies finding anything useful.) This 'phone call gave Bruno much hope and also told him where Elena was. (By then they had returned from the villa where they had taken refuge after their apartment was bombed, and were living in an apartment in Borgo Pinti around the corner from their old apartment but still in the same complex.)

He remained hidden for two more months, suffering intense hunger and thirst as there was no water in the old town because the Germans had also destroyed the water and electricity supply. (The occupants of Gherardesca were more fortunate because there was a borehole/well and hand-pump in the garden. However, there was such demand on this borehole that the women had to queue for hours to fill a brandy bottle with water while the men pumped. This was enough to clean teeth, sponge vital parts and wash underwear sparingly.)

By the 20th of August 1944 the remaining Germans were moving up to the Gothic Line (which stretched for 320 kilometres across Italy from Pesaro on the Adriatic to Massa Carrara on the Tyrrhenian Sea) and Bruno decided that it was safe to begin moving about more freely. He became increasingly anxious to check on Elena and her family and went to look for them on the 6th of December, perhaps spurred on by memories of their St Nicholas party when he had first got to know them.

On arriving at their old home, he found the door to the apartment open, but the apartment empty. Then he spotted a note on the doorpost saying that they had moved into an apartment around the corner because of the damage to their first home.

When he reached the new apartment, the door was also open. He ran up the stairs and found himself in the midst of a huge and raucous party. The Dutch flag had been hoisted and the sitting-room was overflowing with Allied officers from various branches of the forces and, touchingly, he recognized some of the friends and guests from the St Nicholas party of four years previously. There were also some notable absentees, including the Einsteins. A few Dutch friends were present but the rest, he discovered, had already returned to Holland. As he walked in, the realization hit him for the first time that the war was really over and Florentines were free to admire the victorious troops.

There was Toly distributing dolci (NAAFI cookies) and when he finally spotted Elena, she was surrounded by "splendid, mustachioed, khaki-clad figures" and was "luminous" with all the attention being bestowed upon her. He describes her as "Regina de la Festa" or the "*Queen of the Festival*". Bruno noticed that she seemed to be particularly taken with a strong-looking, khaki-clad man sporting a carrot-coloured moustache (George, of course) and suddenly the tea lost its pleasant flavour.

Lucia took his hand in hers as he stood in the corner and proceeded to fill him in on the terrible events of the last year. Barend and Orso had spent the year in hiding with a Catholic priest. A farmer had delivered a message from the priest that they were all right. In September of 1943 their apartment had been bombed and Lucia and the girls had been taken in by the Dutch artist, Wijnand Otto Jan van Nieuwenkamp, and his wife.

Wijnand, born in Amsterdam in 1876, owned the villa Il Riposo dei Vescovi (*'Bishops' Rest'*), a national heritage. This enormous villa and garden had been used as a halfway house or resting place for the church elite when they journeyed between Florence and Fiesole in the sixteenth century. The fountain from which they revived themselves can still be seen in the grounds. Wijnand had bought the property in 1926 and renamed it Villa Nieuwenkamp, but it goes by both names.

According to the Villa Nieuwenkamp website, the villa was built on top of a farm building which was owned by the Abbey at Fiesole. It remained a humble dwelling until the 19th century when it was transformed into a much more majestic habitation. During this gracious period it hosted many grandees and notables including Henry James who wrote a wonderfully evocative description of Florence viewed from Il Riposo.

When Wijnand bought the property it had been sorely neglected. He poured his heart and soul into the restoration of the villa and the grounds. The website states: *"The five-hectare garden is divided by a 230-metre-long avenue lined with cypress trees, and is on several different levels organized as a series of terraces edged with box hedges, cypress trees and laurels connected by stone steps that follow the contours of the slope. At the point where the avenue leading off from the villa is crossed by side paths, stand various stone elements. Firstly two female busts, followed by a fountain on several levels and then an elliptical glade ringed by cypresses and edged with circular seating; a fountain, positioned against the boundary wall, forms the backdrop to the end of the walk. Nieuwenkamp decorated the park with statues, busts and archaeological finds."* (Another source refers to a Solomonic column.) *"These include a bronze gong at the side of the building, a statue of Buddha, next to which is the artist's own tomb, and large conches and jars made of Impruneta terracotta that adorn the wall around the tennis court. Nieuwenkamp wrote two whole books about his villa and all the changes and additions he made both inside the house and out in the garden, work that he illustrated in great detail by more than a hundred superb drawings."*

Wijnand died in 1950 so when the Van Praags stayed at the villa much of this work was already in place, including the very big pool at the rear, or northern side, of the house. This pool is right up against the house outside the large salon from where it can be viewed from the full-length windows of the salon. It looks very glamorous and enticing.

He must have been a man of enormous energy, determination and resourcefulness as some of these installations are huge. The gong, for instance, stands considerably higher than a tall man.

Wijnand specialised in porcelain base-relief and had done a large work in Holland which covered an entire wall, a copy of which was in the villa. It depicted coffee picking in Indonesia where he had spent a great deal of time. The family legend was that this was because he needed to escape there for periods of up to two years every time his wife had a new baby! His nickname was the 'Wanderer'. Back in Holland he had also spent much time on a river boat.

His Indonesian existence was commemorated in the villa in the magnificent carved doors which he had installed. Bali was where he spent most of his time in Indonesia and according to an article by Georges Breguet, he was the first European artist to take an interest in traditional Balinese painting. He wrote what Mr Breguet refers to as *"the most important early book on the island Bali en Lombok (sic) (1906-1910), which included pioneering ethnographic and archaeological studies."* Wijnand had not received any formal training and was self-taught.

The Nieuwenkamps had two daughters, one of whom was also married to an artist who did woodcuts. After the Germans had fled, this poor man climbed a fig tree in the villa garden to pick a fig. The tree had been booby-trapped and as he reached for the fig, his hand was blown off.

There was no difficulty in finding space for the Van Praags and their possessions in the Villa as some of the rooms were so large that a single room could accommodate their entire Florentine apartment. The room they were allocated was 165 square metres. They were paying guests and also shared their rations. There were a number of other guests, including a brilliant and highly-strung American concert pianist who had found herself stranded when war was declared. When the bombing was bad she played the piano as loudly and dramatically as she could, in an attempt to drown out the thunder of the bombardment.

Their host, Wijnand, too, had a noisy eccentricity. This was an inclination to fart after dinner. This charming habit was given greater emphasis by the drumming of his fingers on the furniture and la-la-la-ing loudly to cover the sound. The smell, however, could not be disguised in any way. The girls found this highly entertaining and had some trouble controlling their giggles. Lucia would silence them with a stern look.

*   *   *

Back to the party celebrating the departure of the Germans: when Bruno finally got to talking to Elena, they discussed the future – that the Old World was finished and that reconstruction was going to be very difficult. He claims that Elena asked what was going to happen to them personally and he replied in the words of a popular ballad that "nothing good was going to happen" as his own prospects for the future were modest and Elena was going to start a rich new life in a "land of gold".

He told Elena that she had saved his life whilst he had been in hiding on the Italian-Swiss frontier. Starving and tormented by lice and cold, he had felt that he was losing his mind and simply wanted to die. It was the memories of Elena and the letters she had written to him while he was in the army that had kept him going. (Elena says that they never even exchanged a kiss and he had certainly never told her that he loved her. The letters, too, were concocted by Elena with much help from Toly when she ran out of inspiration. She would sit outside the toilet door writing whatever Toly was inspired to tell her to write whilst Toly was occupied inside the toilet. Many such letters were composed to a number of young men away fighting.)

After the war Bruno resumed his career as an accountant and took over his father's fabric factory. In 'The Pink Book', in true accountant fashion, Bruno tells us that he had done some calculations regarding his future and concluded that "it would have taken ten years to start a family". Precisely what he meant and who, or what, the "it" referred to, we don't know. However, he did marry in 1953 and had two sons.

At the party, Bruno realized that his chances were up and graciously gave Elena his blessing. Later, he brought her a gift of very fine, blue woollen fabric to be used for her wedding dress. He was very proud of the fact that the original wool had come from the Cape. Dear Bruno really was a gentleman.

In the tailpiece to 'The Pink Book' he says that a friend to whom he had told his wartime story, asked what news he had had of Elena. He said that for some time he had been able to keep up with her news but when Elena's parents died all contact was lost until years later when he bumped into Agnese.

He was in a hospital in Florence for an operation and heard the name 'Van Praag'. He asked the receptionist where the person of that name was and she pointed Agnese out to him. (She had resumed her maiden name after her second husband died.)

Agnese assured him that there were diamonds and gold in South Africa, but 4000 metres underground, and that one had to check under the beds for snakes (not entirely a fabrication because Toly had found a green mamba hanging over her baby's cot at Palmleigh-on-Sea while she was staying with Elena when her husband was away in Northern Rhodesia).

Bruno notes that the friend asked whether his feelings for Elena weren't just infatuation. Bruno denies this on the grounds that one couldn't retain those feelings after going through the pain and suffering he had experienced, if they weren't feelings of real love. The friend also asked if she was really as beautiful as Bruno claimed. Bruno showed him a photograph, telling him to look for himself and asking him if the pain hadn't been worth it.

He concludes 'The Pink Book' with a delightfully 'Brunoesque' touch: he has a pocket arrangement at the back of the book and he writes above it: "Dear Reader, pull out this slip of paper (a picture of Elena framed in a tyre – greatly valued in war time) and you can judge for yourself."

Elena saw Bruno again on a visit to Florence in 2001. She was staying with Agnese at the Palazzo della Gherardesca in their old apartment which Agnese had continued to occupy. (As part of post-war Italian legislation, no tenant could be evicted from any apartment they had occupied during the war.) He seemed a little vague and had managed to get himself lost in his own city on his way to see her. It was then that he told her that she had saved his life during the war. When he died in 2005, his wife 'phoned Agnese to give her the news.

CHAPTER 9

As far as food was concerned during the war, the Van Praags also managed to eke out their rations with supplies that Barend had saved from his shipping days. They had tinned food consisting of vegetables, a bully-beef type meat, and 'galette', or '*dog biscuits*', which the sailors had used instead of freshly-baked bread. The tinned food and biscuits tasted increasingly delicious as the war went on and eventually became treats.

Barend also discovered a trattoria established by a partisan who operated under the guise of being a Fascist. During the week the fare was quite mundane and in keeping with official food restrictions. However, Sundays were a different matter altogether. The owner used the black market to keep his restaurant supplied with very good, but very expensive, food which included wonderful steaks and hearty helpings of pasta. This quisine only made its appearance on the Sabbath.

The trattoria was housed in a warehouse/factory-like building and was furnished with benches and long tables. The open kitchen was at one end and on Sundays the chef/owner kept up a running dialogue with his patrons, often holding up the steak for inspection and approval before cooking it.

Barend would escort his family there when he felt they needed a pick-me-up in mood and nutrition. They regularly had their main meal there, which must have cost Barend a fortune, especially on Sundays.

On a Sunday, when the trattoria was supposed to be closed, they would knock on the roll-up garage door and then stamp about impatiently and nervously, trying to look innocuous, until someone responded to the knock. They would then have to identify themselves before the door would be raised to allow them in. It was all very cloak-and-dagger and sociable.

On one occasion, Elena declared that she couldn't finish her plate of pasta. A good-looking young man with gorgeous eyes, who was also a regular customer, told her that he would like to marry her because she would be so cheap to keep. Elena was never particularly bothered by a lack of food. Toly, however, always knew where the best restaurants were, and in better times, knew exactly what each restaurant had on its menu.

The same young man popped back into their lives at a most opportune moment. Elena and Toly were walking down a street one day when a street battle broke out between the Fascists and the partisans. They were well aware of the dangers of being caught in the streets in the midst of a 'rastrellamenta' or more domestic political difference of opinion such as this one, but some urgent errand had had to be run.

There was nowhere for them to seek shelter from the bullets that were raking the street. The pasta man happened to be there and he grabbed them both and pushed them towards a doorway. Once safely inside, they all lay low. He would peer out every now and then. Eventually he declared that the coast was clear and they went on their merry ways.

On another occasion, Toly had gone out to buy bread when she was caught in a rastrellamenta. When the warning cry, "Lupo! Lupo!" went up, Toly suddenly found a baby thrust into her arms. A desperate father had done this, thinking the baby would be safer with a woman and enabling him to escape more easily. Toly had no alternative but to take the baby home. The father arrived later to fetch his child but one wonders what would have happened had he been captured. Elena says they would, no doubt, have kept the baby.

Allied bombing had been taking place for quite some time and was initially focused on disrupting the work of the factories on the outskirts of Florence. These factories, largely paper and fabric factories, had been taken over by the Germans. (Perhaps this was why Bruno felt that his future was so uncertain as his father's factory was one of these.) The procedure was to drop little parachutes to which strong orange lights were attached and which lit up the whole area. This would be followed by a bomb, and then twenty minutes later by another bomb in a different sector. This bombardment could go on for four or five hours at a time. The objective was to destroy factory routine and disrupt the sleep patterns of workers to make them less productive. It was this routine which the girls found such a nuisance when they were trying to cook on their ancient and temperamental stove and their efforts kept being interrupted by the air-raid sirens.

The Americans began bombing in January 1943 and their primary target was the railway-yard which lay not a kilometre away from Gherardesca. This was a particularly important station as Florence was situated on the main line connecting northern and southern Italy and was also the junction of a line coming from the west. The Americans flew very high, in formation, and used carpet bombing in their attempts at destroying the railway-yard. They made a terrifying noise and their aim was atrocious: not one of their bombs landed on the yard. It was a different kettle of fish when the British and South Africans took over the task. They flew much lower, dropped their bombs and scarpered. Their aim was perfect: no target was missed and the whole station was destroyed.

When the bombing in their vicinity was bad, they would stay with Orso's future family in the centre of Florence. Here they were afforded extra protection by sleeping in the passage. The passage was lined with end-to-end mattresses and the arrangement generally meant a festive occasion for the young people. Every trip to the loo was an opportunity for horseplay because they had to climb over each other to get to the toilet.

Early in 1943, with the Germans' occupation of Florence and the Fascists' increase in rastrellamenti (which had driven Bruno into hiding), plus information that the Fascists were targeting the Van Praags, Barend, who was 62 and had already suffered a heart attack, and Orso decided it would also be wise to go into hiding.

The Bussellis (their wine-farming friends in Radda in the district of Chianti) helped to organise this and made arrangements for them to lodge with a peasant family. However, this didn't last long because Barend's fastidiousness was severely offended when he found his peasant hosts boiling their undergarments in the same pot they used for cooking. It didn't help matters that the washing of the underclothes only took place once a month – and that wasn't because they possessed an abundance of underclothing which would have sufficed for regular changes!

Father and son moved to a parish in Sansepolcro where the priest, Don Gino Saragoni, took them in.

Barend adopted the operatic name of 'Nabucodonozo' and Orso became 'Luigi'. Barend took over the bookkeeping for the parish. The peasants were in the habit of tearing lire notes in half and placing a half-note in the collection plate on a Sunday. It was Barend's job to pair up the halves and stick them together when the second half arrived on the following Sunday. Orso became an altar boy!

Barend and Orso were very aware of the danger their presence posed for the priest. The priest in a neighbouring parish had been found with weapons for the partisans hidden beneath the altar and he was summarily shot.

Don Gino became a close friend and after the war spent his annual holiday with the family for years.

Barend, Orso and Don Gino were also constantly aware of the possible presence of spies as the partisans often lodged Allied soldiers with willing priests until they could organise their escape. Of course, the Germans knew this and tried to infiltrate spies into the residences of priests. At supper one night Barend became disturbed by a so-called British officer whose English, he thought, had a hint of a German accent. He told Orso to fetch a kitchen knife to dispatch him. Elena can't imagine how the gentle Orso would have managed to do that. Fortunately, the officer heard them talking to each other in Dutch and revealed that he was a South African. They told him how close he'd come to having his throat slit.

Their stay with Don Gino came to an abrupt end when they were arrested by the local carabinieri who accused them of being British paratrooper spies! A more unlikely pair of paratroopers one could hardly wish to find.

They were forced to take a long march in the snow to the nearest village. The ever-resourceful and imaginative Barend told Orso that he would fake a heart-attack and they would take whatever opportunities this diversion provided. Barend's previous experience of a heart-attack enabled him to put on a convincing show. He collapsed in the snow and lay there gasping and clutching his arm. Orso rushed to his side in the greatest of consternation and helplessness, his display made easier by the frightening realism of Barend's performance.

The carabinieri, themselves feeling the effects of the cold and being anxious to return to the comfort of their police station, showed not a jot of sympathy, nor made any move to assist. Orso was ordered to march on or be shot. Forcibly lifted to his feet and prodded in the back with rifle butts, Orso was marched along the path, grief-stricken and calling out to his poor old dad left to 'die' in the snow.

Making a quick recovery and getting up once he was sure the carabinieri were out of the way, Barend wasn't sure of what his next move should be. He didn't want to impose himself on Don Gino again for fear that the priest was being watched but he couldn't hang around in the bitterly cold snow for too long. Fortunately, the partisans found him soon afterwards and helped him to make his way back to Don Gino.

Orso was taken to the village where he was imprisoned in the local jail. A message was sent to Lucia and the girls and Lucia went into action.

Before the war the family had had an association with a Dr Alfino, a very kindly and dignified elderly man who was in charge of the Office for Foreigners in Florence and was, therefore, well aware of their status as civilian internees. Lucia went to see him and he received her most graciously. He very quickly ordered Orso's release.

When he was released early in 1944, he returned to his family's bosom - stinking to high heaven. He had had an interesting Christmas: as the only inmate of the prison he had been required to attend the local Christmas party because none of the carabinieri was prepared to miss the fun by staying behind to guard him. He spent the evening confined to a chair and watching his captors getting progressively drunker and more raucous. Very Italian!

Dr Alfino advised Orso to remain at home but to be as unobtrusive as possible. Don Gino also felt that it would be safer all round for Barend to return home as German and Fascist action against the partisans in the rural areas was increasing dramatically. Dr Alfino assured them, should they have any more unpleasantness, that he would be able to extricate them but they should not take any chances. As a precautionary measure Orso and Barend stayed away from the windows, which were kept shuttered anyway, and never went outside. The carabinieri who had captured them, were told, by the partisans, to leave the Van Praags alone. The order was reinforced with the threat that their own families would not be safe if they tried to interfere with Barend and his family again.

In the same way as Lucia had ridden to the rescue of her husband and son by approaching an old acquaintance, Toly, too, was required to make use of an old connection. Elena can't remember what this crisis was all about. What does survive clearly in her memory was Toly's rescue operation.

Before the war in Genoa, Toly had been courted by the brother of one of her teachers. This man was much older than Toly and this was the reason Barend had given him for not allowing him to negotiate marriage. They had parted cordially. When the Van Praags arrived in Florence, who should they discover holding high office in the government of Florence but the self-same man and, for a short period, he seems to have acted as a temporary mayor. When they had arrived in Florence, Barend had said that he could be a very useful connection and they should remain on good terms with him.

Now Toly dressed up and went to see him. He was delighted to see her. The upshot of this particular incident was that Toly regularly reminded her family that she had risked her virtue in order to save them. They weren't suitably grateful because they said she'd thoroughly enjoyed her Matahari role.

In the midst of their anxiety about Barend and Orso, Elena became very ill with a raging fever and terrible abdominal pain. She had acute appendicitis and was rushed into hospital for emergency surgery. Painful and frightening as the experience was, it did provide a kind of reprieve from her normal daily anxieties and the nuns were very caring. One little nun was particularly pretty and younger than the rest. This was Sister Cecile. Whenever a male visitor arrived for Elena she would make sure she got to her ward first to warn her and surreptitiously hide the bedside photograph of Elena's current beau – just in case. She also went out of her way to encourage Elena's appetite, regularly making her favourite crème brulée. For such kindnesses people are remembered.

On the 25th of September 1943, while Barend and Orso were in hiding, the girls were all at home and their little family doctor was paying them a social visit. They heard planes coming over but felt no alarm as the planes sounded very high. Elena and Toly were standing at a window in Orso's bedroom overlooking the garden, trying to see what was flying over. Initially Elena thought they were stuccas because of the high-pitched whining sound she could hear. The planes were flying in formation and they were able to count thirty-three B-52's. They circled three times.

The next minute a bomb fell right into the garden, hitting the top of a tree and exploding. They called Agnese, who was in the kitchen, to join them. As they were standing there another bomb was dropped in front of the apartment on the street side of the building. They all started to run for the exit, only pausing to grab their handbags, each of which contained the individual's passport and ten guilders, from a drawer in the entrance hall. It was after this that Lucia made the pouches which they wore under their clothing, day and night.

As Elena reached the door to the staircase, the fanlight, a huge, ornate piece, was blown backwards into the apartment by the percussion of a bomb landing in the street outside. Elena lost consciousness but when she came to, they gathered themselves up and ran to the shelter in the garden. The fanlight had landed on her shins which had been lacerated but she was oblivious of the blood streaming down her legs as they ran. ("Bloody sore later on," she says.) She was also deaf for a month afterwards.

There was a large room just inside the entrance to their apartment. This room was used for storage. In it were wardrobes used to house their winter clothing, the doors of which were kept locked. Later they found that the blast had somehow forced the doors open. Dust and concrete had been sucked in and the doors had sealed tight again.

They made a habit of leaving their windows open in case of bombing and they found that all the right-hand windows of each room had been blown out. But the canary was still singing! All-in-all, five 25kg bombs had landed in the garden.

Agnese was hysterical and nothing they did could stop her hysteria. The little doctor told her to stop it and then slapped her face twice. That brought her to her senses. Elena remembers, with amazement, how she had given no thought to her family and just ran. It was also crazy to use the staircase as this is usually the first area to collapse. They all knew this but it didn't stop them.

Terrible destruction had been wrought in the area. Five houses down the road, on the Viale Giacomo Matteoti, the whole front of a building had been blasted away and a maid was left standing in the remaining half of a kitchen up on the fourth floor.

The scene was chaotic. The air was filled with dust and debris. The inhabitants of Gherardesca and the neighbouring buildings were milling around and there was little co-ordinated effort to restore order, establish the safety of the buildings, or control the movements of the populace. It was pretty much up to individuals to decide what the next steps should be. The little doctor attended to Elena's legs and administered first aid wherever he could, assisted by a couple of nurses who lived nearby. Agnese was still flapping about but had more or less got herself under control – she didn't want another dose of the little doctor's particular brand of first aid for her histrionics. Lucia was a centre of calm and, with Toly, began to consider their options.

They realized that the apartment was too damaged and unsound for them even to consider camping out in the rooms.

Once a semblance of calm had been restored, Lucia, Elena and Agnese made their way back into the apartment – up the same treacherous staircase. The place was a shambles but there was no time, and no point, to consider cleaning up. Apart from their clothing, they needed to pack up as many of their smaller goods and furniture as they could. What to take was a problem because they didn't know where they were going and, consequently, what they would need. They also didn't know what would happen to the apartment or how safe it would be from looters.

Lucia, in her methodical way, began identifying what needed to be rescued and organising the girls to pile their possessions at the windows so that they could lower the bundles down to the street below. By now they had come to their senses and realized that the staircase should be used as little as possible.

Toly, in the meantime, had taken it upon herself to find accommodation. She had remembered the Nieuwenkamps at Villa Il Riposo dei Vescovi and had somehow made contact with them. They had agreed to take the Van Praags in. She had also found a small truck somewhere. When she returned, they began the arduous task of getting everything through the windows and loaded on to the truck.

And then it started to pour with rain, after three months of severe drought!

Orso's future father-in-law, little Papa Alberto of the post office and telephone exchange, came to help. As they were passing a mattress through a window, he had a hand on either side of the mattress, trying to hold it and direct its fall. Determined little man that he was, he didn't let go in time and started to slide through the window on top of the mattress. The girls had to hang on to him by his legs and then drag him back into the room where they all collapsed on the floor, engulfed in laughter.

As the girls continued to struggle to get the larger and more awkward pieces of furniture through the window and then load them on to the truck, a strapping young man happened to stroll by. He offered his help, for which they were immensely grateful, and trotted off to fetch a friend. He turned out to be a parachutist who had gone AWOL and was in hiding with the friend whom he'd gone to call.

The secret compartment which Barend had built in the stairwell had to be broken open to rescue the family silver and other treasures. Fortunately, this was not the main staircase but the one leading up from the cellar and maid's room.

The parachutist and his friend went with the girls to Il Riposo where they helped to unload. This was just as well as they struggled to get the furniture into Il Riposo as the stairs were so narrow and twisting. The largest pieces were left in Florence and recovered in the days which followed.

Later, in Milan, after Elena had met George, she was with George's driver to collect a javelin for George when she heard her name being called – it was their parachutist!

There was very little to do at Il Riposo to occupy their time. What did help them while away the time was the company of the other guests whose eccentricities were always entertaining.

Many of the Gherardesca families had to abandon their homes and this included the family from Genoa whom they had befriended. They, too, left on the day of the bombing and the Van Praags never saw them again.

A few months later, the Van Praags were able to return to Gherardesca when an apartment became available at 106 Borgo Pinti, around the corner from their old apartment at Number 1, Viale Giacomo Matteoti (previously known as 'Principe Amedeo' but which underwent a name change at the hands of the partisans).

After their return from Il Riposo, the girls and Lucia would walk to the centre of Florence every day and remain there from nine o'clock until one, during which time most of the bombing took place. They would spend the morning near the Ponte Veccio on the Arno in the assurance that the Allies would avoid bombing this very important historical structure. This belief was well-founded. The Germans, too, left it alone and even when they were leaving Florence, and bombing every important installation they could find, including all the other bridges across the Arno, they did not touch the Ponte

Veccio. However, they did destroy all the buildings on either side of the bridge to hamper Allied passage.

What is intriguing and fills one with amazement, is the way all these bridges were reconstructed after the war, to the precise pre-war design and using all the material from the old bridges, much of which had to be fished up from the depths of the water. In one case, only the hand of a particular statue remained unrecovered!

It wasn't long after their return to Gherardesca, that Orso and Barend were also able to come home.

After the return of the menfolk, Barend was inspired to 'toughen up' Orso. One of his methods was to make Orso stand with him in the garden, outside the bomb shelter, in order to watch the lights of the bombing. Orso endured this patiently and uncomplainingly while his sisters sat inside the shelter, flinching on his behalf every time they heard an explosion, and roundly criticizing Barend. Although Orso took this treatment, when he was returned to his sisters they could see how jittery he was. If Barend had thought this trick would work, it didn't. All it did was make his daughters very angry with him for bullying Orso.

Barend still spent a great deal of time plotting the movements on the various front lines. He had acquired an easy chair for his den, and this he positioned so that he could fiddle with the knobs on his wireless in comfort. His very large atlas always lay open on a round table in front of him. He would pick up as many stations as he could and listen to news reports in every language he knew which included French, German, English, Dutch and Italian. He couldn't speak Russian but he could identify the names of Russian towns. He would then cross-reference the various reports and try to sort out fact from propaganda in deciding where the real front lines lay. He used a red pen, a blue pen and a pencil to mark the information in his atlas.

This activity eventually occupied him from seven in the morning until midnight, and became his life and lifeline. Lucia often had to remind him to turn the radio down, especially when he was listening to the English news with its very distinctive signature tune.

One day they were raided by the Ovra (Italian Internal Intelligence Agency). The investigators simply rang the doorbell and walked straight in. No one was allowed to move as they searched the apartment. They all sat frozen as these men made their way through their home.

Barend was in his den listening to the wireless when they arrived. He managed to switch it off but it was still hot. The Ovra demanded to know what he had been listening to. He told them that it was Mussolini's speech and they wanted to know what Il Duce had had to say. He gave them some story which seemed to satisfy them but, nevertheless, they confiscated his radio.

Barend felt as though they had confiscated his life. They would have taken a great deal more, however, had they noticed his atlas. Fortuitously, for once it had not been lying open on his table and they had overlooked it, together with all its incriminating markings! The penalty for what he had been doing was a firing-squad.

Thereafter, Barend began to take his morning exercise, and the purchase of his cigarettes and newspaper, very seriously! He would pay a visit to the grocer, the butcher, the green-grocer and the pizzeria, a destination of which he was particularly fond because the pro-partisan shopkeeper was especially helpful. At each of these stops he went into the back of the shop where he was able to listen to the news.

Later, when the Germans were ensconced in the Gherardesca garden, he would mooch around their campsite picking up whatever information he could on their radios. He went largely undetected because they didn't realize how acute his German was. If the wireless wasn't switched on, or was not on a news station, he would even have the audacity to ask the Germans to tune it to a news broadcast in Italian or German and then, as soon as they were out of earshot, he would switch to the English news. If he came under suspicion, he just pretended to be a doddery old man who was hard of hearing as he fiddled with the dials.

Toly had a talent for dealing with sticky situations and seemed to get some sort of thrill from flirting with danger. Perhaps it was her mathematical, problem-solving brain that gave her pleasure in working out solutions and then putting them to the test. Possibly these risky situations also gave her an opportunity to exercise her acting abilities. They certainly gave her the chance of using her powers as a femme fatale.

One such opportunity to use her talents arose in the rescue of Carlo, the son of old friends.

Carlo was a doctor and had been drafted into the Italian army. He was based in Florence. The Van Praags received a frantic 'phone call from him one evening, early in 1944, saying his unit was being sent to Germany the next day and he was desperate to avoid this.

Toly once again rode to the rescue. She braided her hair, crown-fashion, around her head and, looking a very innocent and very distraught young woman, she went to the barracks. She pleaded her case to the sentries: her fiancé was being sent away the next day and she didn't know when she would see him again, and what was she going to do without him? They melted and allowed her in.

When Carlo appeared, she flung her arms around his neck and whispered that he should play along. They clung to each other and then slowly began to circle the grounds, talking intensely and embracing often and tearfully. As soon as they got near the gate, and Toly saw that the guards weren't watching them, they sidled through the opening and bolted.

That was the last the Italian army saw of Carlo. The Van Praags donated his uniform to the partisans and Carlo became a permanent, if not always welcome, guest.

CHAPTER 10

It was shortly after Carlo's arrival that the Germans encamped in the grounds of Gherardesca. In the meantime Barend prepared official-looking letters exempting Carlo and Orso from the army in case they were raided, on the grounds that they both suffered from tuberculosis. It helped that everyone was underweight. Orso did have a weak chest, possibly an after-effect of the 1918 'flu from which he had nearly died.

Barend had become quite adept at producing such official-looking documents. When he created one such letter for an elderly Italian woman about her son who had been taken in a raid, he told her to say, should anybody ask where she had got the letter, that a little man with a narrow moustache which ran from his nostrils to his lip, and a fringe of thin, straight hair which flopped into his eyes, had issued the letter.

Carlo did little to ingratiate himself and his subsequent actions and attitudes eventually made them view him with loathing and contempt.

He was paranoid about being arrested and refused to use his medical skills to help anyone in case any such assistance should lead the authorities back to him. When a neighbour caught her finger in a heavy door and bruised the nail very badly, he was most indignant that Barend should ask him to help. This incident wasn't as desperate as the shooting of the Red Cross nurse, though.

Partisans were hiding within the Palazzo della Gherardesca, across the garden from the Van Praags' apartment. Another group of partisans was in hiding across the road in the Viale Giacomo Matteotti. The men in this latter group were crying out for water and the nurse, in full Red Cross uniform, tried to cross the road from Gherardesca, carrying a bucket of water for them. As she crossed, a Fascist sniper fired at her and she was hit in the leg.

She was carried up to the Van Praag apartment and Carlo was asked to help. He refused.

Somehow the family managed to patch up the wound and Elena accompanied her to hospital. This was a very frightening trip as they had to make their way on foot, fearful of being shot and with the nurse barely able to walk. She had to lean heavily on Elena and their progress was extremely slow.

Food was extremely short and there were no more visits to the trattoria as the streets were too dangerous. It was now that they discovered that Carlo was getting up in the middle of the night and stealing their precious rations. When he finally left, Orso discovered that he had also helped himself to a gold pen given to Orso by his aunt.

Shortly after Barend and Orso returned home, Toly responded to a knock on the door one day. She opened it to find a German officer standing there. He demanded accommodation for six men. She explained that the apartment was full and they had no room to spare. He stepped aside without saying a word and she was confronted by two soldiers with their submachine-guns aimed at her. She had no choice but to let them in. They took over the sitting-room and dossed down on mattresses at night which the girls had to tidy away during the day.

Barend was made the unofficial liaison officer between the Germans and the other residents who had also had these unwelcome guests forced on them. In addition to foisting themselves on the residents of Gherardesca, the Germans had taken over the garden as a camp-site and parking area. Barend was instructed to inform the permanent residents that if anything untoward happened to a single German, everyone in Gherardesca would be locked in and the whole place would be dynamited.

When Toly was tidying the sitting-room one morning, she found bullets under a pillow. Convinced that this was a set-up, she made sure that she handed them back to the German when he returned that evening.

Naturally the Germans wanted to know what Orso and Carlo were doing in the apartment and why they weren't serving in the Italian army. They presented the Germans with Barend's letters of exemption claiming that they both suffered from tuberculosis. No further questions were asked.

As the Allies were progressing northwards towards Florence, and the Germans had not yet left Florence, Toly found herself in yet another predicament. She had travelled south to see their friends and suppliers of their wine, the Busellis, in Radda in Chianti, about an accounting problem. On her return journey she was travelling in a bus when it was strafed by an Allied plane. Pandemonium ensued with excitable Italians hurling themselves to the floor or trying to smash through windows as they clutched their children, chickens, baskets and bundles, all the while screeching at the bus driver, the bomber and their deity.

The bus ground to a standstill and they were ordered off. Fortunately, there was a ditch alongside the road into which they scrambled for cover. Cowering, they heard a plane returning. As it circled overhead, Toly looked up. It was so low that she could see the pilot. She waved to him and he waved back.

Toly was first out of the ditch and then began the very long trudge home. Not long after she had started walking, a German tank came trundling along the road and she flagged it down. When it stopped, she asked for a ride and was duly helped up.

Lucia heard the tank rumbling along the street. This wasn't an unusual occurrence but when it clattered to a halt outside the apartment, her curiosity drew her to the window. The sight of her eldest daughter graciously being handed down from the tank by the tank commander nearly sent her into orbit!

Lucia was livid with her. Apart from the unladylike clambering in and out of the tank, Lucia couldn't believe that she had been associating with the Germans, endangering herself, and laying herself open to accusations from the partisans of consorting with the enemy. Toly merely saw her actions as a practical solution. Trust her, too, to pack a flirtation with a British pilot and a German tank crew all in to one day.

The Germans were now using every underhanded means they could find to further their aims in their desperation as the Allied pressures increased. This included covering their vehicles, especially those carrying armaments, with the Red Cross flag. Elena saw this herself. As she was looking into the street from her bedroom window, the flap on the back of a 'Red Cross' truck flew up, revealing its load of bombs.

She also never forgot the sight of an Italian tripping in front of a convoy of tanks. A tank simply rolled over him as he lay helplessly in the street. This was followed by the rest of the tanks until there was nothing left of him.

Another well-used and effective trick was for the Germans to intersperse themselves with the yellow convoy trucks used by the Pope to send food supplies to beleagred Florence. This made it very difficult for the Allies to strafe the German vehicles and sometimes the Pope's vehicles were hit.

One such truck driver had been hit by a bullet which had ripped open the length of his forearm. The Pope's trucks were also parked in the Gherardesca garden overnight and the wounded driver was brought to the Van Praag apartment for help. Once again Carlo refused to help, wailing that he would be shot if he were caught. Toly told him to shut up and get on with it: if he were caught and shot he would have plenty of company because all six of them would be shot too, for hiding him. The driver expressed his gratitude by giving them a very precious, and much appreciated, bottle of olive oil.

The Germans didn't provide them with much to laugh about and they constantly had to be aware of their actions. Elena in particular, struggled to curb her ebullience to avoid being a danger to herself and her family. She was in the kitchen one afternoon, belting out a song at the top of her voice. Orso raced into the kitchen, told her she was a bloody fool and asked if she wanted to get them all shot. She had no idea what he was talking about until he told her that she was singing (or caterwauling) the Marseilles, used as the unofficial Russian anthem, or 'The Workers' Marseilles' – surrounded by Germans who were not feeling very kindly towards the Russians at that stage of the war.

They were woken by a great deal of shouting in the garden one night. It turned out that one of Germans had been asked for the password. When he couldn't remember it, he was shot by his own side. All the occupants were ordered to attend the funeral in the garden the next day. They made sure that they wore dark glasses so that their twinkles of merriment and derision couldn't be seen.

It was a matter of honour not to ask any of the Germans for anything and this was a principle to which they stuck religiously but there was one occasion when Elena did ask for something: this was powdered opium without which her constant nervous state caused her chronic diarrhoea.

Elena was in the garden one night in early August when she heard the pitiful cries of a wounded German soldier. He was in a truckload of wounded men who had been left in the garden for the night. This callousness and neglect was probably a result of the panic and chaos the Germans were experiencing as they prepared to retreat ahead of the Allied onslaught, but Elena didn't know this then. The rest of the men were quiet but he was calling, „Wasser, bitte, Wasser." She stood stock-still, frozen by her hatred for the Germans. And then, as she began to move away, she was overcome by compassion. She couldn't ignore this heart-rending plea of a suffering human being and fetched a glass of her precious water, opened the truck flap and held out the glass saying, „Wasser." The glass was seized by someone, the water administered, presumably to the beseeching man, and silently returned.

The following day the Germans suddenly packed up and left the apartment and the garden. As they were preparing to leave, Orso and Barend went on the prowl. They found four precious, brand-new, tyres and a barrel of very good red wine which the Germans had overlooked. Moving quickly, before anyone missed the booty, they hid their loot in a cellar. Later they donated the tyres to the Red Cross and took the wine home where it was greatly enjoyed. In time they received a letter from the Red Cross thanking them for the tyres "stolen from the Germans".

The Germans who had been accommodated in the apartment, left a loaf of bread behind in the kitchen. Possibly it was a token of thanks but Lucia wasn't taking any chances. As useful as it might have been, she was convinced that it had been poisoned and refused to allow her family to touch it.

On the whole, their German guests had caused the Van Praags little trouble. They did create more work, took up a lot of space, invaded their privacy and disrupted their family communion. However, they were always courteous, tidy, never familiar and not once did any of the girls feel uncomfortable or threatened in any way.

After the Germans pulled out of the garden, a hush settled over Gherardesca which lasted until sunrise. Then a voice was heard shouting, "The Germans have gone!" Windows were opened, questions were tossed back and forth and disbelief resounded from all quarters, including from the hiding partisans.

*   *   *

This momentous day was Friday the 4th of August 1944. Vic Alhadeff, in 'South Africa in Two World Wars', quotes the reporter, Victor Norton, who was writing for the 'Cape Argus': *"Before first light on Friday morning light tanks of a Transvaal armoured regiment moved up, and the entry into Florence began under fire from German snipers who covered the approaches to the river crossings. Moving through wildly cheering crowds of civilians, the New Zealand armour and infantry moving into the city on their flank ... Near the banks of the Arno it was difficult to manoeuvre through the dense crowds, who swarmed round the tanks, trucks and Jeeps to kiss the soldiers, shake their hands and press gifts of flowers and wine upon them ...*

"The South Africans entered Florence just before the New Zealanders. It was a fitting ending to a great advance of nearly 200 miles from Rome. For more than a fortnight the South African forward troops have been subjected to the heaviest shelling they have yet experienced since they joined the Allied drive, and they have been opposed by some of the best formations in the German Army."

Two hours after the Germans fled Gherardesca, they were replaced by the Allied Indian Division. They, too, ensconced themselves in the Van Praag apartment and camped out on the floor of the sitting-room.

The Van Praags had learnt to shrug their shoulders like the most insouciant of Italians and they simply fell back into the routine they had adopted for dealing with the Germans. There were only two real differences: the atmosphere was generally more relaxed and informal and Lucia no longer worried that their food had been 'booby-trapped'.

However, Lucia was confronted by the deed of one Tommy which left her incredulous and shaking with rage and indignation. This unfortunate lad reported to her that her toilet wasn't working properly as the waste pipe was too small to accommodate the 'waste' he had deposited. When she discovered that he had abused her bidet, she told him, in no uncertain terms, what she thought of his breeding and education and made him clean up the mess himself. Despite the fact that her English was shaky, he was left in no doubt as to what she meant.

Another guest who really offended Barend was a lieutenant in the Indian Division. Barend had been saving some Napoleon Brandy for the first Ally to set foot in the apartment. This lad was John Smith (real name!) and he was offered a very precious tot of the brandy. When he asked for water to be added to it, Barend was almost apoplectic.

Also on the day of their arrival, the Allies in the garden were calling for water. Lucia, filled with bonhomie, stood on the balcony tossing apples to them as she had no water.

The battles between the Germans and the Allies were now being fought at very close quarters. Within the confines of Florence itself, German snipers were very active. One morning the Van Praags were woken very early by British officers, John Wilson and Clive Bullock, who told them to get dressed quickly because they were expecting to have to retreat.

They always slept in their underwear so it was a quick and simple matter for Elena to pull a dress over her head and be ready. She then went to open her shutters and spotted a sniper running across the park opposite (the Piazza Donatello) to hide behind a tree.

She called to one of the soldiers in the apartment, then flipped up the lower shutter and stood supporting it so that a marksman could shoot him. The marksman fired and she watched as the German flopped to the ground like an apple falling from a tree. This image has stayed with her along with feelings of great unease at her casual role in this man's death.

The battle continued to rage around Gherardesca for some time. The family was pulled away from the windows and their places were taken by more British soldiers. They hovered in the passage, finding the situation ever more surreal. Having seen the Germans depart from Gherardesca in such a hurry, they had thought they wouldn't be seeing much of them again. Crouching now, as far out of harm's way as they could, it was hard to believe that the firing was growing louder and coming more rapidly when it should have been diminishing.

As the 'Battle of Gherardersca' continued to rampage, the Brits couldn't hold their position. They decided it would be prudent for everyone, including themselves, to evacuate the apartment. The only way out was via the ladder from the balcony into the garden. This was the same ladder which the family always kept handy in case the apartment was raided by the Fascists and Orso and Carlo had to make a quick escape. Down they clambered under the supervision of their erstwhile saviours.

The infantrymen took up new positions and the Van Praags made their way to the nuns across the garden. From the convent they escaped into the Via Gino Capponi. It was relatively quiet on this side of Gherardesca but they were all very jumpy in case the fighting spilled over into this street.

They thought that their best option was to flee to the centre of Florence. Here they hovered about in the streets, listening attentively to the fluctuating sounds of gunfire.

Later in the morning Barend noticed that the shooting had stopped. They strolled back to Gherardesca, taking their time to enjoy the morning and discuss every aspect of their recent adventure. Back at home they found Clive Bullock. He was distressed at having lost one man but was also very grateful that he hadn't lost more.

Elena asked him what time the battle had finished. He replied, "Let me think: we had breakfast at ten. By about eleven or eleven-thirty everything was over."

As the Allies ensconced themselves in Florence, the Van Praags were able to move about with greater freedom but the danger was not yet entirely over.

They were all out together one day when they were overheard speaking Dutch to one another. A group of partisans, who had confused their Dutch with German, surrounded them and tried to force them into a nearby cellar. They were besieged by aggressive, shouting partisans who began to prod and push them with rifle butts towards the cellar.

Barend knew that going into the cellar would be fatal and he put up a determined resistance. He made the whole family take out their passports, which they still kept on them at all times for just such an occasion as this. As the family waved their Dutch passports at their captors, Barend insisted that they be taken to the British headquarters for their passports to be verified. His vociferous demands eventually got through to the partisans and they were marched along to the British HQ where an officer checked their passports. The Van Praags were delighted when he sent the partisans packing with several fleas in their ears.

CHAPTER 11

Job opportunities with the Allies began to come their way. In August '44, Orso went for an interview for a job with the Civil Labour Unit because he could speak English. The Civil Labour Unit utilized Jews, the medically unfit, and anyone who didn't qualify for action. Elena was with him because she was on her way to see the dentist and had to be escorted by Orso. An American captain of Italian descent, who spoke very good Italian, interviewed Orso.

When the interview was over, this man turned to Elena and asked her where she was employed. She replied that she wasn't allowed to work away from home. He informed her that as she was an ally, she was compelled to work as she could be trusted and was needed. She was told to bring her father with her to see him the following day. He needed a secretary and an interpreter for an Englishman, Major Boris Gooseman, who headed the Civil Labour Unit in Florence. She said that she couldn't speak English. However, he discovered that she could speak French and she therefore qualified, as Major Gooseman could also speak French and they would be able to communicate. The added advantage of employing her was that she could type secret documents which were not to be seen by civilians because she didn't understand a word of English so didn't know what she was typing.

Major Gooseman had a glass eye. He was a very kindly character and they got on extremely well together. At tea-time every day they were both provided with muffins from the NAAFI. What Elena didn't know at the time, was that Major Gooseman was paying for her muffins out of his own pocket.

When it was very cold, it was the Florentine habit to fill a little pottery container with glowing coals and then cover the coals with ash. These little pottery heaters (called 'veggi') could be carried about and used throughout the day. They could also be hooked on to bentwood frames and placed in beds to heat them. The frame was called 'The Priest' and Orso's wife's family joke was to ask if one wanted the priest to share one's bed – one of the jokes of the nights spent sleeping in the passage when the bombing was fierce.

One afternoon, after lunch, Elena was sitting in Major Gooseman's easy-chair, feeling very relaxed and cosy with her veggi at her feet, and she dozed off. He simply left her to enjoy her nap.

On another occasion Major Gooseman really seemed to be out of sorts with her and she couldn't work out what she had done wrong. He simply wouldn't talk to her and looked the other way when she entered the room. Eventually she asked someone how she had upset him. She was told that he was mortally offended by the thick, woollen stockings she had chosen to wear for warmth. She replied that there was nothing she could do about her horrible stockings as she couldn't afford silk stockings. He doubled her salary on condition she always wore silk stockings.

Elena also suffered from chilblains, which at times were so bad that she couldn't even get her feet into her shoes, and was forced to wear her rubber overshoes instead. Major Gooseman didn't seem to have had an opinion about this state of affairs.

The Major was well aware of Elena's naïvety. He told her about a very pleasant evening he had spent with an attractive female officer. He said that they'd had a lovely evening, including a good dinner, and then they went to bed. Elena, like a clot, asked him what they did then. His response was, "We sat in bed and sang hymns," to which she said, "Oh, that was nice." He rolled his eyes. It was some time, and a good deal of experience later, before she got the joke.

They were also good at playing practical jokes on one another. Boris, however, always held the ultimate winning hand. In his office was a set of tall, rickety shelves. When Elena had outwitted him once too often, he would pick her up and plonk her on top of the shelves. There she would have to remain, helpless because the shelves weren't attached to the wall: she couldn't jump down without toppling the whole structure. She would have to wait until he relented and lifted her down. On one occasion someone came into the office and found her precariously perched up there. To this man's enquiry, Boris waved a dismissive hand and said she was being punished because she was behaving very badly that day and would have to remain there until her attitude and unruly behaviour were remedied.

Toly had also found employment. She worked for the British Military Police and this was how she met Charlie Pretorius. She had just left home one day, on her way to work, when she saw a South African officer and his driver in a Jeep. They were trying to ask some Italians for directions and weren't having much luck. She said, in English, "Can I help you?" The officer replied that it was wonderful to hear English and asked if she knew how to get to the British Military Police Headquarters. As this was where she worked, she cheekily told them she would show them if they gave her a lift.

Charlie was a major with the South African Military Police stationed in Florence. The British Military Police and the South African Military Police had offices on opposite sides of the same corridor so Toly saw a great deal of Charlie and his driver, Corporal Ernst Taljaard, whom she eventually married.

Charlie had requisitioned a villa, one of a few which formed a boundary of the Gherardesca garden and the Van Praags invited him to visit, to talk about his family and show them his family photographs. Charlie was a devoted family man and a good husband, never deviating from the marital straight and narrow as so many servicemen did.

Other South Africans they met belonged to the Tank Division of the South African Sixth Armoured Division. Charlie brought three young men to visit them. He had told them about this Dutch family who were very hospitable and loved entertaining and they would be able to communicate with each other.

One of these men was Danie Theron, who was good-looking, but the girls were a bit put off by the fact that he had false teeth. Then there was Neelis van der Westhuizen, who was blond and blue-eyed and a 'proper Boer'. He took a fancy to Agnese but when he heard that she was a Catholic he said

"Liewe Here (*Dear Lord*) – I could never take a Catholic home: my mother would kill me!" and that put paid to any budding romance there.

The third chap was someone whose name Elena and Agnese can't remember but who was generally known as 'the drunk'. He arrived at the apartment one evening, much the worse for wear. Lucia said, "Myne jonge, come here," and proceeded to take him in hand, force-feeding him black coffee and then taking him to Orso's room where she put him to bed to sleep until he was sober enough to be returned to his barracks in a less dishevelled state.

Renzo Busseli, the son of their wine-producing friends in Radda in Chianti, was another occupant of the Van Praags' apartment. He was studying in Florence and needed accommodation. Of course the girls had heard the rumours about Scotsmen and their kilts so when they were visited by a Scotsman wearing his kilt, the girls got Renzo to sit on a low stool opposite this man, whom they had nicknamed 'Peepo'. Renzo was tasked with catching a glimpse beneath the kilt so that he could report to them. Perhaps the wily Scotsman outwitted him: there was nothing salacious to report, or Lorenzo couldn't bring himself to describe the scene, but they got no information out of him.

Whenever the Van Praags were expecting guests, the younger generation knew that they couldn't have any coffee because there wasn't enough to go round. It was, nevertheless, offered to them and they came up with a variety of excuses: "Oh, no, thank you. I couldn't fit another thing in!" and so on, drooling in the meanwhile at the wafting aroma.

Sugar and salt rations were also still very limited and Elena made the dreadful mistake one month of pouring the newly-arrived salt ration into the sugar container and vice versa. They had to go without sugar and salt for the rest of the month.

Food shortages continued to be a problem. Elena's gums began to bleed and a doctor told her that she had to eat a lemon a day. The problem was that lemons were astronomically expensive with one lemon costing ten shillings. Of fresh vegetables, only spinach and cauliflower were available and dried foods, such as split peas, were full of weevils. Barend continued to complain loudly about the weevils and Lucia continued to hide his spectacles at mealtimes. Orso still made comments about getting free protein to which Lucia would tell him to, "Shut up and eat!"

The appearance of white bread was greeted as a very special occasion. They had an Italian friend who heard that white bread was available on the other side of the Arno where the British were billeted. He made a special trip to collect a loaf and brought it back to share with everyone.

An elderly Dutch friend had a daughter who was dreadfully ill from malnutrition. When the British arrived, Lucia helped this old lady to get her daughter into a British hospital but it was too late to save her and she left behind two young daughters of nine and ten. The same old lady managed to summon the spirit, not long afterwards, to serenade the arrival of the South African troops as they crossed the Arno with a rendition of 'Sarie Marais', the folk-song held dear by so many South Africans.

Two American officers also visited them from time to time. One was of Dutch extraction. It was he who noticed the sorry state of their footwear. He returned later with two pairs of beautiful leather shoes for Barend and Orso. He also noticed Elena daydreaming one day and asked her what she was thinking about. She said she was dreaming about eating a pork chop – he brought her a dozen!

Barend and Orso, as heavy smokers, were ingenious in their antics to find something to smoke. Eventually they were making cigarettes out of dried camomile flowers. Elena, too, had her methods. She had a silver snuffbox in which she kept all the left-over tobacco she could salvage from the butts left behind by their guests. In fact, as soon as their guests left, they all made an undignified dash for the ashtrays to retrieve what they could. The girls were at a serious disadvantage when the guest was a boyfriend as the respective daughter would have to see the visitor to the door while the rest of the family scrambled for the ashtray.

Elena became an expert roller of cigarettes using typing copy paper. She would offer her cigarettes with a choice: with or without her sealing spit.

Barend knew a farmer from whom he bought tobacco leaves. He would dry these in the oven or the sun. He then added brandy to improve the taste and soften the tobacco. The leaves were rolled up tightly, hung to dry, and then cut finely as a sausage would be sliced. The tobacco was then ready to be rolled into cigarettes.

When cigarettes could be bought, they cost a shilling a cigarette on the black market. Family etiquette dictated that if visiting officers offered them a cigarette, they were never allowed to accept more than one. On one of George's visits he brought Elena a whole carton! She gave a packet each to Barend, Orso and Toly and hid the rest in her room. While she was busily finding a spot to secrete them, she heard a noise at her door and discovered Barend trying to spy on her hiding-place through the keyhole!

Elena, 1945

George, in uniform, during the war.
The autograph reads: "Yours Always, George".

Elena competing on Racci in the National Equestrian
Competition at Nervi in April 1939.

Newspaper photograph of Elena and Giancarlo competing in a half-
section championship at Marassi (May 1939) which they won.

The press photograph showing Elena in her moment of glory after winning a show-jumping competition at Marassi on 5 April 1938. She was the only woman competing against 24 men.

Elena and her winning team

Elena and her basketball team: Elena is the second girl from the
left in the back row. Agnese is on Elena's right. Elena thinks
that number 9 is Luce Einstein and number 8 is Cici Einstein
and that their cousins, Lorenza Mazzetti, is front left, and Paula
Mazzetti, is number 6. Their Fascist coach and manager seem
oblivious to the fact that almost their entire team is Jewish.

Barend

George, back left, in his final year at Victoria High School, now
Graeme College, in Grahamstown. The Hirsch Shield is the annual
inter-schools athletic competition still held in the Eastern Cape.
This photograph is published with the kind permission of Graeme College.

Elena celebrating her ninetieth birthday at the Port Edward Country Club.

CHAPTER 12

With the arrival of the Allies, the girls' social lives improved dramatically.

Toly and Elena often attended dances and parties organised by Major Gooseman and his staff. These occasions usually took place at the large villa where Major Gooseman was billeted. They also attended dances at a nearby hotel.

On one occasion Major Gooseman asked her if she would like to dance with a good-looking American. She agreed and after a short time, the American asked if she would mind being held a little closer. Her normal response to any English question was, "Yes, yes, yes," not understanding a syllable of what was really being asked. This time she very quickly got the gist and leapt away from him exclaiming, "No! No! No!"

One evening in October '44 the girls had been out with Major Gooseman and his officers. On their return home, they saw a strange cap hanging up in the entrance hall and asked Lucia who it belonged to. Charlie had been visiting and had brought another South African along with him. This man was also a captain in the military police and was based at Prato, but had come to Florence on rest and recuperation. Charlie had told him that he was going to visit a Dutch family with three attractive daughters and he decided to accompany him.

In the course of the evening it emerged that Charlie didn't have room to accommodate him for the night. This didn't seem to worry the man greatly but when Lucia and Barend offered him mattress space on the sitting-room floor, he accepted gratefully. Elena was annoyed to discover that her parents had taken in yet another stray and complained that she wouldn't be able to go to the toilet in peace because he would hear her.

By the next morning she'd forgotten about him. As she wandered into the dining-room for breakfast, she was surprised to see a strange figure standing at the French windows looking out over the garden. His back was to her and he was fastening the buttons at the back of his battledress. Her irritation of the previous night returned briefly but the figure was tall and athletic, and this caught her interest. Then he turned to face her. The remains of her annoyance slid away.

There was a fraction of a moment before the social niceties intruded, when they looked at each other and registered the other's existence. Something indissoluble fastened in each of them as their eyes connected. Elena's neck tingled and she felt the telltale rosy fingers of a blush creeping around her neck and up her face. A blister of indrawn breath seemed to have lodged somewhere behind her breastbone and her pelvis tightened. None of this had she ever felt before.

George's blue eyes were mesmerizing but what had flashed between them was far more than that.

And then the rest of the family began to drift in for breakfast and Elena's levitating moment had to be put aside for the social conventions of sharing a meal with a guest. General conversation took over and they had very little chance to say anything to one another. Perhaps that was just as well because Elena needed time to digest what had just happened to her and polite chatter was beyond her capabilities. Filled with nervous energy, fear that he just might not come back, and frustration at not having the chance to utter a single meaningful word, she was very reluctant to see him leave.

As soon as George was out of the door she rounded on Toly, who, of course, had also been mightily taken and knew how to make an impression. She had sat beside George at breakfast, had chatted gaily and had been very attentive to his every need. Normally Toly's fancies were her own affair and there had never been any competition between them with Elena not being particularly interested in Toly's beaux. But this was different. She told Toly that this man was the one for her and she would not countenance one out-of-place move from Toly. Toly retreated graciously.

When she thought about that moment afterwards, she had the impression that the light in the room had grown sharper and the sounds of clattering kitchen utensils had become clearer. The rest of the day she spent in a haze, only speaking when spoken to.

George, too, felt the effects of aftershock. In contrast with his more usual policy of silent discretion about matters romantic and personal, he told Charlie about his meeting with Elena and enlisted Charlie in a scheme to see her again.

Charlie was most obliging and invited the whole family to an outdoor cinema evening at his villa. This was a make-do and novel form of entertainment which had caught on with many Allied servicemen. Such evenings were informal and had an air of festivity. Deck chairs had been set out and Charlie carefully engineered the seating arrangements, leaving a vacant chair next to Elena.

Elena assumed that the chair was for Charlie when he had finished organizing the proceedings.

Just as the film began to roll, from the corner of her eye, she became aware of a figure edging past the knees of the other guests. When he paused beside her, she glanced up. It wasn't Charlie at all. It was George and her breath caught.

Despite her overwhelming conviction that something important had passed between them on their first meeting, she couldn't be absolutely certain that their meeting had meant the same thing to him. But here he was!

Outwardly she maintained her decorum while inwardly seething with bubbles of nervousness, anticipation and jubilation. The film passed in a blur – all Elena's attention was focused on the being next to her – so close that she just had to stretch out her little finger to touch the fabric of his sleeve. Tempting as that was, there was still a chasm of protocol to bridge before any such familiarity would be possible. She had to content herself with stealing glimpses at his profile, noting the tanned, taut skin, sliding her gaze down his sleeve to a lean, athletic thigh – trouser-leg pulled tight by the bend of the knee – large, slender hands and long, blunt-tipped fingers.

Conversation was stilted, hampered by Elena's intense shyness, a burning desire to make the right impression, and the fear of her gaucheness driving him away. George hadn't put so much effort into the planning of this campaign to be driven off so easily and the evening progressed along its bumpy, but joyous, path.

Part way through the film he reached out and she felt his fingers close over hers. She held her breath, not wanting him to take his hand away, and too afraid to stir. He gave a gentle squeeze which reassured her enough to return it and flick a glance in his direction. There were those eyes again, looking straight into hers, affirming the mutual attraction. The corners of his eyes crinkled with warmth and humour. It was all she could do to stop herself reaching up to touch the lines. Instead, she held his hand between both of hers. She found herself gradually inclining towards his shoulder. What the movie was about, she never really knew: her entire focus was on their hands.

The film was over far too soon. It was a wrench to stand up, fold away the chairs and make polite conversation. George tucked her arm into the crook of his elbow and escorted the Van Praags home. They refrained from their usual mockery.

Thereafter he visited whenever he could. The family happily accepted him as a regular guest. They all liked him and enjoyed his company. They had already become used to the differences between Dutch and Afrikaans and conversation flowed easily. Barend was a gifted raconteur and they all enjoyed a good story.

It was rare for Elena to have the luxury of knowing when George would be able to call because he couldn't predict the demands of his duties. The flip-side of this situation, though, was the absolute surprised delight of finding him on the doorstep if she answered the ring of the doorbell. If anyone else in the family answered the summons, it was equally exciting to look up from whatever task was engaging her to find George in front of her.

Privacy, of course, was an exceptional treat. With such a sociable family and fairly crowded living conditions, it wasn't easy to find a space where they could restrict their conversation to themselves. Social convention also always dictated that they be chaperoned on any outing. The Gherardesca garden was a godsend because they could wander the park without raising eyebrows. There were usually other residents taking the air in the park but it was large enough not to have to talk to too many people and to be able to find a quiet corner to themselves. To find a sunny nook and while away an hour in pleasant, peaceful surroundings and gentle flirtation was bliss.

George was also the bearer of gifts. He had a discerning eye for stylish goods and fine craftsmanship – probably inherited from his mother who was an esteemed dressmaker whose evening-gowns were in great demand. The first of his gifts he presented in November on her birthday and this was a highly prized pair of silk stockings and a handbag. The stockings might have been regarded as a rather intimate first gift under different circumstances, but the privations of war pushed any such qualms Lucia might have harboured into the background.

Then came a greatly treasured bar of soap. Soap had become a rare commodity and Elena guarded her cake jealously because it had to be used for washing and as a shampoo substitute. She always made sure it was well hidden from her sisters.

The soap was followed by other 'luxuries' like toothpaste and two American pure woollen army blankets which were beautifully soft and fine. They were khaki green and Elena had one dyed brown and made into a coat. The other one she still has. Throughout their lives together George chose gifts with a mixture of thoughtfulness, sensitivity and practicality.

George's arrival in her life brought much, much more, though. Overnight her shoebox life was transformed. The war had forced the family into constant and close confinement with each other and even with outsiders whom they had to absorb into the family circle. As with the Italian doctor, some of these people weren't even very likeable. And then there were the German officers camping in their living quarters and compelling them to watch their every move and word. The daily struggle to put together a meal was another encumbrance.

The presence of George in her existence suddenly removed all the growing tensions and irritations of daily survival. Her tiny world became a glowing, new universe. Everyone was viewed with greater tolerance and patience. Tired, old family jokes took on a new funniness. The rhythm and pace of the days lost their tedious uniformity.

Major Gooseman was very nosey about George's appearance on the scene and when a huge bunch of flowers accompanied by a card, written in French, arrived at the office, Boris took it upon himself to read the card first. He asked Elena why she wanted to go out with a "pig of a South African". She replied that she'd rather go out with a South African pig than a British dog. Perhaps she had learnt something about men by then and certainly how to deal with her Major.

If George's presence had given Elena a new universe, she had become the centre of his solar system. He had never really experienced a strong and permanent emotional pivot, always having relied on himself for his emotional stability. His entire upbringing, education and career had revolved around physical activity and achievement and he wasn't much given to introspection about matters of the heart. He had been brought up to 'get on with the job' and deal, in a practical manner, with whatever came his way. For the first time in his life there was another human being at the focal point of his every day, other than the strict fulfilment of duty, or achievement of goals he had set for himself, or somebody else had set for him.

Not that he was lacking in experience of the rituals of flirtation and courtship, but there had never been any woman who had brought the kind of permanent glow to the most mundane of duties that Elena brought to him now. There was also the sense of her joyous being in his life which filtered through the most harrowing and arduous of assignments. What was it that someone said about love turning a nursery rhyme into an ode?

*   *   *

To better understand the George with whom Elena fell in love, it helps to know something about the people and life from which he had come.

George Samuel Jennings was born on Christmas Day 1914 (also Lucia's birthday) in Upington, in the far Northern Cape Province of South Africa. The town lies on the edge of the inhospitable and vast Kalahari Desert. At the time of George's birth, the lone policeman in the town, Constable Thorne, rode a camel in the course of his duties.

George's parents were Edgard and Hendrieka Suzanna (née Van Sittert). These were two tough people who both came from long lines of tough people. Hendrieka and Edgard didn't particularly like each other.

Before George was born, Edgard and Hendrieka had had twins but sadly, both babies died within an hour of their birth. The twins were followed by George, and two years later, Hilda. They then had another son, John, but he died at the age of nine months after contracting meningitis.

Their youngest child was Trixie. This delightful little sister survived childhood but her life was marred by great hardship. Her marriage was disastrous as her husband was an alcoholic and a really brutal one at that. She had a daughter, Gay. Trixie eventually left her husband and, against the odds, qualified as an air hostess. Tragically, she was killed on her first flight in 1948 when her plane crashed somewhere in the Free State. Gay was raised by her paternal grandparents who refused to allow her any contact with her mother's family and it was many years before George was able to re-establish contact with Gay.

George was born during the 1914 Rebellion in which many Afrikaners, still bitter about the South African War, were adamant about not supporting the Allied cause. Their resentment was further fueled when General Louis Botha announced that South African troops would invade German South West Africa to wrest the territory from German control. The organization of the Rebellion was somewhat haphazard with fighting breaking out almost simultaneously in the Transvaal, the Orange Free State and, most significantly for George's family, near Upington.

Edgard was away with his commando unit, fighting the rebels, when Hendrieka went into labour with George. She was alone in Upington. It being Christmas Day, everyone was preoccupied with their Christmas festivities and family duties, and there was no one for her to send for. However, even if she had been able to call for help, she was so contentious and independent that she wouldn't have done so any way. Consequently, she delivered her baby herself.

When Edgard returned that evening she asked him to fetch the scissors. He asked what she needed them for and she told him that he would need them to cut the umbilical cord for her. This horrified and repelled him and he couldn't bring himself to do it so she was forced to cut the cord herself. She wasn't best pleased with Edgard anyway: the fact that the rebels whom Edgard's commando unit had been pursuing were her Boer people, also left a bitter taste in her mouth.

Initially George did not thrive and, to add to their woes, Hendrieka received news that they were under threat from the rebel forces and needed to flee Upington. Once again Edgard was on commando. She, George and a domestic worker fled on foot. They were forced to cross a river in flood to escape. George's nanny balanced him on her head to keep him clear of the swirling waters over the submerged causeway.

Safely back in Upington, George was taken to their doctor who said that he was starving. It was little wonder that Hendrieka was unable to feed him under those harrowing circumstances.

She found a wet nurse who stayed with the family for many years. His nurse came to regard George as her own. As an adult, George visited the old lady. He was greatly touched when she gave him 20 cents to "buy himself some sweeties".

The Van Sitterts were 'trekboers', that hardy, semi-nomadic tribe of Dutch descendants who refused to conform to any system of established government. Before the dawn of the nineteenth century they had explored far beyond the recognized frontiers of the Cape Colony.

Hendrieka's mother was a herbalist and midwife. By the time Hendrieka was born they had not yet settled down to living in one place and were still nomadic. When Hendrieka was four or five, whilst they were on trek, she fell ill and it didn't look as though she was going to survive. She was too ill to continue the journey and her father had to push on to find fresh grazing for his cattle. He left her and her mother camped out under a tree near water somewhere, fully expecting to return and find that his daughter had died. She didn't.

Hendrieka's parents always remained extremely self-sufficient, even when they had given up their nomadic lifestyle and had settled permanently on a farm. Hendrieka recalled their tradition of slaughtering a cow, a pig and a sheep, all on the same day. This vast quantity of meat then had to be processed before sundown. The meat that wasn't made into biltong (salted and dried) was stored in an outside cool-house. This building was constructed of a double wall of aerated bricks, lined with coke. Water trickled down from a tank on the concrete roof through the walls, creating a very effective cool-room. Nothing went to waste and they even continued to make their own candles and soap at a time when these products were readily available in shops.

George's father was descended from the 1820 Settlers and he came from an equally tough mob.

The Settlers were all of British stock. Of the 90 000 applicants only 4000 were selected for their good character, skills and potential hardiness. They were an exceedingly diverse group drawn from all walks of life and social rank. What they had in common was a burning desire to escape the desperate economic privations of post-Napoleonic Britain and create a better life for themselves and their descendants.

What the Settlers didn't know was that they were to be used as a human buffer between the Cape Colony and the advancing Xhosa tribesmen. What the authorities didn't know was that they weren't going to be dealing with meek and mild individuals who would quietly submit to their autocratic dictates. It was the independence of mind and spirit and indefatigability that not only ensured the Settlers' survival, but also enabled them to make an inestimable contribution to the character and development of their new land.

Theirs were the dreams and hopes that would be shared by so many post-World War Two European settlers.

George's great grandfather, James Jennings, was born at Deverill Longbridge, near Warminster in Wiltshire in 1817. He was only three years old when he arrived in Africa with the 1820 Settlers.

James, his mother, Mary, who was 30, and his 28-year-old father, also called James, boarded the Weymouth on the 21ˢᵗ of December 1819. By the time they reached Spithead, just outside Portsmouth Harbour, James senior had fallen seriously ill. The captain decided that the little family would have to be put ashore. James senior was taken off first and transported to the shore by longboat. He was admitted to the Royal Hospital Haslar which served as the naval hospital.

Before Mary and little James could follow, a storm blew up making it impossible for them to be landed. There was Mary, desperately worried about her gravely ill husband, trapped on the heaving deck of the ship with her little boy clutched to her chest. No amount of pleading with the officers could persuade them to allow her to return to land and the tide was turning. The Weymouth set sail with them still aboard. Feeling bullied and at the mercy of officialdom, she could do nothing but hope and pray that James senior would be nursed to health and sail for the Cape later. Purportedly, it was only when Mary arrived at the Cape that she learnt that James had died in hospital. (British 1820 Settlers to South Africa website).

They were members of Edward Ford's party which was made up largely of labourers from Wiltshire. Most of these people had sold all they possessed in preparation for this venture and when they had arrived in Portsmouth, towards the end of 1819, they found that their ship, the 'Weymouth', a naval supply ship and one of the largest ships, had not yet been refitted and was not ready to sail. This placed them in a terrible predicament: they had no spare cash and no accommodation. The Colonial Department did take pity on them (or perhaps didn't want the image of their emigration scheme tarnished) and gave them temporary accommodation aboard a three-decker hulk which was serving as the tender for the Weymouth. Conditions were not easy and one wonders what this state of affairs contributed to the elder James's illness.

The voyage, too, was appalling. Many children under the age of two died on this terrible journey. The ship records show that between the 5th of February and the 25th of February, nine children were buried at sea.

Death and disease weren't their only tribulations. They even had an encounter with a galleon which threatened them with a piratical takeover. They found themselves under fire from this large vessel with intimidatingly lofty prow and stern sections. The Weymouth was forced to heave to. Pandemonium must have ensued amongst passengers and crew. Guy Butler, editor of 'The 1820 Settlers', quotes William Cock, the leader of the Cock Party, who wrote of the incident "*She was quite prepared for battle, … carried several small guns, with a long, brass gun on a swivel, and a rascally-looking crew fit for anything – no doubt a pirate as well as a slaver.*"

Once some sort of communication had been established, the captain of the galleon identified his ship as a licensed slave-ship. What was more revealing of the captain's other career path, though, was his excuse for firing on the Weymouth in the first place: he claimed that he had mistaken the Weymouth for a Spanish merchantman! Why would he fire on a merchant ship if he weren't a pirate? And then a group from the Weymouth was invited aboard the slave-ship. Was this to verify the captain's claim that his ship was a slaver? The notorious stench of slave-ships would have been enough to confirm this without having to board the vessel. Was the invitation some sort of apology? One can't imagine that a guided tour was in the offing or that any sane human being would want to take up such an offer. Perhaps the dreadful tedium of the voyage was enough to make any form of diversion welcome and some passengers actually did pay their assailant a visit.

Mary must have been a redoubtable woman because before the journey was over, she had taken on the care of two more children, Ephraim and Joseph Dicks, whose father had died in Table Bay on Wednesday the 26th of April.

His body was interred ashore. Their mother, Jane Dicks, died on Wednesday the 3rd of May. As the two boys are listed under 'Jennings' in the Settler roll, Mary's fostering of them must have been official and recorded in the ship's log.

Who knows what Mary's thoughts and feelings were by the time they landed in Algoa Bay in May. This was certainly not the green and pleasant countryside which she had known in England. Before her arrival she could not possibly have envisaged the bleak and inhospitable stretch of coastline that was Algoa Bay. The seemingly endless curve of sand dunes might have been spectacular but for her this was a desolate wasteland of continuously pelting sand that infiltrated everything. In addition to the wind, summer was over and the weather was turning cold. Their shelter was a bell-tent which did little to keep out the rain, sand or cold.

The circumstances were not easy for any of the settlers but it must have been an even worse ordeal for a grieving woman with the additional responsibility of feeding and caring for three children, two of whom were very young, in less than sanitary conditions. Also, there was the added uncertainty of her personal situation. These people had arrived as farmer-settlers: each family was supposed to occupy a piece of land, build a homestead and cultivate the soil. In addition to this, there was no infrastructure such as roads and markets. How on earth was she to do all this on her own? There was nothing in England for her to return to and in any case she lacked the financial means of returning. Not for the first time Mary must have felt hemmed in and shoved in the back by fate and the authorities.

Eventually Ford's party was moved off but their destination was vague and they seem to have been thoroughly mucked about. They were moved from place to place until they were finally settled on the right bank of the Lynedoch River on land which is now known as 'Ford's Party'.

They might have felt some relief at knowing where their destiny now lay but their situation was dire. There was little chance of beginning to build for the future, or even envisage a better existence. They were trapped into scratching for the meanest level of subsistence survival.

A mysterious 'Mr F' visited a number of the parties in the early months of 1823 and made the following comments about Ford's Party in his diary on the 3rd of April: *"Hyman and Ford's party are in a truly miserable plight, with scarcely anything to eat, but a few vegetables. I here saw an aged couple in almost a starving condition. On going into their hut, I found the poor woman boiling a little pumpkin soup, which was mixed with some milk. She said this was the only food they had; and their wretched dwelling was neither wind nor water-tight.*

"At a little distance I met what had once been, as I was told, a fine hearty-looking young woman, but now miserably emaciated – apparently about twenty-four or twenty-five years of age. She was leading one child, another following, and a third was on her arm. They were all without shoes or stockings. The woman's dress (if such it could be called), consisted of the remains of an old tent tied about her; the children were clad in the same manner; and the canvas appeared so rotten, that it would scarcely hang on them." ('The 1820 Settlers' edited by Guy Butler)

This heart-rending scene could so easily have been a description of our Mary. In a sense one hopes it was Mary because there is some comfort in knowing that Mary survived such horror because she later married Joseph King whose wife, Ann, died in 1823. Joseph and Ann had had five children: Charles, Joseph, Mary Ann, Phillip and Andrew. Mary and Joseph then produced two more children: Elisha and Eleanor Mary. Joseph was a member of Bradshaw's Party which had settled in Lemon Valley on the Torrens River. They called the district New Gloucester.

Little is known of young James's youth and education but he did develop a passion for this wild, new land along with great hunting skills for which he became renowned in his adulthood.

James junior married Sarah Sanders in Grahamstown in 1838 and they had eleven children. According to the British 1820 Settlers to South Africa website, their first child was Jeremiah, known as 'Jere' who was born in 1840. He was followed by James William, known to the family as 'William', who was born in 1842 and died on the 13th of March 1882. Two years later, on the 4th of September 1844, John was born. Sarah took an eight-year break after

John's birth and her next baby was Emma, who was born in 1852. Emma was followed by Mary and in 1859, George Edward Jennings arrived.

In 1866, when James was nearly fifty, he and Sarah packed up and trekked to the Transvaal, where James began a whole new career. On reaching the Witwatersrand, they stopped on a Boer farm and James asked if the Boer knew of any farming land which was for sale. The man told him that his land could be had for twelve head of cattle. James offered him eight and his offer was rejected. This farm was called Langlaagte.

Ironically, twenty years later, in 1886, the main reef group of Auriferoris Conglomerates was discovered on this very farm by George Harrison and George Walker, two miners who had packed up their tools in the Eastern Transvaal when the diggings in the Pilgrim's Rest and Barberton areas gave out. They had found employment on Langlaagte and made their discovery when out for a walk. This discovery led to the proclamation of the Witwatersrand Goldfields. Langlaagte itself became the first of the vertical shaft gold mines on the Reef and was christened 'Langlaagte Estates'. For four more head of cattle James would have been sitting atop a very rich gold mine!

The man who owned the farm at the time of the discovery of gold was Gerhardus Cornelis Oosthuizen. Whether this was the same man who had offered his farm to James is not certain.

The family finally bought the farm 'Blaauwbank' near the spot where the town of Magaliesburg is situated today. And discovered gold! The horizontal mine shaft they dug into the hillside behind their house was the first proper gold mine on the Witwatersrand and dates to 1874. The homestead and family graveyard still exist and the mine is now a tourist attraction.

I was chatting to my father about the Jennings connection to Langlaagte and Blaauwbank, Langlaagte being of great interest to my father because my grandfather was a blast contractor and mine official on Langlaagte. I discovered that my father knew a great deal about Blaauwbank too. One of his great school pals was a lad called Reggie Nichols. Reggie had an aunt called Mrs Lester. Before her marriage she had been a Jennings and was the current occupant of the Blaauwbank homestead and owner of the original farm.

Reggie and my father spent a great deal of their holiday time in the 1930's on the farm and my father has vivid recollections of the mine and the farm. At that stage the mine was still operational although not highly productive. It had never been a rich mine because it didn't lie anywhere near the main reef. Donkeys were used to pull the coco-pans in and out of the mine. According to my father, mining ceased at the end of the 1930's.

The cemetery, too, was a source of fascination for my father, as was the homestead. This had begun life as a fairly modest dwelling but over the years, as various members of the family married and produced their own offspring, the house had been extended until it was an extremely long, sprawling building.

The name 'Jennings' had not completely disappeared from the region and a family of Jennings descendants owned a neighbouring farm. However, some sort of rift seems to have occurred between them and the Lester branch. Mrs Lester disapproved strongly of some aspect of her relatives' way of life. This bit of gossip was gleaned by my father as he eavesdropped on tea-table conversations between his parents and the Lesters.

James continued his diverse and active lifestyle once his family was settled and his name often crops up in hunting contexts all over Southern Africa where he hunted with such notables as Frederick Selous and Henry Hartley. He died on the 19th of October 1905 at the age of 89.

CHAPTER 13

Where and when George's grandfather struck out on his own is unclear but he must have settled in Upington at some point because George's father was born there in about 1880. Edgard was a bookkeeper for a law firm in Upington and he bred and trained racehorses on his farm outside Upington. The farm was well supplied with water, being on the Orange River, and able to exploit the canal system established in 1921 as part of the Orange River Scheme. The farm was on the road to the 'coloured' township outside Upington and Edgard and Hendrieka established a trading store and butchery and had a petrol pump on the property.

When George first went to school in Upington he rode the four kilometres on horseback. Later he did this on a bicycle with his shoes suspended by their laces around his neck. This was Hendrieka's means of saving the shoes from being used as brakes.

When he was a little older he and his sister, Hilda, who was two years younger, travelled by train to the town where Hendrieka's parents had settled. This was a long and complicated journey for two little children. They had to change trains at De Aar. To prevent their losing their tickets, they carried them in pouches suspended from thongs worn around their necks.

They attended a convent school and boarded with Hendrieka's mother, whom they referred to as 'Mingy Granny'. Her parsimony, no doubt, was a hangover from her frugal Trekboer days but difficult for the children to understand. At some point George ran away and hitched lifts from 'coloured' people in their ubiquitous donkey carts. When he finally got home, he was given a hiding and sent back immediately.

George's father was alternately a dictatorial, domineering father and free and easy. George learnt to drive when he was seven when his father made a habit of getting him to garage the car. Perhaps the most effective teaching was knowing what would happen if he bumped or scraped the car.

When he was fourteen an incident occurred for which Hendrieka never forgave Edgard.

The great friend of George's childhood was a young coloured boy, Jonas, who became Edgard's jockey when he reached adolescence. George and Jonas had practically grown up together and had spent endless days in each other's company, doing what veld-raised boys do – riding, exploring, hunting and camping together – and consequently developing a silent understanding and empathy which only the veld can breed.

Edgard had a magnificent but unpredicatable, temperamental, and sometimes vicious, stallion. Edgard had forbidden George from going near him. As George was a very competent rider, afraid of nothing, this animal must have been very frightening.

George was away at boarding-school when tragedy struck. The horse threw Jonas and then trampled him to death.

On George's return from school, he took the horse out and rode the devil out of him. When his father discovered that he had disobeyed him, he took a sjambok to him and flayed his back to the point where he had to take to his bed. George remembered lying on his stomach while his mother applied ointment to his back. She was weeping silently but he could feel her tears dripping on to his back.

His own much-loved horse was called 'Vierklawer' because of the star on his forehead which was in the shape of a four-leafed clover. It turned out to be a very well-chosen name. Vierklawer was out grazing, with his back legs hobbled, when the Orange River came down in spate. Poor old Vierklawer was swept away and George was heart-broken. However, three months later a starved and decrepit horse arrived on the farm. To his wonderment and delight, George discovered that it was Vierklawer! The poor creature was still encumbered by his hobbles.

George claimed that his athletics career began with his having to run after the car after opening and closing about thirty farm gates between Upington and the farm. There was certainly no waiting for him to catch up.

For his high school education he was sent to Victoria High School in Grahamstown. The name of this school was changed to Graeme College in 1938. Here, he maintained, his running ability was further encouraged by having to sprint from the sports fields, uphill, back to the boarding establishment, in order to avoid being last in line for food. He played good rugby and cricket and excelled at athletics, especially in track events, earning the Victor Ludorum.

George could be a handful. When he was seventeen he 'borrowed' his father's car and found his way into a highly-restricted diamond mining area in the desert. The area was rich in alluvial diamonds and he had collected a tobacco pouch of diamonds when he was spotted by a policeman – probably Constable Thorne. By then Constable Thorne had been given wheels and he gave chase but couldn't catch George. He also couldn't identify the vehicle because of the dust cloud George left in his wake.

A few days later George was awaiting his turn in the barber-shop when he overheard Constable Thorne telling the barber about the bastard who had been stealing diamonds and who had eluded his best efforts to catch him. George sat with his hands in his lap and his shoulders shuddering with barely-contained merriment.

He couldn't tell Elena what had happened to the stones because he forgot all about them when he returned to school. No doubt Hendrieka found them and disposed of them quickly and quietly: the penalties for the illicit possession of uncut diamonds were dire.

He matriculated in 1932. His father wanted him to go to university but he wasn't interested. He chose, instead, to join the police where he believed he could exploit his love of sport. This he succeeded in doing and, while ordinary policemen were on the beat, he became a physical training instructor.

In his class were some very interesting characters who were to make their mark on South African history. They included both Leibbrandt brothers. These two were both champion boxers. Sidney Robey Leibbrandt was the South African heavyweight boxing champion in the 1936 Olympic Games.

Robey's admiration for Hitler grew beyond control through his Munich experience. He made known his commitment to Nazi Germany and underwent training by the Germans as a paratrooper and saboteur. The Nazi objective was for him to return to South Africa to stir up as much trouble as he could for General Smuts's government. The code name for this operation was 'Weissdorn' or 'White Thorn'. His aim was to take over command of the Ossewa-Brandwag, an underground Afrikaner movement of people who deeply resented any South African support of Britain, and who supported all things Nazi. This was to be followed by the assassination of General Smuts and a coup d'etat.

Once his training in Germany had been completed, he sailed for home from the south of France in a tiny yacht, the Kyloe. He was accompanied by an officer who was in command of the Kyloe, and a radio operator called Dorner. He quarrelled with both but was especially distrustful of the officer in charge. He was supposed to land at Lamberts Bay on the West Coast but instead demanded that they land him at Mitchells Bay which is slightly north of Lamberts Bay. He took with him the radio transmitter, which was hidden in a tin marked 'flour'. For all his heroic and arrogant attitude, he didn't appear to manage things particularly well from the outset. He even succeeded in overturning his dinghy between the yacht and the shore.

Despite these foul-ups, he managed to stay at large for six months. At one point while he was on the run, and in the company of his brother, the authorities were about to pounce. To escape, he and his brother joined a procession of mourners and in this way managed to elude their pursuers. During this time he stirred up a great deal of controversy and excited a significant number of rabid anti-British supporters. He was finally captured on the 21st of December 1941.

George said that boxing against either of the brothers was a terrifying experience.

Of course, boxing was a compulsory part of the training so there was no escape. He also joked that he was particularly concerned about preserving his looks from their fists.

Also in the class was Hendrik ('Lang Hendrik' because he was 6'5" tall) van den Bergh who became head of the Bureau of State Security (BOSS). This was the organisation which was so hated by liberal students and anti-apartheid dissidents in the 60's and 70's. In 1963 he established South Africa's first secret intelligence-gathering organization. This was the forerunner of BOSS, which he founded in 1969. He was heavily involved in the 'Information Scandal' in which state funds were used by the ruling National Party for propagandist purposes, including trying to improve South Africa's image overseas.

Rocco de Villiers, who became deputy commissioner of police, was another classmate.

After George died, one of George's infamous student associates contacted Elena and invited her to visit him on her next trip to the Cape to see Toly. He boasted that he had a magnificent property, worth millions, on the West Coast. Elena decided to take him up on his offer and arranged for him to pick her up from the airport.

The approach to his house was a sandy track and her first glimpse of his home, as they came over a rise, was anything but magnificent – it was a shack. This inauspicious start did not bode well and things didn't get any better. He had a German shepherd called Rex and every time poor Rex barked, he yelled at him, "Rex get back in your blerry box!" Supper on the first evening of Elena's stay consisted of a small slice of stale pizza. The next morning Elena went shopping for groceries for which he was gracious enough to allow her to pay.

By the following morning his confidence had obviously accumulated and he decided to pay her an amorous early morning visit – in his underpants. When Elena's more genteel rejections of his amour failed, she said to him, "Rex, get back in your blerry box!" This had the desired effect and shortly afterwards Toly arrived to rescue her.

Enough about George's deplorable old classmates!

In about 1938, George left the police and joined the army, which he regarded as a 'proper' career option. Here, too, he was an instructor. He continued to enjoy his athletics and discovered a new talent. He had a friend who threw the javelin. George was helping him by fetching and carrying his javelins during a training session when George decided to hurl one himself – and threw it far further than the pal had ever managed.

At the Royal Scottish Gathering of The Federated Caledonian Society of South Africa in 1939, he won first prize for throwing the javelin and broke the South African Javelin Record, becoming the SA Champion and qualifying to represent South Africa at the 1940 Olympic Games, which, of course, never took place.

And then George did something that he lived to regret. He got married! He had been to a party where he had got rollicking drunk with his girlfriend's sister and then spent the night with her. In their inebriated state of sentimentality, they decided to get married the following day. It being 1942, and there being numerous marriages taking place in a hurry because men were being sent off to fight, getting married in such a rush didn't present any great obstacles and the deed was done – a disaster before it had even begun.

The pair lived in a flat in Pretoria. Lily was slovenly and fat, neither of which sat well with George, and then he discovered that she had other appetites which were also out of control: she had no control over her spending habits and loved a good party. She owned more than a hundred pairs of shoes! George also got very tired of funding the lavish drinks parties she hosted in their flat, often when he wasn't even present.

As a physical education instructor he was not compelled to go to the front but in desperation to get away from Lusty Lily, he applied to go north. The Allies had just been defeated in North Africa and he joined the second group of South Africans to be sent to North Africa. He was in the artillery at the time.

Major Bob Dreyer was in charge of the military police in Egypt and he offered George a captaincy in the military police, attached to the South African Sixth Armoured Division. Later Bob would become the chief of the South African Military Police in Italy and would be based in Rome.

George took part in the Battle of El Alamein and talked about the bombing in the first wave of attack beginning at midnight. He said it was so bright that one could read a newspaper in the light of the bombing. He would experience exactly the same thing in the Battle of Monte Cassino.

George developed a passion for Jeeps and first encountered them in Egypt where he managed to roll one in the desert in response to an American's challenge that it was impossible to roll a Jeep. Later, in Italy, George found himself at Monza and took the opportunity to race a Jeep around the famous track and pretend that he was the victor. He finished the course standing up behind the steering-wheel with fist raised in a victory salute to himself and the loud imaginary applause of his adoring crowds.

From Egypt, George was sent to the south of Italy and landed at Taranto. It was from this point that the Allies gradually made their way northwards to Monte Cassino.

Monte Cassino was a Benedictine monastery which dated back to the sixth century. It was filled with innumerable works of art and ancient artefacts. High on its mountain-top, it had a view across the Liri Valley. At the foot of the mountain lay the town of Cassino. The monastery and town had the unfortunate distinction of lying on the only militarily-feasible route to Rome, or what was known as 'Route 6' ('Italy's Sorrow' by James Holland page xxxvii). It was essential for the Germans to hold Monte Cassino in order to keep the Gustav Line intact. The Gustav Line extended from slightly north of the mouth of the Garigliano River on the west coast, through the Apennines, to the mouth of the Sangro River on the Adriatic.

It was George's job, along with his corporal, to reconnoitre and mark the route for the 6th Armoured Division. This meant that he was always stationed close to the front of the action.

To better understand the difficulties faced by the Sixth Armoured Division, and consequently the enormity of George's responsibilities and challenges, it is worth quoting war correspondent Victor Norton writing for the 'Cape Argus'. His report is recorded in Vic Alhadeff's 'South Africa in Two World Wars'. *"It is not easy to give an idea of the real strain and achievement in this kind of war, which involves hours and hours of steady forward movement against anything the enemy can do. The armour has to face anti-tank guns skilfully placed on winding roads, mines, bazookas and phosphorous bombs, and the infantry is seldom out of contact with snipers, small-arms and machine-gun fire, shell fire and incessant mortar fire."*

At Cassino George had to make a daily trip along a section of Route 6 to check on the men under his command. Travelling along this route meant always being under sniper fire from Monte Cassino. He became adept at driving the route in such a fashion as to make himself an unpredictable target. He varied his time and speed and zigzagged all over the place.

On occasion, he also had to drive Major-General W. H. Evered Poole along the route. Poole was head of the 6th Armoured Division. For this service to the Major-General, George was mentioned in dispatches by Poole.

The Allied attempts to take Monte Cassino began in January 1944. By Valentine's Day the US 34th ('Red Bull') and 36th ('Texas') Divisions had been decimated. The trees on the mountainside were shredded and splintered – a sight of absolute desolation – and the Abbey still gazed out like a "monstrous eye" *('The Lost Evidence: Battle of Monte Cassino' BBC History Channel)*.

It was occupied by a few monks who were sheltering a multitude of refugees. The Germans claimed that they had not occupied the Abbey but this was belied by Allied reconnaissance which reported seeing groups of Germans entering and leaving the monastery. Defending the position was easy for the occupants who needed only one man to defend against six trying to climb up to the Abbey.

The Red Bulls and Texans were replaced on the mountain by the 4th Indian Division and the 2nd New Zealand Division. On the 15th of February, at 09.30, 147 B17 heavy bombers, under the command of General Alexander, began an unearthly bombardment of the monastery. Witnesses describe the attack as having the ferocity of an earthquake and being able to feel the shock in one's bones, with chunks of the edifice being tossed in the air. The Abbey was destroyed – and still the Germans held the position.

The Allies made no attempt to secure Route 6 or the Abbey, and the Germans quickly regrouped and built up their rock defences. By the 11th of March all action had ceased around Monte Cassino and the extreme weather conditions weren't helping the Allied effort either. All this changed on the 11th, the day which saw the third attempt on the part of the Allies to take Monte Cassino.

General Alexander launched an air assault on the town in the form of four hours of carpet bombing. A quarter of a million shells were fired on this little town and there was nothing left. However, the Allied cause had not done itself too many favours by causing so much damage because the New Zealand infantry follow-up, which began at midday, was severely hampered as all the roads had been destroyed and the New Zealanders couldn't get their tanks into the town. The hidden alleyways created by the building rubble provided marvellous hiding places for the defenders and forced the New Zealanders into close combat.

By the 12th of March, progress had been made up Castle Hill towards the Abbey but control of the town had not yet been achieved. The 1st and 4th Platoons of the Essex Regiment had been given the unenviable job of trying to reach the Abbey and reinforce the Ghurkas. They had to follow white tape, which had been laid by the New Zealanders, but the tape had been cut in many places and they could only see the tape by the light of the bomb flashes anyway. They held out against the German paratroopers holding the Monastery at horrendous cost.

The scene was described as "a place of slaughter" and the screaming "unbelievable" ('Italy's Sorrow' by James Holland). On the 29th of March a truce was called. Incredibly, the German paratroopers borrowed stretchers from the Essexes to fetch their own wounded and return the Allied wounded.

Five thousand Allied soldiers were dead. Monte Cassino had become synonymous with misery and horror.

With D-Day only two months away, all the Allied commanders planned a decisive action involving all 28 divisions at their disposal. Their final attack was further delayed when the Germans hit their main ammunition dump at Cassino. The explosion was so enormous that it took with it several other storage depots, including the meat store. George recalled seeing bits of sheep carcass flying in all directions. Naturally, it took some time to reassemble the ammunition supply.

The Polish Corps, in the vanguard of the 8th Division, saw this planned action as their chance to reassert themselves after the devastation they and their people had suffered at the hands of the Russians and the Germans.

On the 11th of May at 23.00 hours, the Allies began a bombardment of every known German outpost on the Gustav Line whilst two Polish divisions attacked the Germans on Monte Cassino. Battles raged along the Gustav Line for thirty hours. By the 17th of May it had finally been breached after five months of struggle.

In the meantime the Poles had been pinned down on Cavalry Mount. The taking of Monte Cassino was no longer of strategic importance, but for the Poles it was a matter of critical national honour. They continued to fight like wild men to get up the slopes to the Abbey. Reportedly they relied heavily on vino, schnapps and whisky to keep up their morale and were always slightly sozzled. They refused to give in.

On the 18th of May they continued their advance up the perimeter of the Abbey wall, constantly expecting to be attacked, but the Germans had withdrawn under cover of darkness. At 10.20 a.m. a bugle sounded inside the Abbey – the Polish call to arms – and from this vantage point they were able to watch the American advance on Rome. The pennant of the Polish

12th Lancers fluttered above the Abbey. Two thousand Poles had died in this attack.

The next Allied objective was to defeat the Germans south of Rome. General Mark Clarke was particularly keen for the Americans to be seen as the liberators of Rome and to trap the Germans before they could reach northern Italy. However, his grandstanding allowed the Germans to escape northwards to establish the Gothic Line and prolong the struggle. Clarke's actions proved vainglorious as D-Day took place 48 hours later.

In all, 180 000 men died at Monte Cassino.

It is sacrilege of the worst kind to name a casino 'Montecasino' when so much human suffering took place there. There might be a bar space and an 's' missing from the name, but the word play shows the grossest of insensitivity and unforgivable ignorance.

*   *   *

All through the first half of the month of October, the South Africans were moving towards Monte Sole where the Germans were well entrenched on the massif, having established themselves very effectively in the caves at the top of the mountain. They had also created machine-gun nests so impregnable that they couldn't be routed from any direction.

As part of setting themselves up so cosily, they had conducted a brutal rastrellamenta at the end of September and beginning of October, over a period of about three days, to eradicate the partisan threat. The population in every village and settlement was rounded up and annihilated. No farm house was left untouched. By the time they had finished, seven hundred and seventy two people, mainly civilians, had been killed on Monte Sole *"making it the single worst massacre in Western Europe during the entire war"* according to James Holland in 'Italy's Sorrow'. He adds that *"One hundred and seventy four buildings had been burned to the ground."* Monte Sole would remain, forevermore, largely unpopulated. Those little communities would never be the same again.

Somewhere in this vicinity, George and his sergeant, Stan Conker, came across a deserted village. They couldn't understand why the village was so quiet – there was no sign of a child, a dog or any beast. The whole place was enveloped in an eerie silence.

George sent Stan ahead into the village and Stan approached the village church - which was his normal practice in a strange village. From a distance he realized that it had been set alight and was little more than a burnt-out shell. As he drew near he discovered something far more shattering. This was something from which he would never fully recover.

Outside the building were the bodies of infants and children, all with horrific injuries, largely to their heads and faces.

Inside the church were the bullet-riddled bodies of the village women and old men.

When George arrived he found Stan on his knees in a state of dazed horror.

It took them both some time to gather themselves sufficiently to piece together what had happened.

The Germans had rounded up all the adults, mainly women and old men, and locked them inside the church. They had then gathered all the children outside the church and bludgeoned them to death with their rifle butts. Many had been swung round by their feet and had their heads smashed against the stone of the church walls. This was confirmed by the bloody testimony on the walls and the corners of the building. It was conjectured that this method of execution was used to save precious ammunition. In the meantime, their helpless families had had to listen to the cries and thuds. And then it was their turn. The adults were gunned down inside the church and the building set on fire.

What memories does a man take away from a scene like this? Does the memory fragment itself into isolated images such as a child's ball made from rags and held together with twine? A tiny rag doll no bigger than a woman's hand? A lost shoe? Is this fragmentation the mind's way of coping and moving on? The trouble is that these images can't ever be banished and continue to boil unpredictably to the surface, no matter where the witness goes or however long he lives.

War zone photographers seem to have a particular penchant for finding and focusing on the abandoned fragment, the reminder that before the tragedy, children played and were loved and cared for, mothers prepared vegetables for dinner and fathers tended gardens and enjoyed a drink. These images might provide a mental 'sliding away' from the abomination of mutilated innocents but they also hold a terrible poignancy. It is often in what the pictures don't say, the absence of brutal, in-your-face depiction, that a terrible poignancy lies, a poignancy which is somehow sharper, and encompasses even more sorrow.

CHAPTER 14

George and Stan never openly discussed with each other what they had endured together in that little village. George did not want to have children of his own and perhaps this event had something to do with his attitude. His own photographs (and he loved photography) were always living things – a grey-bearded old man on a bench, Elena's youthful hands, and birds, lots and lots of lovely bird studies.

Stan was broken by this experience. He had left his own little girl in Durban, a child with whom he was quite besotted. Elena only met Stan after this experience. By then he was in the habit of peppering every second sentence with a blasphemy and she had some quite entertaining incidents in which George pushed poor old Stan to the edge of his precarious grip and would then hear his explosion: "J___ C___, George, are you trying to bloody kill me?"

The particular incident which aroused Stan's ire to the point of apoplexy occurred some time later, in 1945, when George was billeted on the shores of Lago Maggiore near his headquarters. The area had taken on a very festive air after VE Day and there were regular parties in the villas around the lake which were occupied by Allied officers. In order to get to the various parties as quickly and conveniently as possible, George had requisitioned an outboard motor boat. Presumably it was also used for more serious military purposes. The Italians from whom such boats were borrowed were evidently very happy about the arrangement because the boats were reconditioned by the army and returned in far better condition – if they hadn't been written off!

One afternoon George invited Stan to join him for a joyride. As they were approaching the dock at the end of their outing, George told Stan to stand in the bow holding the rope in readiness for leaping on to the dock at the appropriate moment, to tie up.

Unfortunately, George miscalculated his approach and realized that he was coming in much too fast: he was about to crash into the wall. Without any word of warning to poor Stan, he threw the motor into reverse. Stan went flying into the water where he was confronted by a forward-moving boat with an angry propeller heading straight for him. He began kicking out at the hull with all his might in a desperate attempt to shove the boat away.

Thankfully he came to no harm and emerged behind the boat, spluttering and spitting and fit to kill George. George was not the least bit remorseful and nearly split his sides laughing. Stan still hadn't forgiven him when they met up with Elena later. He said to Elena, "J___ C___, Meidjie, don't you go anywhere with that bastard. He'll kill you!"

A few months later Stan disappeared. When Elena asked George where he was, she learnt that he had finally had a complete nervous collapse and had been sent home to Durban.

By the 10th of October 1944, the South Africans had reached the Monte Stanco massif, south of Monte Sole, and proceeded to wrestle it from the Germans over the next week.

Monte Pezze was taken next, on the 16th and 17th of October, and by the 23rd of October they had reached Monte Salvaro. All that remained was Monte Sole. This progress was made at enormous cost in lives and injuries.

Allied losses for October in the four US Divisions averaged five hundred and fifty men a day and desertions had also increased markedly. Many of the men were feeling that they were stuck in these mountains for no good cause as Italy was no longer a campaign of any significance in Europe. September and October had seen the highest number of casualties of the whole Italian campaign and even exceeded the dreadful toll of Monte Cassino.

By the 31st of October the Fifth Army was no longer pushing north, although the front continued to be active throughout the winter months.

It had been decided, with Eisenhower, that Allied activity in this part of the war arena would consist of a two-pronged approach, with one branch continuing in Italy, and the other across the Adriatic on the Yugoslavian coast. General Alexander's immediate aim in Italy was to force the Germans to retreat to the River Adige in north-east Italy. However, this would probably not be possible before spring but part of the preparation for this was to take Bologna and Ravenna.

Ravenna was to be taken first by the Eighth Army, while Fifth Army troops were withdrawn from the front in shifts to be rested in order to be ready when their turn came to capture Bologna. This was scheduled for the 30th of November.

All these plans depended, though, on weather conditions. If conditions deteriorated badly none of this would happen and the Fifth and Eighth Armies would have to sit tight for the winter.

The relevance of all this to George, of course, was that these plans determined the extent of his active involvement in finding the routes to be taken by the Sixth Armoured Division. Consequently, by the end of October he had a little more free time on his hands as the South Africans were embroiled around Monte Sole and the Allied commanders were in talks about their next moves before winter really set in.

The Fifth Army was planning to renew its offensive on the 1st of December but very quickly this was changed to the 7th of December and still nothing much happened.

In the meantime, from the end of October to the end of November, George and Elena saw each other as often as possible.

On the afternoon of the 22nd of November, George arrived at the apartment quite unexpectedly. Elena was surprised and delighted at the visit but as she led him into the apartment she noticed that he seemed a little restrained. They went through the usual social niceties with the family who always warmed to George's presence. A little later he suggested that they take a stroll through the Gherardesca garden. This wasn't unusual but it was a chilly autumn afternoon and dusk was closing in.

There was nothing that Elena could put her finger on but clearly all was not right with George that afternoon. As they strolled towards their usual sheltered spot, Elena held on to George's elbow and upper arm in the way that was becoming pleasantly familiar and which provided her with warmth, comfort and closeness but that afternoon also communicated some sort of tension to her.

She was feeling increasingly nervous as they seated themselves on their bench. It wasn't in Elena's makeup to anticipate bad news but by now she was trying to figure out what George could possibly have to tell her which could be disturbing him so much. Could he have been transferred to somewhere out of reach? Was he being repatriated? Had someone died?

He took both her hands in his and looked into her eyes. It was a look which seemed to reach right into her but also felt very distant. As George began to talk, it took Elena a moment to focus on what he was actually saying to her: she found herself hearing George telling her that he was married. And what did Elena do?

She laughed!

Perhaps it was shock. Maybe it was relief. But it definitely wasn't what George expected. Then she stood up, spun around in a pirouette of sorts, pulled him up off the bench and performed a not-very-dignified jig. It was clear that his marital status mattered not one to jot to her and he grabbed her in a bear hug of relief and gratitude – for her understanding, her complete lack of rancour – and for just being her!

As Elena nestled against his chest – a now familiar and favourite spot – she was aware that her attitude might be unconventional but she had such a sense of oneness and harmony with this man, such a feeling of rightness, that she knew they would overcome any and all obstacles to be together. It certainly wouldn't take a marriage certificate to keep them apart or together.

Elena must have realized, of course, that her family wouldn't take kindly to the news and it would cause some kind of upheaval, or perhaps she was so taken up in the moment that she couldn't give too much concern to it. She had never been one to worry about the future and had a particular talent for living in the present and relishing every moment of it. Perhaps this wonderful gift was now more evident than ever before. She didn't tell anyone about his marriage, including Toly, and nobody detected any concern or change in her, so possibly this is more evidence that she really wasn't particularly bothered.

George came to see her on the 27th of November, her birthday. He was back on the 29th of November, a Wednesday, and they, accompanied by Toly, took a jaunt to Prato where George was still stationed.

It must have been soon after this, in early December, that George's headquarters were moved northwards to Castiglione dei Pepoli where he would be based for the duration of the winter and through the beginning of the Spring Campaign. Accommodation in Castiglione was good but the base camp he had to use beneath Monte Sole was a peasant house which was so bitterly cold that icicles hung from the roof – inside – and he had to stuff paper into the keyholes and other crevices in a vain attempt to keep out the draughts.

Many Allied officers were still calling on the Van Praags on a regular basis and no doubt George's name occurred frequently in conversation. As protective and proper parents, Barend and Lucia were listening attentively (and probably instigating a lot of the conversation). One afternoon in December Major Gooseman sent Elena off on an errand to post Christmas cards and told her that she could go straight home afterwards.

When she reached the apartment she was delighted to find that George was there visiting her parents. Her delight was short-lived when she realized that the atmosphere was distinctly chilly. There was no sign of the usual cheerful chat about inconsequential things. There was no lighthearted banter or laughter. Barend looked unusually stern but one look at Lucia's face really put the wind up Elena. Her mother was tight-lipped. Lucia also had a peculiar way of tensing the skin beneath her eyes which made her eyes look slightly narrower and which signalled extreme displeasure.

Elena looked from Barend to Lucia and then to George and for moments nobody said a word. Finally Barend broke the silence.

The rumour that George was married had reached their ears but they had hoped against hope that there was no truth in the rumours, or that there had been some mistake. In the meantime, George had decided that he himself had better enlighten them about his situation. He had chosen that afternoon to see them without Elena being present. He assured them that his marriage had been over long before he had left South Africa, his separation was official, and that he'd volunteered for active service to underscore the fact that the marriage was dead and gone. There was no question about his determination to marry Elena as soon as his divorce was finalized and he was hoping to hear that the decree nisi had been granted in the very near future.

The Van Praags liked, respected and trusted George and had no doubt about his sincerity. Nevertheless, they reacted with understandable outrage. Once Barend had told Elena what was going on, Lucia turned to Elena and said, "Jij mag niet de jonge man meer zien!" (*"You may not see this young man any longer!"*) to which Elena replied, "Maar, Moeder, ik hou van hem," - the bizarrely understated Dutch way of stating that she loved him.

George continued to declare his honourable intentions and Elena simply said that if they refused to let her see him at home, she would see him in the streets. This really affronted their sense of propriety and eventually they realized the futility of the ban.

Given the times and the values of her parents, this was quite a concession for them to make. They did, though, have years of experience of their headstrong daughter. Although quite proper in her own way, Elena was not easily swayed once she'd made up her mind. And so Barend and Lucia must have given a grudging blessing.

What Elena didn't know, and what George only revealed to her years later, was that that afternoon Barend had told him that he, too, had been married previously and because his first wife had been unable to have children, the marriage had been annulled!

*   *   *

December of 1944 was a very festive season. Florence was free and although the Allies still faced serious obstacles in clearing the Germans out of the rest of northern Italy, and probably wouldn't be able to complete the task during the winter months, Allied command had had their important conferences and there seemed to be a renewed sense of purpose and focus. And it was Christmas time and a much more hopeful one than Florentines had experienced in a good few years!

On the 6th of December the family had their own celebration – their traditional St Nicholas party. It was this very occasion that Bruno talks about in 'The Pink Book' when he came looking for the Van Praags after being in hiding for so long, and found himself vortexed into great merriment with Elena in the middle of a group of very attentive Allied officers and all aglow at being the centre of their lavish attention, particularly the attention of one tall, good-looking captain: this was Bruno's 'Queen of the Festival' and the tall, good-looking captain was, of course, George.

Toly, too was making the most of the occasion and was practising her English, of which she was so proud. She got herself involved in a conversation with an officer who asked her what her father had done before the war. She said, "He owned sheeps," to which the officer asked, "How many sheep did he own?" She said four, and he asked, "Where did he keep them? In the garden?" She said, "No, of course not. He kept them in the harbour." He then wanted to know if they hadn't drowned. She said they had, because they had all been sunk. The penny eventually dropped!

The girls still had all their pre-war ballgowns and their precious furs – carefully stored – and all the necessary accessories. Their day wear might have dwindled to very little that was respectable enough to be seen outside their home, but their evening wear was none-too-shabby. Unpacking these treasures must have brought a great sense of restoring happier times.

On the 16th of December Charlie Pretorius (the captain in charge of the military police in Florence) hosted a big dance at the villa requisitioned for his use, and which was also situated in the Gherardesca garden. This was one of a group of villas which formed a section of the boundary of the garden.

Consequently, it was just a short distance from their apartment and could be approached through the garden or via the street. It was here that George usually stayed when he was in Florence. The 16th of December, the Day of the Covenant in South Africa, was possibly as significant for the South Africans, especially at this stage of the war, as St Nicholas Day was for the Van Praags. Charlie's villa became the venue of any number of dances and celebrations which Elena and George were to attend.

They weren't able to spend Christmas Day together (both George's and Lucia's birthdays) but he was back on Boxing Day and again on New Year's Eve.

In January, George presented Elena with a broad, silver-linked bracelet of wonderful Italian craftsmanship and which is often on her arm in photographs of special occasions. No gold was available in Italy because Mussolini had forced every last ounce of gold out of his citizens for his war effort. People had even had to give up their wedding rings. Lucia had replaced her ring with an iron band, which was the normal practice. The jewellers, however, had continued to exercise their skills with whatever material they could find.

On Sunday, the 4th of January, George took Elena and Toly to Castiglione. Whilst they were having tea at the villa where he was billeted, Toly wanted to go to the loo but was at a loss as to how to approach the matter with decorum. Elena tried to sidestep but Toly said, "He's your boyfriend. It's your job to ask him." They decided the politest approach was to use their usual Italian expression for moments such as these and they told George that they would like 'to wash their hands'.

He sent for his batman, passed on the message and the batman disappeared, which mystified them. He didn't come back for some time but George said not to worry – he was getting things ready: more mystery. Eventually he returned and showed them to a room where a basin of water had been poured and towels laid out – but there was no sign of a loo! They had no option but to ditch that euphemism.

Thereafter, George was always very solicitous of Elena's needs, making sure that 'facilities' were available. His precautions led to more confusion and hilarity on the occasion when she had to be driven somewhere in an open

Jeep by George's sergeant. George had told the sergeant to make sure he offered her the opportunity to visit a 'restroom' at some point on the journey. The sergeant asked her if she would like to 'powder her nose' to which she replied, "Why on earth would I want to powder my nose when I'm covered in dust anyway?" Eventually he said to her, "Please, Meidjie, die Kaptein sê jy moet gaan piepie!" (*"the captain says you must have a pee!"*), blushing furiously as he told her this.

Incidentally, it must seem rather odd, and perhaps pedantic, that the specific dates of so many of the meetings between George and Elena are recorded, especially in the light of the fact that Elena was hardly the sort of character to keep a diary. What she did do, though, was to keep a record of their growing romance, (and intimacies – in code) in pencil, on a scruffy little piece of paper. She still has this piece of paper. It is kept in a lovely little wooden box with a secret opening – the same box in which it has always been kept. This box was a gift to her from the Busseli daughter – the Busselis from Rada in Chianti who kept the Van Praags supplied with red wine. For me, this little scrap of paper is an icon signifying the illimitable human spirit in which life and love continue, despite the horrors and sorrows that humans visit upon themselves in war.

Throughout January there were no major changes in Allied positions on the front. Things only really began to move again from the 19th of February. The object was for the 10th Mountain Division to get rid of any enemy presence across two mountain ridges so that the front line could draw level with the South Africans and the 1st Armoured Division across the Monte Sole massif. This operation lasted until the 5th of March and created a six-mile front which was seen as good preparation for the Spring Offensive.

As the South Africans were pretty stationary during this time, George had reduced scouting activities. He wasn't completely free of responsibilities but his time was more flexible. He was given leave from the 3rd of February to the 12th of February but this seems to have been extended, judging by all the outings they shared in February.

On the 9th of February they paid a visit to the Busselis in Radda in Chianti, accompanied by Lucia. They bought a barrel of the Busselis' red wine. When they got home this had to be siphoned into carafes which were then plugged with screws of paper because corks were unavailable. Agnese, who didn't drink wine as a rule, got herself quite tiddly by siphoning too enthusiastically.

George and Elena, being horse lovers, had of course talked about their shared interest and varied experiences but riding out together seemed a far-off dream. However, George was never shy about doing his damndest to turn dreams into reality. He scouted around until he found a decent livery stable and then began organising a ride which turned into a rather special occasion.

Elena was thrilled at the idea and resurrected her old riding outfit. It gave her immense pleasure to unpack the breeches and jacket that Barend had so generously had tailored for her. They were much too large for her now but she pinned and tucked and moved buttons so that her svelte waistline was emphasized and she thought she cut a dashing figure. She also spent a happy hour buffing her precious boots. What added to her anticipation was the fact that this outing would be unchaperoned because Toly couldn't ride!

George, in the meantime, on the 11th of February, had arranged for the horses to be ridden from the stable-yard to a stretch of parkland in Florence through which the River Arno ran. He fetched her from the apartment and they drove to the park where the sight of the horses waiting for them brought a lump to her throat. Memories of her old friends, human and equine, flooded back and she was silent for a moment. These horses weren't fat but they were in good condition and someone must have worked hard to protect them and keep them going through the privations of the war.

She stood back, watching George as he checked her horse's girths, the fit of the bridle and bit, and shortened her stirrup leathers, accurately assessing the length she needed. His long, blunt-tipped fingers moved confidently and quickly. She would always love watching George at work, absorbed in a physical task, skilful and sure.

He gave her a leg-up, which she didn't need, but she had no desire to assert her independence. She found it very pleasant to make the most of his masculine concern after the sometimes brutal competitiveness of the boys she had ridden against.

To sit astride a horse again and breathe in that horsey aroma, was wonderful. The aesthetic appeal of viewing a long elegant, arched neck, and the flicking, scimitar ears in front of her, was something she'd almost forgotten. That moment always gave her a kind of metaphysical thrill: that she and horse had briefly been lifted to a plain beyond ordinary existence, one in which they were inseparably bonded in the moment, and predestined to achieve an impossible goal together, working as some mystical unit. Perhaps it was in such a moment that an ancient conjured the image of the original Sagittarius. (Perhaps, too, it's not accidental that Elena is a Sagittarian.)

No rider can stay in that transcendental ecstasy for more than a moment unless she wants a rude awakening. To be out riding again, and in George's company, returned her to the present very quickly.

They had to keep to a walk and, at most, a brief trot because the park was too confined for a canter, let alone a gallop. This didn't matter at all. It was such a pleasure to ride alongside George and view him in this new light. His hands were light and steady and kind. His firm seat, unconsciously and perfectly centred, (in contrast with the Italian seat which is slightly more forward) and the suppleness of his long, lean torso, didn't go unnoticed. His knee and thigh, on a level with her own, had a companionable familiarity. She found herself straightening her shoulders and tensing her tummy muscles in the hope that her own presence wasn't going unnoticed by George.

They also managed to fit in three dances from the 14th of February to the 19th – really making the most of the St Valentine's season. The dances were held in various villas occupied by the Allies and military police, and at the clubs which were coming to life again.

Friday the 22nd of February was a momentous occasion in that George was allowed to spend the night in the apartment, in Orso's room, as a family guest. He had been given a double promotion: promoted from dossing down in the sitting-room where casual visitors and stray officers were accommodated, and being acknowledged as a respectable suitor. He left the following morning but was back in Florence by Sunday the 24th of February.

On the 3rd of March they again attended a dance at Charlie's villa followed by another riding outing the next day. There was more dancing on the 8th of March and Charlie hosted yet another dance on the 12th of March.

Charlie's villa was a favoured venue. Because it was only a short walk from the apartment, and in the precincts of the Gherardesca garden, parental vigilance about curfew was more relaxed. Elena enjoyed being escorted to and fro by George. There was something romantic about the leisurely stroll in either direction.

On the way there, there was the pleasure of feeling all dressed-up and glamorous and anticipating an evening of fun and romance. The villa also boasted a terrace overlooking the garden where the two could enjoy quieter, more private moments during the evening. Enfolded in George's arms on that terrace, Elena finally learnt what proper kissing was all about!

They were both accomplished dancers and were usually the first to take to the floor. As George's arm circled her waist and her hand settled in his, she felt herself become quite weightless, dandelion-down, in his confident grasp. They seemed to share one torso while her legs and feet lost their own volition, floating wherever George led. Having spent so much time dancing with her sisters and other girls at their afternoon dancing sessions to while away the time in Gherardesca, Elena had a tendency to try to take the lead with less competent men but this was never a problem with George. She relished the extravagant and showy turns and flourishes they managed, at the same time being able to focus on each other's faces. George had a particular twinkle of approval and amusement for moments when their moves were especially clever. She never tired of looking up at him, waiting for those flashes which were for her alone and which she treasured.

The end of each evening at Charlie's establishment also came to be a special time. Moving from the brightly-lit, smokey rooms, the noisy chatter and gales of laughter into the quiet, chilly, darkened viale or Gherardesca garden felt, to Elena, as though they were being enveloped in their own private cocoon. Her pleasure was complete when George would slip his arm around her waist beneath her fur coat and draw her close as they walked. It was a time to savour the evening: the dancing, the entertainment, and laugh about the wilder and more idiotic antics of inebriated men and their desperate attempts to impress a woman.

In the meantime, the Allies were conducting vicious air attacks on the rail and road links through the Alps between Verona and Austria. This was the Brenner Route which was very heavily defended by German anti-aircraft guns. The Allied bombardment, which took place between November '44 and March '45, was causing chaos to German supply lines and the Germans were unable to restore them. This would prove to be an enormous problem to them when the Allied onslaught was resumed in the spring. Later, Elena and George would travel the incredibly beautiful Brenner Pass with its majestic mountains and gleaming lakes. George would be able to use his treasured Leica to capture the scenery and numerous pictures of Elena (often in conversation with cows) against this backdrop.

While the Brenner Route was being lambasted, the fighter-bombers of the Desert Air Force were targeting bridges, roads and railways on either side of the River Po. These activities helped to clear the Germans from an important section in front of the advancing Allied infantry.

On Saturday the 17th of March George took Elena to a big dance in Prato and visited her again on Sunday the 18th in Florence.

Their dancing continued throughout the following week: on Wednesday the 21st, Friday the 23rd and Saturday the 24th. On Sunday they went to Lucca, an area which provided lovely country drives. George was back in Florence on Tuesday the 27th and they returned to Lucca on Saturday the 30th for a dance. On Sunday the 31st of March George took Lucia and Elena to Lucca.

The intensity of their feelings for one another was galloping apace. The pressure-cooker atmosphere of war probably added to this, as well as the worry Elena experienced when George was away from her. Just thinking about George made her heart thunder and whenever he actually appeared in front of her, for the first few seconds, she always felt that it was about to explode through her chest cavity. She had also rapidly developed an abiding trust and confidence in him. With all this circulating through her, this relationship was destined to move on to another level, despite the strictures of her very conservative upbringing and the social taboos surrounding sex for girls of her class.

Where to find any real privacy, though, was a major obstacle.

To the rescue came Charlie's villa.

In a quiet corner of the garden, close to the villa, was a caravan. It had been parked there to provide additional accommodation for visiting officers but was rarely used. George and Elena noticed it. Telling each other that they merely wanted to have a look inside, but both knowing that there was more on the agenda than that, they planned a visit and George procured the key.

As George wrestled with the stiff lock, Elena stood behind him, every nerve-ending tingling with nervousness and anticipation. She'd learnt a great deal about herself in the short preceding months but was still alarmingly naïve. Fortunately, George wasn't. When he finally got the door open, he stepped up into the caravan and turned to take Elena's hand to help her up. He drew her towards him and quietly closed the door on the outside world.

And thus began a lifelong, passionate, and fulfilling sex life for both of them.

When George was dying he expressed his deep sorrow that he was no longer able to play his part in what had been a very rich aspect of their lives together.

George, of course, had had to teach Elena a great deal, her rearing having actively prevented any real knowledge of what went on in a marriage bed. Elena was a very avid pupil and she brought an acute sense of fun to their activities.

CHAPTER 15

Preparations for the Spring Offensive were very close to completion in the first week of April but until the Offensive was properly launched, George's main task of finding suitable routes for the 6th Armoured Division was limited and he seems to have been involved in running shorter errands. This was possibly why he was able to come to Florence so often.

Again on Saturday the 7th of April they went dancing and visited Orso and his wife, Gea, for lunch on Sunday.

At about this time, before the Allied main attack began, George did something really hair-raising. The Germans made a practice of booby-trapping as many buildings as they could when they were retreating and while they still had the time and means to do so. George and his sergeant came across a double-storeyed house which common sense said must have been booby-trapped, and George was dared, or dared himself, to snaffle something from the house. He climbed up to a first-floor window and, using a stick, managed to hook a pillowcase off a bed. Elena still has the pillowcase.

General Clark's plans for the Spring Offensive included aiming the Fifth Army towards the west of the River Reno, and then north to the Po, while the Eighth Army would focus its main attack through the area which became known as the 'Argenta Gap' on the western edge of Lake Comacchio. It was finally agreed that the Eighth Army would launch its attack on the 9th of April, followed by the Fifth Army's launch on the 14th of April. By the 15th of April the Fifth Army had succeeded in taking the elevated positions overlooking the Reno Valley, Highway 64, and Vergato in the Reno Valley.

The job of the South Africans in all this frenetic activity was finally to capture Monte Sole (which lay to the east of the Reno Valley). George was at Castiglione throughout the battle and witnessed the entire event. He also came close to getting himself wiped out. He was standing next to another officer when this man had his leg blown off.

The Germans had previously proved themselves impossible to dislodge from the caves on Monte Sole with ordinary tactics and bombing. However, at midday on the 15th, the Allies turned to what appeared to be some form of petrol bombing or incendiary device which caused huge plumes of black smoke and sucked the air out of the caves, forcing any surviving Germans into the open. George reported that when the Germans ran out of ammunition, some resorted to hurling stones in their desperation. Later in the afternoon the initial bombing was followed by fighter-bomber attacks which obliterated any unfortunate Germans below who had somehow survived the earlier onslaught. (Holland page 511)

By the morning of the 16th of April the South Africans had claimed Monte Sole and the battle was finally over.

The South Africans who had died at Monte Sole were buried in the cemetery at Castiglione dei Pepoli, a little slice of South Africa in Italy because this land had been gifted to South Africa. George took it upon himself to photograph every cross. The monks tended these graves for many years and as far as Elena knows, they continue to do so. A mass was also said for the South African soldiers every Sunday.

The cemetery continued to be used for the burial of South Africans who died elsewhere in Italy in the following months. Towards the end of 1945, Elena accompanied George to the funeral of a lieutenant who had died as a result of a road accident near Genoa.

He had been drinking and was driving a Jeep ahead of the one in which George and Elena were travelling. George had warned him to go slowly as the road was dangerously curved. They watched in horror as he lost control. The vehicle veered wildly across the road and crashed into a low barrier wall. He was tossed out of the Jeep and soared through the air before plummeting head-first into the wall.

The two leapt out of their vehicle and rushed to his side. He was unconscious and breathing shallowly. They stabilized his head and neck as best they could and carefully loaded him into the back of their Jeep where Elena sat with him, trying to keep his body as still as she could. They rushed to the nearest Italian hospital. It was a fear-filled, harrowing journey. Elena found herself praying desperately.

At the hospital they were met with the intransigence of Italians who were reluctant to treat him because he was army personnel and they didn't want to get involved, or be answerable to army authorities. George was very insistent that they treat him. He finally resorted to threatening them with what would happen to them if they didn't treat army personnel to the best of their ability, the increasingly riotous and angry confrontation being translated in two directions by Elena. Eventually the Italians thought better of the situation and wheeled him away.

Spattered with blood, dusty and dishevelled, George and Elena waited in the little entrance, seated side-by-side, on a hard wooden bench. George held Elena's shaking hands as they prayed and hoped for their foolhardy friend. However, there was nothing that could be done to save him.

It fell to Elena to sort out his possessions. She had often undertaken this task but this time she found it particularly difficult because she had known and liked the man and because of her involvement in the accident.

Amongst his things she found the button collection he had been gathering for his wife. This was too much for her. As she sat on his bed amidst his spartan belongings, she was overcome by the pointlessness of his death and the needless heartache and loss to his loved ones. Holding the buttons made Elena very aware of his wife, his loving and his life, all now over, and she was filled with the deepest anguish. She cleaned his uniform and packed it. Then she placed the buttons and the photograph of his wife at the top of the parcel and it was sent home to South Africa.

Although he had been killed near Genoa, he was buried at Castiglione. Elena was the only woman in attendance and, as it was bitterly cold and wet, she was wrapped in her furs and doing her best to look elegant in silk stockings and heels. She was carrying a large bouquet of flowers and feeling great sorrow at his loss. Lost in thought about his wife and family and their grief, her reverie was rudely interrupted when her feet suddenly slipped from under her on the steep slope down to the graveside. She could do nothing to stop herself and slid wildly all the way down the slope, on her bottom, in front of all those men.

Once the Allied offensive had got going again, George's main task of marking the route to be followed by the 6th Division, was resumed. Near Milan, he and his sergeant were physically engaged in indicating the route by placing white flags along a road, when they looked up and saw a column of German armoured vehicles and trucks, an entire division, coming towards them. Panic-stricken, they had nowhere to go and no time to take cover, so simply remained where they were.

To their utter astonishment, the vehicles continued to trundle towards them without a shot being fired. When the leading vehicle, a gleaming car in which six officers were seated, drew level with them, they were greeted very courteously by the German commander. Every man and piece of equipment was immaculately turned out and the soldiers on the trucks were all standing in perfect rows. The commanding officer asked where he could find the Allies as they wished to surrender. And they had made sure that they would do it in style! George pointed in the direction from which he had come and then watched as they pulled off and continued on their decorous way.

George managed a brief visit to Florence on the 19th of April as the Allies began moving towards the Po River behind the retreating Germans. The Germans began their attempts to cross the river from the 21st of April but were unable to get their equipment across the Po. Everywhere there were abandoned and burning vehicles. Some had been driven right into the river. Whether the Germans had set light to their equipment themselves out of desperation and frustration at not being able to save it after having kept it going under such difficult circumstances, or whether Allied bombing had done this, is not certain. In the light of George's experience, it would seem that the latter was the cause of the destruction.

Many of the Germans had long since run out of fuel and in their desperation to save their equipment, they had harnessed horses to pull their vehicles. George came across a heart-rending scene at the Po.

The South Africans crossed the Po at a point to the south of Legnano, according to James Holland, so it must have been at this spot, at some time around the 22nd of April and certainly before the 27th of April (when the last of the South Africans crossed the Po) that George was faced with this awful scene. He must have been one of the first there.

The bridge had been destroyed and everything on either side of the bridge had been obliterated but what remained indelibly etched on his memory, were the sights and sounds of the injured and dying horses. They had been used to tow the vehicles and had been bombed along with the machinery.

Apart from the broken limbs, many had been terribly wounded. Some had been disembowelled. There were screams of agony and the suffering of these poor, dumb creatures was pitiful. George and his sergeant could do little more than walk amongst them and shoot them to put them out of their misery. It was a nightmare picture which would never leave George.

Once across the Po, the 6th Armoured Division, together with part of the Eighth Army and the New Zealanders, moved north-east towards Trieste. It may have been during this time that George, scouting ahead of the 6th Division, came across a seemingly abandoned house and pushed open the door. Sitting around a table inside were five or six German officers. They were taken completely by surprise. This gave George the crucial second in which to open fire on them before they could shoot him. He shot all of them.

When Elena questioned him on how he felt about the event, he said that he felt very little then or subsequently: it was a matter of the loss of their lives over his life. However, Elena knew that it was a subject best avoided.

*   *   *

In the meantime, over this period at the end of April, Mussolini was trying to make his escape. According to James Holland, on the 25th of April he went to Milan in the hope of surrendering to the socialists. One of his conditions of surrender was that he be allowed to retreat to the Valtellina, a valley in the Alps, and keep three thousand of his Blackshirts with him. For various reasons, not least of which was the ludicrousness of his demands, the talks broke down and in the midst of much confusion in Milan, on the 26th of April, Mussolini fled in a northerly direction, hoping to reach the valley of Valtellina. Clara Petacci, his mistress, was, of course, included in this cavalcade. Headed in the same direction, but travelling separately from each other, were Alessandro Pavolini, the Fascist Party leader, and Elena Curti, Mussolini's illegitimate daughter.

Mussolini travelled via Como and on to Argegno on the western side of Lake Como. In the meantime, his daughter had caught up with Alessandro at Argegno and they continued, together, northwards to Menaggio where they found Mussolini skulking in an old school building.

The following day, on the 27th of April, they continued their journey northwards, together. A number of German troops travelled with them. At this point, Alessandro, Mussolini and his daughter were all travelling in Alessandro's armoured car. Just beyond Musso they had a puncture. Whilst trying to repair the tyre, they were surrounded by partisans who eventually agreed to allow the Germans to continue to the Alps but they refused to allow any Italians through. However, the German commander offered to smuggle Mussolini, and only Mussolini, through, but he would have to be disguised in a German uniform. Gallantly, Mussolini jumped at this opportunity.

After they had left, the remaining Italians in the party came under fire, and all, excepting Elena, surrendered or were shot. Pavolini and Clara were amongst those who surrendered. Elena had remained in the car and now she found herself entirely alone. Eventually she decided that she must try to get away but as soon as she crept out of the car she was caught by a group of partisans. Although she was armed, for some inexplicable reason, the partisans took her to the town of Dongo and let her go in the main square.

The rest of the party was not nearly as fortunate. When Mussolini reached Dongo, he was apprehended. Pavolini and Clara were also taken to Dongo. On the 28th of April they were all executed in Dongo. The sixteen bodies were taken to Milan where they were offloaded in the Piazzale Loreto. Here the enraged populace took their revenge on the corpses, showing them every possible indignity and finally hanging them upside down from butcher's hooks at a petrol station in the square. This, according to my Elena, was a traditional indignity practised by Italians on their disgraced leaders.

It was at this point that George came on the scene. He found the suspended bodies. They had been extremely badly beaten and disfigured with Mussolini's notorious face barely being recognizable. In the midst of this horror, George was deeply affected by the action of a British officer who gathered together the folds of Clara's skirt. In an effort to give her some small dignity, he pinned the folds so that they no longer flopped over her head.

According to Agnese, when the bodies were taken down, they suffered more abuse at the hands of the local populace. Where they were all buried, we don't know, but Agnese thinks that Mussolini was buried near his wife's home. However, his brain was removed before burial and sent to America to be studied! Incidentally, Mussolini's wife was seen as an innocent party and continued to receive a state pension until her death.

I have a little addendum of my own to attach to George's experience of coming across Mussolini's and Clara's bodies. Before I got to know Elena, our very enthusiastic history master at school, Patrice Pousson, raced into my classroom one day to show me a photograph which one of his matric pupils, Warren Barrow, had included in an assignment. This was a picture his grandfather had taken with his little box camera at the same scene. In the picture Claretta's skirt had already been tidied up. There were a couple of officers standing near the bodies. Slightly to the left of the bodies, on the right of the picture, was a tall, slender officer I am convinced was George. This conviction could be the distortion of wishful thinking, though, because I don't have the picture.

When Elena told me about George's involvement, I spent days searching Patrice's very dusty and chaotic storeroom. I sifted through hundreds of old assignments and got very excited when I finally found the pile belonging to Warren's year. The feeling was akin to that of an archaeologist finding a piece of rare artifact – and then finding nothing more! I then tried to track down Warren but with little success until I bumped into him at a wedding in Cape Town. However, this, too, was a dead end. He didn't have the picture and his parents had sold up and emigrated to New Zealand and there was little likelihood of their having taken it with them.

*   *   *

As the Allies continued to chase the Germans north of the Po, George was once more deployed in finding routes for the Sixth Division. He and his sergeant were approaching a wooded area which they feared would be a perfect ambush site and so were on their guard.

They spotted a figure sitting beneath a tree and were doubly perturbed. The figure, however, made no move. He was wearing a German uniform and made no sign of seeing them as they approached. They left their vehicle and stealthily approached on foot. He continued to sit absolutely still. Then they noticed that he had squatted down to relieve himself and was holding a letter. He must have taken the opportunity of a moment's rest to read, or reread, his letter. He was stone dead.

His death must have been instantaneous because there were no signs of distress in the way he was sitting. The letter ended with the words: „Hans, Du bist meine Liebe und mein ganzes Leben." (*Hans, you are my love and my whole life.*)

On the 2nd of May the New Zealanders captured Trieste from the Germans who had been holding out against the Yugoslavian supporters of Tito. The German forces in Italy surrendered unconditionally on the 3rd of May. This signified the end of the war in Italy but certainly not the end of the struggle to restore order to a devastated land and people.

Recorded in 'South Africa in Two World Wars: a Newspaper History' by Vic Alhadeff, *The Friend* printed the following:

'An official statement on the position of the Sixth South African Division was issued in Cape Town this afternoon. It reads: "With the surrender of Axis armies in Northern Italy and the cessation of fighting in that theatre, the task of the Sixth South African Division has been completed. The Allied plans for the garrisoning of Europe and for securing and administering the Mediterranean lines of communication to the Far East have already been laid down, and these plans do not require the presence in Italy or in the Mediterranean zone of the Sixth South African Division. It has been agreed by the Allied military authorities that it would be to the advantage of all concerned if the South African troops were repatriated from the Mediterranean area as soon as the necessary transport facilities are available."'

Vic Alhadeff goes on to say: *"Major-General William Henry Evered Poole, CB, CBE, DSO, held a massive victory parade at the motor-racing track at Monza. He stood on the dias with Frederick Sturrock, South Africa's Minister of transport and Acting Minister of Defence, as thousands of military vehicles drove past. The procession lasted three hours."*

Elena says that George was not at this parade. Whether or not he was involved in sussing out the track for this grand occasion we don't know. Perhaps he just wanted to visit the track for his own satisfaction but it was round about this time that he grabbed the opportunity to race around the track, with no witnesses, to be able to claim that he had 'raced at Monza'.

Alhadeff also records Major-General Poole's speech given at a parade near Milan where he spoke to representatives of all the units of the Sixth Division. His words reveal the depth and character of this great leader. If this speech had been better heeded by all South Africans in the years to follow, so much suffering and heartache could have been avoided.

"Today is May 4, 1945. Exactly one year ago today our division went into action north of Cassino for the first time. It has been an enormous honour for me to have commanded this division. Let us carry out this great comradeship and ésprit de corps that we have forged on the battlefields of Africa and Italy through adversity

and victory - that comradeship forged in the fire of war — and carry it with us into our country after demobilization, so that we can stand together in peace as we do in war, that we stand together against the cancer of racialism and that we help build our nation on sound foundations, (having) routed those attempts to imitate a rotten Reich, the type of which we have now annihilated."

Hindsight makes his words tragically ironic.

*   *   *

George's role in Italy was not yet over. After demobilization of the Sixth Division he would stay on as part of the mopping-up operations and the efforts to restore dignity and order to Italy.

On Sunday the 6th of May, George gave Elena an engagement ring. It was a striking pale blue sapphire in a silver setting.

The following day, Monday the 7th of May, Europe celebrated VE Day and George and Elena travelled to Genoa to take up their new duties.

CHAPTER 16

The Civil Labour Unit to which Elena was attached was transferred to Genoa and if Elena wanted to continue to work for them that was where she had to go. Accommodation was not a problem as she was able to live with her favourite cousin, Rafaele.

Unfortunately, Major Gooseman had been transferred elsewhere so she would no longer be working for him. She was now employed as a telephonist and she found the attitude of the British officers in her office most disagreeable. Perhaps they had grown used to the desperate compliance of Italian women, especially in their sexual availability, and thought that any young woman in Italy was up for grabs. They were far too familiar and insinuating and made Elena feel very uncomfortable. They were also constantly entertaining prostitutes.

Elena experienced very few lewd or suggestive comments regarding her relationship with George. There was only one such incident and the comment wasn't made directly to her. She and George were at a club with a group of officers. When Elena left the table to go to the restroom, one wag passed an off-colour remark about her. George invited him to take a stroll outside with him. By the time Elena got back to the table George had returned. She asked where the fellow had disappeared to and George told her that he had been very tired and had gone to take a nap – induced by George's fist, but he didn't tell her that bit.

By early June she couldn't bear the behaviour of the British officers any longer and she contacted one of George's sergeants. This man was in charge of the rest camp for the South African Military Police in Rapallo, a lovely coastal resort near Genoa.

The sergeant came to fetch her immediately. He stormed into the room where she was working and in typically South African fashion he asked her, "Meidjie, moet ek hulle donder?" (*Meidjie, must I give them a beating?*) She told him that that wouldn't be necessary. He instructed another telephonist to tell the captain that Miss Van Praag was leaving. She didn't even wait to collect her pay.

Elena hadn't been able to contact George so when he arrived to inspect the camp on the 3rd of June he was amazed to find her there.

The villa in which the centre was housed was a three-storey structure called Villa Sette Archi, or the Villa of the Seven Arches. It belonged to two brothers by the name of Cacciabue who owned a leather factory in Milan. In the past the brothers had used the Villa as a weekend retreat but their wives had occupied the house during the week.

One of the wives had found herself a lover. Her sister-in-law was fully aware of this and aided and abetted her in cuckolding her husband. This seems to have been a fairly common practice with Italians who had a special sign for cuckolded husbands: the index fingers held above the head and waggled about. When this Cacciabue husband found out what was going on, he immediately booted his wife out of the home and the family. So incensed was his brother on his behalf that he also got rid of his wife for having kept her sister-in-law's secret.

Elena had earlier been instrumental in the requisitioning of the Villa for the military police. She had been with George before her permanent arrival in Rapallo when he was looking for a suitable house. When they found Villa Sette Archi, it was Elena who informed the six Italian families who were squatting in the house that their time was up and they were being evicted. They had been placed there by the Italian government because of the desperate shortage of accommodation. Had it not been requisitioned, the Italians would have had the right to remain there for the rest of their lives.

Contrary to expectation, the Cacciabues were delighted to have had their villa requisitioned by the military as they knew they would eventually get it back and it would be properly maintained. The Italians, though, were none too pleased with Elena and voiced their displeasure vociferously. The Cacciabue brothers expressed their gratitude to her in regular gifts of wine. They also presented her with some sumptuously soft leather in red and black which she had made into shoes that she wore constantly. She was wearing these shoes on the day of her wedding. The only shoes available on the market at the time were made out of cardboard and were next to useless.

This was a most beautiful house, judging by the photographs Elena has. The picture of the dining-room, taken at Elena's birthday celebration organized by George, shows an enormous and very elegant room with soaring ceilings and plaster-embellished wall panelling and cartouches. It was a dining-room which could well have graced a very smart hotel. However, the war had taken its toll and, if one looks closely, the peeling paint is evident.

George's arrival on the 3rd of June coincided with his leave and they were able to take a trip to Vercelli. On their return, they passed through Torino which was renowned as a fashion centre. It was here that George bought Elena two glorious silk dresses. These were the first new dresses she had had since the outbreak of war. She was still pitifully thin but in George's photographs of her in these dresses, she looks radiant.

Elena's clothing was worn out and difficult to replace. Because she worked for the military police, she was entitled to wear a uniform which she now requested. She was given a man's winter and summer uniform. These she took to a dressmaker and had altered to fit her – and most stylish they were too, especially with her red leather shoes which she always wore with the uniforms.

This trick of having men's clothing remade to fit her wasn't a new scheme. Before the war she and Toly had helped themselves to a couple of pairs of Barend's trousers and had them altered by his tailor. They both looked very chic in their trousers and when Barend admired them, he commented that he had very similar pants – and then realized that they were his pants!

After his leave, George returned to Stresse where he was now based. Here he, too, was billeted in a magnificent requisitioned villa which had belonged to a very important Fascist. When Elena visited on Sunday the 8th of July, George showed her around the villa.

One of the bedrooms was kept locked. It had been the bedroom of the Fascist's mistress. When George opened the room for her, Elena was stunned by the opulence, luxury and sheer beauty of the room. From the magnificent paintings on the walls to the exquisite Brussels lace bedspread, the perfumes and cosmetics on the dressing-table and the sunken marble bath – everything was a feast and delight to the eye – and Elena was allowed to touch nothing! George wouldn't even let her sample the Chanel No. 5. When she'd gazed her fill and twisted her innards with unfulfilled avarice, George locked the room again. What she yearned for most was the lace bedcover.

When the Allies eventually vacated this villa, the partisans stripped the house of everything they could carry and burnt it to the ground, including all the contents of that glorious bedroom.

In the meantime, while Elena and George were doing their bit for Italy's recuperation, life continued to barrel along in the Van Praag apartment. Despite his heart-attack and generally poorer health, Barend had found a renewed sense of purpose and a role in helping people to get back on their feet. The Dutch ambassador in Rome appointed him as the Honorary Consul of the Netherlands in Florence and all forms of aid to Dutch citizens were channelled through him.

Large trucks of goods began to arrive from Rome. Boxes and boxes of foodstuffs were carried up to the Van Praag sitting-room where they were stored. Needy Dutch citizens could come to the apartment and, on presentation of their passports, be given food parcels.

There sat Barend and Lucia amidst hundreds of boxes, like Father and Mother Christmas, dispensing largesse and good cheer. The apartment was once again abuzz with voices.

Those who came to them for help often told tales of dreadful hardship and loss. It wasn't always easy for the two to remain cheerful and optimistic about a better future when they were constantly exposed to such suffering.

However, they also met a set of intriguing and eccentric characters who needed Barend's help.

There was the American pianist whom Lucia had got to know when she and her daughters were living at Il Riposo dei Vescovi after their first apartment was bombed. This woman still hadn't been able to get back to America as only military personnel could access transport. She was extremely elegant and a great showman who delighted in entertaining. Even at Il Riposo dei Vescovi, when her nerves were shredded by the sound of bombing over Florence and she used to try to drown out the sound by playing great, heavy chords, there was something of the extravagant entertainer about her.

Then there was the representative from the International Refugee Organisation. He was a Haitian and he had a pitch-black complexion. He was as exotic and exuberant in dress and conduct as he was in appearance. He always wore gleaming black patent-leather shoes with white spats. A conservative dark suit was jazzed up with a stiff-collared and pink-striped shirt. Further adornments included a gold watch-chain and fob and a multitude of rings. He was accompanied by his very pretty Creole wife and his deaf mother.

His mother, too, was noteworthy. Because of her deafness she used an ear-trumpet which she swivelled in one's direction during conversation. The current speaker was expected to lean over and bellow into the horn.

Two more memorable characters were a Dutch couple who had spent much of their lives in China where the husband had been a tea-taster. His wife always dressed in Chinese clothing which included Mandarin-style baggy trousers. This garment wasn't very flattering and made her rear-end resemble that of an elephant. These two always caused a stir in public with people turning to gaze at them in the streets. The family knew that they were approaching when they saw the Italians turning and laughing. They must have been a treat in post-war drabness and the uniformity of military apparel. Mrs Tea-Taster gave Elena a most beautiful piece of antique, embroidered silk.

Another long-standing friendship existed with the wife of Prince Nazibuko, an Abyssinian of great importance in the Abyssinian government before the Italians invaded Abyssinia in 1939.

The conquering of Abyssinia six long years previously had been greeted with great jubilation by the Italians. School children had sung songs in celebration. They had also enthusiastically collected silver chocolate-wrappings to raise funds intended for the feeding of the Abyssinians. Mussolini claimed Italy had found its 'place in the sun'. Elena's present home is called 'Un posto al sole' (*A Place in the Sun*), partly as a tongue-in-cheek dig at Mussolini. The Italians built hospitals, schools and roads in Abyssinia. Even Prince Nazibuko, according to his wife, had been delighted with the improvements.

However, these happy relations proved short-lived. When war broke out, members of the Abyssinian government, including Prince Nazibuko, were imprisoned in concentration camps and their families were declared civilian internees, in the same way as the Van Praags had had their freedoms curtailed. And so it was that Princess Nazibuko and her children found themselves in Florence. Toly was teaching at a Catholic school in Florence and Princess Nazibuko was looking for someone to give her son extra maths tuition. Toly undertook the job and the Princess used to bring the boy to the apartment for his lessons. She was a woman of great beauty, charm and culture and a strong friendship developed. After the war, when it was possible for the Van Praags to resume something of their previous standards of entertaining, she was often an honoured dinner guest.

Lucia was also well occupied, in addition to her normal household demands: she had become involved in the resettling of concentration camp inmates who had managed to survive the war and who had been repatriated to Florence. This not only involved finding accommodation for them, but also trying to scrabble together some of the basic necessities of life because they had been stripped of everything. They were without clothing, furniture or household utensils. Very few were lucky enough to have had neighbours who had salvaged any of their possessions and held them in safe-keeping for their improbable return. There were also very few people who had anything to spare after their own wartime ordeals.

The Van Praags' own financial situation was precarious and all this work they were doing on behalf of others, contributed nothing to their own coffers. Despite his age, Barend wasn't prepared to pension himself off just yet. He found employment in a marmalade factory, working for a Signor Torelli. And then Barend came up with a plan to export juniper berries to America for the manufacture of gin. Signor Torelli thought this a good idea and gave Barend his blessing and support. Barend went ahead and made all the arrangements and established contacts in America. The physical side of the business was handled by the marmalade company but Barend dealt with the administration.

The Americans were in the process of making compensation payments for the suffering inflicted on the populace. Barend accepted one payment and thereafter refused to take any further aid.

Barend's health continued to be a concern and even with an improving diet, he failed to regain any weight. It was then that it was discovered that he had tuberculosis, probably picked up while he and Orso were in hiding. He did, however, respond well to treatment and within six months was cured.

* * *

Shortly after Elena's arrival in Rapallo, the military police appointed her to run the Rest and Recuperation Centre in Villa Sette Archi. George was able to return to Rapallo every weekend to see her. She could never be sure of the exact time of his arrival but always, as the weekend approached, she felt a fizz of anticipation.

A favourite place for her to sit on a warm afternoon, in the lull between serving lunch and beginning dinner preparations, was on the verandah. This was a beautiful spot. It was furnished with cane and had a classically-tiled floor. The seven arches from which the villa took its name, framed the serene view. This was where she often waited for George. It gave her the greatest pleasure to look up and see his tall, loose-limbed figure striding towards her. Often he would grab her and swing her up into the air before she knew what was happening to her.

There were times when he arrived exhausted and they would sit close and companionably, regaining their equilibrium and sense of one another. She cherished the softness of his expression as he looked at her, the humorous curve of his mouth and the way he would stretch his legs out and spread his arms, inviting her into his space.

Elena and I were paging through an old photograph album when we came across a photograph of George sound asleep on a narrow canvas camping stretcher. In the picture he is lying flat on his back with one arm, elbow crooked, above his head. It is a picture of total ease. Elena's comment about the picture was, "My lovely man!"

Other friends also made fairly regular visits to Villa Sette Archi. One such was Speedy Botha. He happened to be there at the same time as one of the Cacciabue brothers was visiting. Signor Cacciabue was an older man and was accompanied by a very lovely, and much younger, woman. Ostensibly, she was some kind of personal assistant but their relationship clearly involved much more than mere secretarial functions.

Speedy was bowled over and, with the arrogance of youth, he was convinced that he could get Signor Cacciabue sufficiently drunk to take advantage of his lovely mistress. He set to with a will – but no matter what he tried, it had absolutely no effect on the wily old Italian. Eventually Speedy was so drunk he could barely stand. Signor Cacciabue got to his feet and announced his intentions to the assembly: "Goodnight! I am going to the bedroom now," and with that he smugly took his lady-friend by the elbow and the two of them ascended the staircase.

Speedy had a reputation for trying hard but he wasn't always successful. He took a great shine to Toly and said to her after a lengthy (for Speedy) pursuit, "God knows, I want you!" Poor man – all that did was add to the Van Praag entertainment arsenal.

Elena seems to have used a great deal of ingenuity in running the villa and was most concerned about presenting the best menu possible. It was a matter of pride that the men in her care enjoy tasty meals. It wasn't easy to provide much variety when her larder was stocked with army rations but she was adept at cheating any system or obstacle placed in her way.

Rations had to be fetched from Genoa and for this she had at her disposal a truck and military police driver. Having an official army driver was most useful for her nefarious purposes because the MP driver couldn't be stopped and searched and so she was able to transport goods which weren't strictly classed as rations.

One such deviation from regulations was to get the driver to call in to a liquor factory she had discovered. From this source she bought alcohol at cost price. Once a week she hosted a party for the men staying in the villa. She had an Italian barman who did a roaring trade on her behalf and the profits she made from the gin, vodka and brandy sold at the parties, she ploughed back into improving the food.

The rations were very limited and consisted mainly of bully beef, tinned mixed vegetables and cabbage, and a quite generous allowance of coffee, tea and sugar. She sold the extra coffee, tea and sugar on the black market and, together with her bar profits, bought fresh fish, better meat, and fresh vegetables from the local Italians.

Elena also did her best to oblige the men in fulfilling their dietary requests but she wasn't always successful. One group of men was desperate for the taste of mieliepap – a longing for the comforts of home. She, of course, had no idea what they were talking about, but when they explained that it was maize-meal made into porridge, she thought she'd grasped the concept.

She only had yellow maize-meal which she used for making polenta. She didn't think that the yellow meal would be a problem and perhaps the men would appreciate an Italian take on their national dish. She was suitably gratified by the cheering which greeted her announcement that pap would be served for breakfast. She was so proud of her efforts and couldn't wait for their reaction to tasting her offering. As each man was served, the room grew quieter – but it wasn't the silence of appreciation! The men were not impressed and refused to eat this disappointment. Being Elena, though, she didn't give up and tried to educate them in the various delicious ways polenta could be eaten - salted and covered in a bolognaise sauce or fried and eaten cold - but this made no impression on these sons of Africa.

She also wasn't above committing the occasional crime to keep her kitchen well supplied and her Italian cook was a handy ally. The odd tyre or can of petrol would go missing when rations were very low, or particularly boring, and when the black market could supply something more nutritious or delectable. When, on occasion, George grew suspicious about the standard of the cuisine, or the level of petty theft, Elena told him that if he wanted a decent table he had better develop a squint.

On one occasion when two tyres went missing, the investigators in the military police caught the Italian who had bought them from Elena. He told them he had bought them from an "American nurse". George realized immediately who the culprit was and when he arrived at the villa he wanted to know when his betrothed had morphed into an American nurse.

George, too, wasn't immune to her thievery and complained about how heavy on fuel his Jeep was.

Elena's safety was a great concern to George. The partisans regarded anyone who had any contact with the Allies or the Germans as being a collaborator and the women were particularly vulnerable. If a woman suspected of collaboration was unlucky enough to be caught by the partisans, the very least she could expect was to have her head shaved. When the partisans captured the female head of the Fascists in Florence, they stripped her naked, shaved her head, covered her in ink, rammed a cucumber into her vagina and left her tied up in the square.

Italian memories were also long and not for nothing were the Italians known for their vendettas. The Van Praags were acquainted with a man who had suffered greatly at the hands of the Fascists when they came to power in the twenties. Anyone who opposed them was in danger of a severe beating and they had a particular hatred for anyone with communist leanings.

This friend was beaten with a heavy wooden baton, probably as a substitute, or symbol, for the bundle of sticks tied around an axe and called a 'fascis'.

In ancient Roman times this bundle was carried before a Roman magistrate, or ruler, to denote his authority. It was this 'fascis' from which the Fascists took their name.

In addition to the beating, which nearly killed the Van Praags' friend, he was forced to drink an entire bottle of castor-oil, also a customary part of the punishment. He saved the contents of his bowels, stored in a bottle, for twenty years. When the Fascists fell in Florence, he went out and found the man who was largely responsible for his torment. When he found him, he forced his erstwhile tormentor to drink every last drop of the contents of that bottle!

Elena and George were out together one day. As they walked along the pavement, Elena overheard two Italians discussing her, saying that she deserved to have her head shaved. Brashly, she rounded on them and told them that they would do no such thing as she was a Dutch citizen and they had no business meddling with her.

George decided that he needed to take precautions on her behalf and arranged for a bodyguard to accompany her whenever she had to go out. He also got her a huge and cumbersome .44 calibre revolver to use if the sergeant on duty at the villa had to go out and leave her on her own. She thought it was more nuisance than it was worth but it was to serve its purpose in an unexpected way. However, that tale will have to wait for a moment.

Elena had struck up a friendship with the man who was running the rest home for South African doctors. He also got his liquor supplies through her. When he invited her to supper she said that she couldn't come because she didn't know what to do about her bodyguard. Consequently, the bodyguard was invited to supper too and they all enjoyed a fine evening.

After the war her host that evening immigrated to Swaziland where he became a pharmacist in Mbabane and owned a number of pharmacies. George and Elena had always assumed he was Jewish and when they visited him in Swaziland he had a mezuzah, or scroll holder, on his doorpost. However, he categorically denied being Jewish and claimed that the ornament belonged to the previous owner of the house. This Elena found strange as the mezuzah is usually removed when the owner leaves to prevent subsequent owners showing any disrespect for the mezuzah and what it represents. Such disrespect is regarded as a grave sin on the part of all involved.

Why he should deny his Judaism remained a mystery but who knows what experiences had led to his attitude. He seemed to have settled into his new life in Swaziland very comfortably. He had even become very friendly with the Swazi king whom George photographed at the house during their visit. The king's children can be seen running around the garden.

It was also at Rapallo that Elena undertook the task of packing up the belongings of men who had been killed, to be sent home to their families. She took great pride in the job and gained some very touching insights into these men. There was the man who had been collecting buttons for his wife wherever he went, and there were many cherished photographs and other momentoes of wives and sweethearts. Of course, there were also the momentoes which couldn't be sent home and she made sure that she removed incriminating photographs and letters from their Italian girlfriends. All their pornography, and there was a fair bit of that too, went into the rubbish-bin.

By now, Christmas of 1945 was coming up and it was arranged that Elena would spend Christmas Eve with her family in Florence and celebrate Christmas Day and Lucia's birthday the following day. She would then travel back to Rapallo late on Christmas Day in time to celebrate George's birthday with him that evening. Her beloved cousin, Rafaele, (nicknamed the 'Count of Buchenwald' after the war because he was so thin) was accompanying her. George had arranged a sumptuous dinner at the Villa Sette Archi for that night. She and her cousin spent a wonderful day with her family but she was also looking forward to getting back to Rapallo to be with George for his special day. However, on their return journey, their Jeep broke down in Sestri Levante. It was probably fortunate that they broke down in this little town because they still had to traverse Passo Del Bracco, a pass which was notorious for banditry.

It was dark by the time the Jeep conked out and Elena made her way to the post office where she managed to rouse someone and asked to make a 'phone call. The assistant was clearly annoyed at Elena's intrusion and told her it was impossible as it was after hours. Elena persisted, telling that it was an emergency. She still refused. Elena's Allied uniform probably didn't make the woman view her any more warmly either.

What eventually swung the situation in Elena's favour was that, being in uniform, she was also wearing her sidearm, the great big revolver George had procured for her. She took this out of its holster and banged it down on the counter, telling the woman that she would shoot her if she didn't connect her immediately. The woman's eyes grew round and her lips drew into a tight little 'o' of shock. Elena got her prompt and full co-operation. As she made her call she kept her eyes fixed on the woman in an intimidating glare in case she should decide to cut her off. All the while she couldn't help the little flicker of triumph at how she had won the battle. Leaving the post office, she wanted to whoop with delight at her wild-west bravado.

After making the 'phone call she and her cousin went to the fire brigade who were very helpful and who got the Jeep going again. They decided to continue their journey as they were bound to meet up with George somewhere along the route. Elena could also hardly go back to the post office and demand to make another emergency 'phone call. In any event, George had probably already left Rapallo.

It was bitterly cold and dark as they bumped and lurched their way up the pass. Elena hunched down in her seat with her arms wrapped around herself for warmth. She was growing increasingly anxious, concerned that their vehicle would break down again and that there might be bandits about, despite it being Christmas Day. At last they spotted the lights of a vehicle coming towards them.

George drew abreast of them at the top of Passo Del Bracco and Elena flung herself out of the vehicle and into his arms. Her relief at his arrival was enormous.

He had abandoned his guests at the villa and had brought the chef with him so that the Christmas and birthday celebrations wouldn't be missed. Arms about each other, they stepped a short distance away from the Jeep to catch up on their day and the chef got busy.

When he called them back to the Jeep, they discovered that this ingenious man, with the soul of a romantic, had decked the bonnet of the Jeep with a white tablecloth and had created a stylish table setting. He popped the champagne and served everyone with roast chicken!

Their eventual journey back to Rapallo was also not without incident. Her cousin suffered from carsickness, and the tension of the day, the rich meal and the winding pass all became too much for him and he was sick in the back of the Jeep.

When they finally got home, Elena immediately went up to her room. She was exhausted after the activity of the day as well as the flood of adrenalin brought on by tension and downright fear. As she got to her room she heard a gunshot. Shocked, her first thought was that George had shot himself! She rushed downstairs again to find George standing in the dining-room holding his revolver, but there was no-one else in sight.

This was one shock too many for the day and she let rip with a voluble stream of Italian (no better language for moments like that) about what he thought he was doing. He did have an explanation: he'd spotted a cat trying to steal a roast chicken from the dining table and he'd taken a pot shot at it to chase it off. The cat had escaped with an indignant yowl (and the chicken), and was completely unscathed – probably because George already knew what his standing with Elena would have been if he had hurt a cat.

And so ended a merry Christmas.

*   *   *

When Elena closed the rest home she arranged for Lucia to collect the left-over rations. Lucia and Agnese were being driven to Rapallo in an open Jeep by William Bates. William had grown up in the Orange Free State and had a dreadful stammer which caused him great torment.

A truck belonging to the American forces hit them and their Jeep overturned. Agnese's thigh was sliced open and Lucia broke her shoulder. Lucia was more upset about the possibility of foregoing her groceries than she was about their injuries and kept saying, "My rations! My rations!" The accident had happened in a forested area very near an American encampment so they were quickly attended to and taken to an American military hospital in Legorna.

She and Agnese loved their hospital stay. They were provided with wonderful meals and were even supplied with bananas – a delicacy they had not tasted in a very long time. They were also able to'phone home every evening. What made them really feel like royalty was being wheeled outside in their beds every day so that they could enjoy the sea view and the sunset. Elena was able to pay them a visit after receiving news of the accident and it was on this journey that she had her bizarre conversation with Lieutenant Rudolph Ollawagen about 'powdering her nose'.

On their return trip from Legorne, Rudolph wanted to visit his girlfriend at a house in Rapallo before he returned to Lago Maggiore where he was based. He also told Elena that the girlfriend was sure to be able to put them up for the night. It didn't take Elena long to suss out this establishment and realize that it was a house of ill repute. Elena was certainly not going to spend the night there. As her own rest home had been closed down, she went along to the South African doctors' rest home and begged a room from her 'non-Jewish' friend.

Amazingly, it would appear that Rudolph hadn't realized what his girlfriend's occupation was. One wonders if such blissful ignorance is possible but would he have expected Elena to spend the night in such a place if he had known? Or perhaps he thought Elena was too naïve to twig. Rudolph and his lass married and she came out to South Africa with him. However, the marriage didn't work out and they were soon divorced. Some of the South Africans did seem to have been babes in the wood.

One such character informed Elena and George that he had met the most beautiful, wonderful Italian girl called Eugenia and that she was a virgin! As soon as Elena met her, and she introduced herself using her Christian name, Elena knew she was not the lady her fellow thought she was as no 'good' girl ever introduced herself this way. The custom was simply to give one's surname. Elena turned to George and whispered, "If she's a virgin then my name's Shirley Temple!" Only when the poor man contracted a dose of gonorrhoea did he realize his mistake. Elena's comment to him was, "Ah, and it was the virgin who gave you this?"

Neels van der Westhuizen was another South African whose girlfriend was a prostitute. She, however, fitted in very well and often socialized with George and Elena. She even met Lucia who seems to have given her approval. After the war Lucia bumped into her and reported to Elena that she was looking wonderful and was very happy as she had achieved the ultimate ambition of many of these ladies: she had become the mistress of some man holding an important office in the caribinieri. This meant that she had been set up in an apartment and all her needs were being taken care of. Lucia's words were that she was a "proper type of whore – a high class whore."

*　　*　　*

After leaving Rapallo and the Villa Sette Archi, Elena was employed by the military police in Genoa. Her office was on the second floor of a huge building known as Lacasa del Ballila which had belonged to the Fascists. It had a theatre where films had been shown (especially of the propagandist variety) and a gymnasium. The building held many childhood memories for her.

During this period Elena bumped into their old fencing master's younger assistant, the young man who had been hired out to fight the older coach's duels of honour. She discovered that he was trying to pick up the bits of his life again by opening a fencing studio but he couldn't find a suitable, and affordable, venue. It gave her great delight to find him a space in La Casa del Ballila, free of charge, and help him get his business going.

On the same floor as Elena's office was the office of the 'Politzia del Buon Costume' or 'Italian Police of Morality'. This office was responsible for monitoring the 10 000 certified prostitutes in Genoa. These women were required to carry an identification document and report to a hospital once a week for a check-up. The military police would regularly raid nightclubs and check their documentation. Although this system was not the brainchild of the military police, it suited their purposes admirably as these women were a useful source of information on criminals and their nefarious activities.

On one occasion the MPs brought in a prostitute and interrogated her about a British soldier who had been stabbed in front of her in some nightclub. They grilled her for hours but she wouldn't utter a word. Eventually they brought her into Elena's office to recover and, possibly, in the hope that she would divulge something to another Italian-speaking woman.

Left alone with Elena, she threatened to commit suicide by jumping from the window. Perhaps she thought this would elicit Elena's sympathy and that she would speak up for her. Elena told her that jumping from the window wasn't going to work as they were only one floor up and all she would achieve would be a broken ankle. Eventually the MPs returned and she still hadn't said a word. When they threatened to hand her over to the Italian police she really started to perform and kept up the tears and screeching as they dragged her away. The MPs evidently didn't have a patch on the Italian police.

This office wasn't all degradation and pain and Elena extracted a great deal of fun from her stay.

There was a group of young Italian policemen who used to congregate every morning at the foot of the staircase which she had to climb to get to her office. Their daily entertainment was ribald commentary and they were astounded and grateful one morning when she stopped to offer each of them a cigarette. As she ran up the stairs she could hear the crackers exploding, the crackers which she had painstakingly inserted into each cigarette. George saw fit to reprimand her: "Meid, it's a serious place this – you can't go around making these sort of jokes." His warning had little impact.

When she found a little shop in Genoa which sold novelties and tricks she was delighted. This really expanded her repertoire.

Elena liked her desk to be kept spick and span and she had a designated spot for every object on her desk. One young man used to come along for a chat and perch himself on the edge of her desk. As he tried to charm her with his trivialities, he would fiddle with everything on her desk and never replace anything. Her requests that he leave her possessions as they were had little effect. Finally, she resorted to a visit to her favourite shop where she found a cunning box of 'cigarettes'. This she left on her desk. When he next visited, he seated himself on her desk as usual and his fingers began drifting about. And then he picked up the box – and was given a nasty little electric shock!

Her practical jokes weren't confined to her office either. When she and George attended a huge dance in Genoa, a South African colonel exploded a cracker behind her, giving her an enormous fright and, worse still, burning her stockings. In retaliation, she put an exploding matchbox with his cigarettes, on the table at which he was seated. When he opened the matchbox, sparks flew out of it and the junior officers at the table roared with laughter – guffaws which were quickly suppressed when they saw the look on his face. He glared at everyone at the table in turn. When he looked at Elena though, she was gazing elsewhere and pretending to be oblivious of what was going on around her.

Some days later, as an apology for her bad behaviour, she took him a cake. He was delighted and cancelled his NAAFI order for tea. Her cake was a beautifully iced block of wood! When she brought him another cake later, he was determined to call her bluff and insisted that she come back at teatime. He also summoned George to join them. Elena was tasked with pouring the tea and cutting the cake and she had no trouble at all in graciously slicing through a real cake. So, the colonel's bluff was called and won by Elena.

The black market was still a problem and George roped Elena in to trap a young South African doctor who was rumoured to be selling insulin which was in critically short supply. She posed as a customer and he sold the insulin to her but when she took it to George, he decided that prosecuting the case was not worth destroying a young man's career. After issuing a stern warning, he dropped the case.

Even Ouma Smuts's Christmas gifts were often stolen and sold on the black market. (Ouma (*Granny*) Smuts was the much-loved wife of South African Prime Minister, General Jan Smuts. She worked indefatigably through the war to raise funds and organize parcels for the South African troops.) These packages contained such comforts as socks, and luxuries like chocolate, shaving-cream and, of course, cigarettes which were contained in cellophane instead of more expensive box-packaging. Both George and Elena received these gift parcels. Unfortunately, the parcels had often seen better days and the weevils had got to the cigarettes. To smoke them they had to block the weevil holes with their fingers, a bit like playing a miniature recorder – but smoke them they did.

CHAPTER 17

Sergeant Rudolph Ollawagen, despite all indications to the contrary with regard to his inability to read women, was an investigator for the military police. In the course of his investigations, he came across a building in Genoa which mystified him. He reported to George that the outside dimensions didn't appear to match the inside and he wasn't sure how to proceed. George's solution was simple and direct: bash the wall down!

Beyond the wall they discovered a magnificent piece of machinery – a Mercedes Benz sports car. It was a two-seater cabriolet with a bench seat behind the front seats. It had an incredibly long bonnet to accommodate the powerful engine. Everything about it was splendid. From the two, chromed and gleaming exhaust pipes which snaked from each side of the engine cowling, to the mother-of-pearl dashboard and the butter-soft, upholstered leather seats, it was, every inch, a masterpiece of motoring engineering and design. George was smitten!

It had been painted in camouflage colours. The building in which it had been hidden was part of a commercial garage and repair shop so George commissioned the business (at his own expense) to respray the car in navy blue, which was far more suited to the car's dignity and beauty.

After further investigation, George and Rudolph discovered that the car had belonged to the German ambassador to Rome. It would appear that this was Baron Carl-Ludwig Diego von Bergen.

The Baron was born in 1872 and had a long and distinguished career in the diplomatic corps. He held the position of Ambassador to the Holy See from 1915. His position in Rome in the Diplomatic College was also greatly respected, his being listed, in December of 1940, as the dean of the diplomatic corps. It was in this capacity that he was given the enormous privilege of delivering a eulogy at Pope Pius XI's funeral in 1939. In this eulogy he encouraged the cardinals to elect a pope who would co-operate with the Fascist governments of Europe. Whether this was an exercise in expedience to appease his own government and the Italian government, or a genuine sentiment, it didn't have the desired effect on Hitler and his cronies: the Baron found himself gradually sidelined because he wasn't seen as being sufficiently supportive of the Nazi vision. His aristocratic background probably also counted against him.

He was suddenly recalled to Berlin on the 27th of February 1943, ostensibly to attend a conference, but he was never allowed to return to Italy. Baron von Bergen had been suffering poor health for some time and died on the 7th of October 1944.

One assumes that when he was recalled from Rome, the Baron must have flown directly to Berlin and had the car driven to Genoa to be railed back to Germany at a later date. By the time Ralph and George found the car, Von Bergen was already dead.

All George needed now was a suitable journey on which to take his car and his girl. And George could never be accused of lacking imagination and initiative.

The journey became a military expedition 'to search for soldiers who had gone AWOL during the closing months of the war'.

They set off in late July. George and Elena travelled in style in the Mercedes and the car turned heads everywhere. For Elena, being seated in that car was the ultimate in sensuous and sensual experiences. Enfolded in the softness of the creamy leather, which still retained its distinctive smell, her legs stretched luxuriously before her, the light constantly playing off the mother-of-pearl dashboard, the grumble and growl of that potent engine at rest and then roaring to life as George took off – was an almighty turn-on.

They were accompanied by an army chef and two other soldiers who travelled in two vehicles. One was a motorized water-tanker filled with petrol and the other was a Jeep which carried all their provisions as no food was available along the route. When they needed a pit-stop George directed the men to one side of the road and Elena to the other. They overnighted in hostelries and hotels, including the hotel in Canazei in the Dolomites where Elena and her family had stayed during their last summer holiday in July of 1939. At each stop they handed their supplies over to the hotel staff to be prepared for them.

Their route took them from Genoa to Milan, then eastwards towards Verona. Just before Verona they headed north, passing Lago di Garda to their west, travelling slightly to the east of Trento, into the mountainous region of the Dolomites and through the Brenner Pass.

The scenery was spectacular but often also desolate and tragic. One little town, called Vado, had been completely shattered with nothing left but the corners of buildings which looked like some mad Englishman's folly. 'Vado' means 'I am going' and the awful irony wasn't lost on them.

George was always captivated by hills, perhaps as a reaction to having grown up in the flat and desolate Upington region. He found it very difficult to bypass such swellings in the earth: he would insist on stopping to climb to the top to see whatever was to be seen. Elena and their three companions were obliged to join him. She was always prepared for such excursions in her flat, red leather shoes but the men had an advantage over her in being able to strip off their shirts when they got too hot.

In the Dolomites their explorations also led to crystal-clear streams and rivers which provided wonderful refreshment in the heat of summer. George was able to indulge his love of photography at every turn.

He had long wanted a Leica and Elena had been delighted to find one for him, at a price she could afford, while she was running Villa Sette Archi. She couldn't wait for him to arrive for the weekend. As he drove up, she dashed out, waving the camera at him. Her surprise didn't turn out quite as she had planned as there he stood, waving a Leica back at her – he had also found one during the week he'd been away!

The Leica had cost her a considerable amount and so she decided to sell it. A South African doctor, by the name of Sadler, took it off her hands but wasn't able to pay her immediately. He gave her a post-dated cheque which she was supposed to redeem in Pretoria when she finally got there. George said she was completely mad and that she had been swindled. Her faith in humankind was far greater than his. When she eventually did get to Pretoria a couple of years later, she took her cheque into a bank and explained the situation. By then it was well out of date but the staff said that they would see what they could do. They contacted her two days later to say that they had spoken to Dr Sadler, all was well, and she could come in to collect her money!

Their journey eventually brought them to Berchtesgaden, in Bavaria, which lies about eighteen kilometres south of Salzburg. Near the base of the mountain on which Hitler's house, 'Eagle's Nest' is built, were huge barracks, air-raid shelters and various military buildings. All these buildings had been bombed out of useful existence in April of 1945 and what can be seen in Elena's photographs are collapsing, blackened shells, criss-crossed with shattered roof beams, fallen-in roofs and gaping holes.

Within the barracks were the remains of Hitler's personal rooms which he used when he was not up in Eagle's Nest. The Allies had made merry with these rooms after they had arrived in May. Hitler's bathroom received special attention. On the blackened walls was a spread of graffiti. Many of the fixtures had been ripped out or broken, including Hitler's toilet which had also been filled to overflowing with excrement. George took a picture of Elena standing in Hitler's bathtub. She is holding a piece of tile in the photograph. She still has this fragment which is a delicate shade of pale blue.

A road winds up the mountain from where the barracks stood, to the tunnel entrance. This was the entrance to the shaft which housed the elevator up to Eagle's Nest. Both the tunnel and the shaft had been cut out of solid rock. Eagle's Nest was not damaged and is currently being used as a conference centre. In 1952 the remains of the barracks were demolished and trees were planted.

To visit Berchtesgaden in this car was something of a private snook-cocking at Hitler and his vicious henchmen for Elena and George. High-ranking Nazis had favoured these cars in their various forms and Hitler had given a small number of the sports variations to a very select group of his valued cronies. Witnessing the burnt-out and crumbling remains of Hitler's carefully plotted fortifications, whilst in possession of a magnificently-crafted piece of German engineering, highlighted the dichotomy of what Hitler could have achieved and the real evil he chose to visit upon the world.

On their return journey, just as they crossed the Austrian border at about midday, the weather was blazing hot and they were parched. Elena happened to glance up at the hillside they were passing and, on a terrace above them, she spotted gaily-coloured umbrellas sheltering tables and chairs. The owner of the house on the hillside had created an impromptu beer garden which was just what they needed.

For Elena and George to sit there, with their three obliging travel companions, and gaze out over the heat-hazed valley, was an interlude to be savoured. The beer had been chilled to just the right temperature and was delicious. All, for the moment, seemed very right with the world and the occasion provided a very satisfying conclusion to their trip.

George became aware that he and his car were being investigated by the military police. He was being accused of having stolen military property. A particularly nosey and determined investigator, who also seemed to resent George for something, tried to charm Elena and invited her out to lunch. All through the meal he questioned her, trying to trick her into inadvertently revealing the whereabouts of the car. Eventually, in desperation as lunch was coming to an end, he asked her directly where the car was. She said, "Oh, I have it here with me. I carry it in my handbag all the time!" He wasn't pleased with her and the occasion ended on a rather sour note.

George was very keen to take the car back to South Africa with him. However, the logistics of managing this, plus the fact that the car was a terrible fuel guzzler, made it a hopeless dream. Consequently, he decided to give the car away. By the time of the investigation he had, in fact, already given the car to a Dutch friend, Jan Lips, who lived in Rapallo. Jan had a motor boat which he always shared very generously with his friends. George felt that he was a deserving recipient of the beautiful machine and would provide a good home for the elegant lady.

Elena was very concerned about the interest the military police were showing in the car but George was nonchalant. Finally, in March 1947, George was arrested, jailed, and told that he would have to appear before a military tribunal on a charge of stealing army equipment. Elena was beside herself, imagining, at the very least, that George would receive a dishonourable discharge, and at worst, face a prison sentence. He continued to be quite indifferent. On the day of his appearance Elena sat in their flat in Genoa, barely able to breathe.

When he finally arrived home, Elena sagged with relief.

He did concede to experiencing some unease at the start of his hearing, the formality of the occasion being designed to intimidate and humiliate. Being made to remove his Sam Browne on entering the court, was what really brought the import of the moment home to him. However, his qualms soon abated. It didn't take much persuasion for the authorities to accept his story and realize that the car had never been military property. The case ended with laughter and handshakes all round and George returned to the flat with a jaunty step.

The tour to Berchtesgaden wasn't the only trip they took in the grand old lady but in the meantime Elena had a very important journey to undertake on her own.

CHAPTER 18

George's divorce had not yet come through but he and Elena were confident that it was imminent and they decided that Elena should take advantage of all the ships transporting men and equipment back to South Africa.

George met the captain of the S.S. Samnes in Genoa and spent a very merry evening with him. In the course of the evening he managed to get the captain sufficiently inebriated to sign Elena on as a stewardess aboard the Samnes so that she could make her way to South Africa. She couldn't sail in a cargo ship as an ordinary passenger because of the added docking fees.

The Samnes was a Liberty ship and when Barend came to see his daughter off, he was horrified that she was to sail in such a contraption. The conventional ship-building method was to rivet the iron sheets which gave the hull a certain amount of flexibility. The hulls of the Liberty ships had been welded as this was a much quicker construction method but it resulted in a rigid hull which did not respond well to very heavy swells. Some Liberty ships had been known to break up under such conditions. No less than five Liberty ships had broken up in the Bay of Biscay alone.

Elena sailed from Genoa on the 6th of March 1946. Only George and Barend were there to see her off. Barend had brought his captain's whistle with him which he began to blow when they could no longer see each other to wave. Elena continued to hear his whistle long after the Samnes had cast off. The vision of his desolate figure standing on the wharf stayed with her for much longer.

The Scots captain and Elena couldn't understand a word the other spoke. What limited English she had picked up was completely confounded by his broad accent, and he understood neither Italian nor Dutch, or even French.

She could communicate with most of the men in Dutch and her rapidly developing Afrikaans.

Despite their lack of verbal communication, they enjoyed each other's company and he made every effort to ensure her comfort and safety. She was the only woman on board and he wasn't taking any chances. The chief steward was tasked with attending her and was the only person allowed to enter her cabin. George had also allocated a military policeman to act as her chaperone but this poor fellow was absolutely useless as he suffered agonies of sea sickness for the entire duration of the voyage.

Each officer took a turn to host a drinks party in his cabin and these events occurred every evening at 9 o'clock. Beer and sandwiches were served and whisky was freely available. Of course, the Scots captain would touch nothing but whisky, unsullied by water. His expression for Elena was, "My lassie, pop me a Scotch!"

He also took a fatherly interest in her which included the right to comment and criticize freely. He didn't like her painted nails, for one thing, telling her in no uncertain terms: "I don't like those bloody nails!"

They only had one stop and that was Tel Aviv in what was still officially Palestine. The Samnes was only in port for a night and a day and her passengers grabbed the opportunity to leave the ship. On the evening of their arrival, Elena set off with a party of officers to visit a nightclub. Her policeman-chaperone was ready to do his duty, not having been able to prove himself in the preceding days. However, even these best intentions were foiled. As they all left the ship, he was stopped by the hypersensitive Israeli security because he was wearing his sidearm. Unable to hand it over, he was forced to retreat to the ship and Elena waved him a merry goodbye as she set off.

The following day the captain took her sightseeing. They had a fascinating and full day viewing old and new. The emerging Israel was vibrant with hope and was making rapid progress: Elena was astounded at what had already been achieved in agriculture with greening fields, acres of hydroponic structures and new orchards.

They arrived back at the Samnes as the sun was setting. The first engineer was livid with them because they were so late. He had already had to fire up the engines and gave the captain a tongue-lashing for delaying cast off.

As they sailed through the Suez Canal and the Red Sea, the temperature began to soar. One evening, early in the voyage, Elena asked for a whisky and water at one of their evening drinks parties. What she was given was a glass full of straight whisky. Whether it was the heat, the alcohol, or her lack of body weight, she doesn't know, but she fainted, to the consternation of the captain and the first engineer. As she surfaced, they were both peering down at her.

The captain's diagnosis was that her fainting was the result of the extreme heat and her thinness. He prescribed a daily weigh-in on the ship's scale, normally used for weighing bags of grain. This consisted of a hook suspended from a spring gauge. It was housed in the coolroom and it was the first mate's job to weigh her every morning. She was a startlingly undernourished 43 kgs. The captain's medication included a compulsory plate of oatmeal porridge every morning. He also went so far as having an air-conditioner installed in her cabin. Elena wasn't so sure that his diagnosis was all that accurate – she thought the neat whisky might have had a lot more to do with her fainting spell.

Bathing amenities were very limited and the water available for ablutions was brackish. There was no bathtub but the very gallant captain provided her with a zinc bath. On the coast of Egypt the chief steward (an elderly and very kindly man) informed her, "Today you are bathing in the waters of the Nile!" - romantic thought. He also made a habit of perfuming her bathwater with lavender.

Despite the air-conditioner, her cabin still became stuffy. And it was lonely. Hence, she spent most of her time on deck with the men. The deck itself was impossibly hot but the tank carriers had been chained to the deck and they provided good shelter from the sun and the frequent drizzle, although they did nothing to reduce the heat. For the most part, Elena and the men spent their time beneath the carriers, playing cards and smoking. This was interspersed with ludicrous games like fining one another a tickey a time for being caught killing a cockroach.

As they sailed down the east coast of Africa they had to contend with some very bad weather. The relatively light Liberty ship, even though she was loaded with tanks, couldn't plough through the mountainous waves. As the ship crested a wave and then slid down into a trough, there was a serious threat to the propeller sheering off if it wasn't submerged. This meant that the engines had to be shut down which created another set of problems for controlling the ship's path. These difficulties, of course, extended the voyage.

One storm was so bad that the tanks in the hold broke loose. The threatened damage to the hull of rampaging tanks meant that they had to be secured without delay, putting the men who were trying to fasten them at great risk of being crushed. This had already happened on another Liberty ship and two men had lost their lives when they were trapped between two tanks. The Samnes's crew was well aware of this horror story and everyone shared some very anxious moments. There was relief all round when the tanks were secured, the horrendous banging from the hold ceased, and the men emerged, unscathed.

Sometimes the sea was so rough that the officers couldn't make it to the dinner table, their seasickness having laid them low. Elena was very proud of her sea-legs when only she, the captain, and the first mate could sit down together.

As they drew closer to Durban the mood grew less languid, despite the continuing heat. The day prior to docking in Durban was spent spitting and polishing everything that could be spat on or polished up. Each man, and one woman, went over personal kit meticulously and every polishable surface on the good old Samnes was also given an extra rub.

The excitement, as they sailed into Durban harbour at sunrise on the 26th of March 1946, was palpable. Every man who wasn't essential to getting the ship docked had crowded on to the deck and Elena, as the lone woman, was given a place at the railings, close to the bow, for the best view of her new home.

210

She had endured the usual corny joshing about the streets being paved with gold but, as she stood on the deck as the ship crossed the Bar, the waters truly were slicked with the gold of the sunrise and the men's silly jokes took on another meaning. Amidst the tumultuous welcome given to the tugboat crew and the pilot as he had come aboard, and the cheers and laughter, there were individual quiet moments of introspection, memories and anticipation for every one of them and especially for Elena.

This was a busy port with a multitude of low sheds. The mouth was the same narrow space it is today but seemed perhaps even narrower than it is now: to the left was the towering Bluff, covered in dense, impenetrable, natural bush and looking very wild and uninhabited to the uninitiated. At its foot lay the abandoned whaling station with its giant iron framework from which great hooks still hung like some monstrous and malevolent child's playground swing. To the right was the concrete defensive battery, still manned as it had been throughout the war, and so close that the men on the battery walls seemed almost within reach of an outstretched arm.

There were few people about so early in the day and certainly no welcoming, waving crowds. Even for the men whose homes were in Natal, there were no families waiting because it hadn't been possible to notify their relatives as to exactly when they would dock. Many of them, of course, still had long train journeys ahead of them, especially if their homes were in the Orange Free State or the Transvaal. None of this seemed to matter much as they provided their own welcoming jollity and the bustle of disembarking took over.

Elena had thirteen large pieces of luggage. Despite the willing hands it took some time to assemble all this in the customs-shed. However, everyone was very jovial, including the particular customs official who was dealing with Elena and her baggage.

At this point, Elena had no idea what her next step would be. She only had one contact number in Durban and no idea of how to use a South African call-box. The number she had, was Stan Conker's. Her lovely, elderly steward found her trying to use the call-box and took over from her while she returned to her luggage.

The customs official made her unpack everything. When they arrived at her pasta machine, he had never seen anything like it and asked her to demonstrate how it worked. In the meantime, the steward had managed to raise Stan who had not yet left for work. Stan was a Durban lad and lived somewhere in the vicinity of Umbilo. Still being part of the military machine, he was employed at the harbour as a military policeman.

Eventually Elena, with her luggage, found herself deposited outside the customs-shed. At this point Stan arrived, hurtling along the quay as fast as his legs could carry him and yelling and blaspheming at the top of his voice in his greeting of Elena. She was enormously relieved to see him and he hugged her joyously. Stan's hullabaloo had hardly settled when another customs official approached the group. He was carrying a clipboard and his frown was at odds with every other face she had encountered that morning.

It was Elena he was looking for and he apologized for his interruption but said that he had something urgent to tell her. And then he dropped his bombshell! He had discovered that she had been listed as an 'undesirable immigrant' and consequently had one week to leave South African shores and return to Italy!

It took some time for the seriousness of this message to penetrate and, as she sank down to rest on her luggage, she was overwhelmed by helplessness. None of it made any sense. Through her family's work with resettling Jews she knew all about being an undesirable immigrant but there was nothing obviously against her name which could have caused this label to be attached to her, especially at a time when the country was actively encouraging immigration. She certainly didn't suffer from any of the obvious disqualifiers such as ill-health or a criminal record. And then she knew who was, in all likelihood, behind this: George's estranged wife, Lusty Lily.

It did turn out to be Lily who had used her military connections to get Elena blacklisted.

Stan eventually gathered Elena and her belongings together and loaded her into his car to drive her to his home where they would settle down to finding a plan. She wasn't thinking very clearly and not much of the young city could make an impression on her. What she did notice as they drove up West Street was the amazing number of shops which were selling salt. There were salt signs emblazoned on almost every large shop-window. All she could conclude was that Durban had suffered a terrible salt shortage during the war and stocks had finally arrived. When she voiced her confusion to Stan, he roared with laughter: the Italian word for 'salt' is spelt 'sale' and this was the beginning of the autumn sale season.

Stan and his wife made Elena welcome. In response to their query about what she wanted to drink, she said that what she most wanted was a glass of real milk.

When they had all gathered their thoughts they contacted Toly who by now was married to Ernst Taljaard and was living in the Cape. Toly swung into action in her usual efficient fashion. Ever resourceful, she contacted a Jewish lawyer she had met in the Cape and he managed to get Elena's stay extended to three months.

Off Elena headed to Cape Town by train. This was also no simple feat as she had to travel northwards to Johannesburg in order to catch a train to Cape Town – a long journey traversing the Transvaal, the Orange Free State and a vast stretch of the Cape Province.

Toly and Ernst were living with Ernst's parents and they accommodated Elena too, while she awaited developments. Ernst's parents lived on a farm and this held some novel experiences for Elena, especially the toilet facility which was a distance from the house and was a pit-toilet!

During the time Elena was with them, Toly and Ernst managed to find a flat in the vicinity of Simonstown. Toly was expecting their first baby and when she went into labour Ernst was at work and Toly and Elena were panic-stricken. They had no transport and the only neighbour who was at home was an elderly, and somewhat doddery, man. He had a car and agreed to get them to hospital. However, his driving was maddeningly slow. Neither sister had a watch and Elena used the kitchen timer to measure the minutes between contractions.

When they eventually got to the hospital, Toly's contractions slowed down and the wait seemed endless. Finally forceps were used and Jacques van Praag Taljaard arrived in the world – yelling and very red. By then Ernst was there. Elena commented on how beautiful the baby was but Ernst had no such scruples and his welcome to his first born was, "Hy lyk nes 'n padda!" *("He looks just like a frog!")* The little fellow was circumcised immediately.

When mother and babe returned home, neither Toly nor Elena had much idea of how to look after him. His first bath had Elena holding his legs while Toly took his arms as they lowered him into the water. And then came the changing of his bandage! They were afraid that it would be sticking to the wound and Elena suggested that Toly wet it before trying to remove it. At this point Toly decided she couldn't cope and called Ernst. He, too, would have nothing to do with it and this left Elena. She managed without too much more fuss and says that Jacques was so good – except that she did receive an eyeful as the bandage came off. She still reminds this now senior citizen of the service she rendered him in his infancy for which she inevitably earns an, "Oh, Aunty Elena, please!"

Toly, as was to be expected, took her usual serious and academic approach to mothering and read whatever she could find. In her research she learnt that vitamin C was very important in infant nutrition and took to giving him tomato juice between feeds. When she saw blood in his stool she had hysterics and phoned the doctor in a panic. When he discovered what she was feeding Jacques, he told her she was crazy. The babe couldn't yet digest tomato and in any event he was receiving all the nutrition he needed from his mother herself.

That wasn't the only unusual child-rearing practice young Jacques endured, but the following memorable exercise had been successfully applied to all the Van Praag children and Lucia had given both Elena and Toly clear instructions on what to do. This was potty-training – from birth!

As soon as Jacques was taken home, his training began. When he woke up he was given a feed and then Toly would position herself on a chair with a potty on her lap. Elena would then pass Jacques to her so that he rested on the potty with his back supported against Toly's chest. He responded appropriately almost from the very start. It seemed that as soon as he felt the chill of the potty against his thighs some reflex signalled what was required of him and he practically never had a soiled nappy! Incidentally, Elena had bought the potty, which was decorated with bunnies. Toly never learnt to pronounce 'bunny' and called them 'boonies' so the potty became known as the 'boony'. As soon as Jacques could make himself understood he would demand his 'boony'.

Prior to hearing the potty-training story from Elena, I had read about this toilet-training method in an article on modern childcare practices and dismissed the idea as ridiculous. When Elena told me what they had done, I was intrigued. Neighbour Margaret is most disapproving and rejects the idea as a form of child abuse.

A year later, in 1947, Ernst and Toly had a second child, a little girl they called Lucille. Their third child was also a daughter, called Erna, who was born in 1953.

Ernst was still in the military police and was transferred to Durban where they lived on the Bluff. They had a short stint in Oudtshoorn and then returned to Durban. Disregarding the short time they spent in Oudtshoorn, they lived in Durban for about nine years, during which time Ernst transferred from the military police to the army. Ernst had not matriculated before the war and set about studying for his matric, which he had little difficulty in completing. No doubt Toly made her inimitable contribution to the project.

He was about to begin studying for a degree when tragedy struck them. Lucille was four-and-a-half and a truly delightful child in addition to her blonde, blue-eyed prettiness. She had inherited Elena's bray. Jacques and Lucille were also great playmates. Lucille suddenly became desperately ill and doctors battled to find a diagnosis. When they did discover the cause of her illness, the news couldn't have been worse: it was rampant leukemia. Within a couple of weeks the little girl was gone.

On the day she died little Jacques was told that she'd gone to heaven. That evening, when he went to clean his teeth, he spotted Lucille's toothbrush.

He rushed to his mother with the toothbrush in his hand and very worriedly said to her, "Ma, Lucille forgot to take her toothbrush. How is she going to clean her teeth in heaven without her toothbrush?"

Ernst took her death very hard. Shortly thereafter he decided to look for a job in Northern Rhodesia. In the months that he was away Toly and the children lived with Elena and George.

Ernst found employment with the Ministry of Native Affairs in the Department of Game and Fisheries where he was seconded to the Kafue National Park. He and Jacques drove up to Northern Rhodesia in June of 1956 and Toly and Erna flew up to join them. Ernst took up his appointment in July and Jacques was enrolled in a boarding-school in Lusaka.

The Park had been earmarked as a national game park in 1924 when the British Colonial Government had moved the Nkoya people out of the area to the Mumbwa District further east. Nothing more appears to have happened until 1950 when it was properly proclaimed. At 22 400 square kilometres, it is claimed to be the second largest park in the world and is Zambia's oldest park. It is situated 322 kilometres west of Lusaka. By 1956 there was still no development and this was the task undertaken by Ernst.

The government supplied the Taljaards with a tent in which to live – and nothing else. However, they seem to have managed quite happily. Ernst's first task was to build a habitable house. This was followed by an office block, staff quarters and all the other facilities needed for such a venture. He was also responsible for building a system of roads.

Once established, they lived extremely well in the luxury that is concomitant with a truly colonial lifestyle. Toly had worked throughout their marriage, usually as a bookkeeper because her qualifications as a chartered accountant weren't recognized in South Africa. In Kafue she was also employed as the reserve's bookkeeper. The two of them made an excellent team. They and their children all loved their existence there. The children enjoyed a wealth of wildlife experiences. One of their most memorable experiences involved two male lion cubs.

The chief game-warden was the renowned Norman Carr who did so much to develop the national parks and tourism in Northern Rhodesia. He was the brain and energy behind the innovation of walking safaris.

The senior game-guard, a man called Chanamina, was out on patrol with his assistant when he found himself trapped between a lioness's den, inhabited by three very young cubs, and their fast-approaching mother. The cubs' mother was known as 'The Smiler' because of a facial deformity. She was the unquestionable leader of her pride and was much admired for her hunting prowess. The cubs were only a day or two old, probably born on the 20th of December 1957, so The Smiler's protective instincts were at their peak. When she spotted Chanamina she didn't hesitate. He had had the presence of mind to realize that he was in a very precarious situation as soon as he had discovered the cubs, and had his shotgun at the ready. As she charged at him he was forced to fire: the shot killed her instantly.

Chanamina and his assistant knew that they had to do everything in their power to save the cubs but this was no easy task as the nearest out-station was Kasempa which was four days' journey away. Chasempa's only alternative was to take them to a mission station. Even this was a day-and-a-half away from their present spot.

At the mission the cubs were fed on powdered milk. By the time Norman arrived, they were all very weak from diarrhoea but managed to hang on until Norman could put them on a proper diet. He left one of the cubs with the game-ranger at Kasempa and took the other two back to the main camp at Ngoma with him.

Getting them through their first months was very time consuming as they had to be fed four times a day. Initially they spent all their time with Norman, even sleeping on his bed. They also travelled everywhere with him. As they grew older he was able to leave them in the camp where they could wander about at will and were very popular with the visitors.

By now their personalities were emerging clearly and they became known as 'Big Boy' and 'Little Boy'. In addition to being physically larger, Big Boy was by far the more dominant of the two. Little Boy also seemed to be a much more sensitive, moody soul in need of greater reassurance. During their first year they were very boisterous and Erna was the recipient of a few nasty scratches. Their self-restraint improved as they got older, though.

Toly also enjoyed their company when they wandered in and out of the office. An English tourist arrived one day and informed Toly that he was visiting specifically to see lions. Toly told him that that was not a problem and to come with her. She opened the door to the room where the boys were sleeping and stepped aside for the Englishman with the words, "There you are!" Toly was suitably gratified by his fright.

Big Boy's trademark activity was to hitch a ride on top of one of the vehicles used by the rangers. This had a canvas top which he found very comfortable as a viewing deck and sleeping platform and he was not the least put out if the driver took off while he was resting atop the vehicle. His equilibrium might not have been disturbed but he always managed to cause a sensation with the tourists.

As the cubs approached the eighteen-month mark, Norman started devising plans to teach the boys greater independence. They didn't seem too keen on this project and some of their antics to reunite themselves with people led to some hair-raising, but very amusing, incidents. Norman relates one incident with a British tourist in his delightful book 'Return to the Wild'.

The man was driving a Land Rover with a canvas top when he saw two lions trotting towards him along the road. He tried to reverse but got stuck. Big Boy just kept coming and leapt straight up on to the canvas roof which collapsed and dumped Big Boy on the poor man's lap. As he was trying to fend Big Boy off, the door flew open and the two of them landed in the road. He managed to escape Big Boy's attentions and raced round the vehicle to try to get back in from the other side – and was met by Little Boy who wanted to slather him with loving licks!

By July of 1960, Norman felt that he had fulfilled his objectives in Kafue and transferred to the Luangwa Valley. He was accompanied by the boys who continued their education. This was a two-way process because Norman was also learning a great deal from them through his observations of their behaviour and their interactions with other wildlife. Norman recorded this wonderful experience in his writing and in a film which was made about the boys.

Ernst, in the meantime, was also stationed at a number of other places including Chilanga, which was near Lusaka, Fort Rosebury, Abercorn, Lake Tanganyka and Lungunia. The work was diverse and interesting. It ranged from monitoring large swamp areas, fishery control, and tsetse-fly control. Finally he returned to Kafue as the acting warden.

Zambia was granted independence from Britain in 1964 but the Taljaards remained until January of 1966 when they returned to South Africa. Ernst and Jacques joined the navy in Simonstown and a little later Toly was also employed by the navy. Initially she worked in stores and then became a translator working in French, English, Italian and Afrikaans. However, they weren't about to settle into a life of urban domesticity just yet.

In 1967 the South African government commissioned the building of three Daphné-class submarines from France. The acquisition of these submarines was felt to be particularly important because of the growing Soviet expansionist threat. Someone was needed to translate the operating manuals from French into Afrikaans and Toly got the job. She and Ernst were sent to Toulon where the submarines were being built. The government provided them with very pleasant, furnished accommodation, generous salaries and travel allowances for frequent trips back to South Africa. Erna attended a boarding-school in Scotland.

Toly worked with a French linguist and an English translator. Her particular difficulty was finding accurate Afrikaans terms for labelling parts of equipment and operational methods which didn't yet exist in the Afrikaans lexicon. One such word coined by Toly was 'loertoring' (*'look-tower'*) for 'periscope'. She also had to satisfy the interpretations of the French and English versions. To do this she needed a fair degree of technical knowledge and this is where her mathematical skills and her navigational experience proved very helpful.

Finally the submarines were ready and the first one, the SAS Maria van Riebeeck, arrived in Simonstown on the 13th of May 1971. She was followed on the 10th of December by SAS Emily Hobhouse and the last to arrive, on the 19th of June 1972, was SAS Johanna van der Merwe. The submarine was escorted by the frigate SS President Steyn, regarded as a 'grey diplomat' showing the South African flag in many parts of the world.

It would be twenty years before a South African naval ship would sail in European waters again, such was the political isolation into which South Africa had thrust itself. The submarines were all renamed in 1999, respectively becoming SAS Spear, SAS Umkhonto and SAS Assegaai. They continued to do service until 2003 when they were finally decommissioned: thirty-two years of service to the nation is an admirable record and Toly's manuals were part of that service.

'Maria'/SAS Spear and 'Emily'/SAS Umkhonto were cut up for scrap after decommissioning but SAS Johanna van der Merwe/SAS Assegaai was given a kinder fate: she was preserved as a museum in the SA Naval Museum in the naval dockyard in Simonstown. Here she is manned by a dedicated team of very knowledgeable, retired navy men.

The preservation of this submarine and the existence of the museum is, for me, a secret and private memorial to Toly – a remarkably intelligent and ingenious woman who made her mark wherever she went and survived and thrived no matter what life threw at her. Her involvement also stands as a reminder of the commitment those post-war European settlers showed to their new home and the great contribution so many made to South Africa's development.

After their three-year stint in Toulon, Toly and Ernst were employed in the South African Embassy in Paris for a further three years. Toly loved this period – the glamour and sophistication of life in Paris were right up her alley.

On their return to South Africa they both continued to work for the navy until their retirement.

CHAPTER 19

George had been informed of Elena's predicament and imminent ejection from South Africa and he applied for leave to return to South Africa. Whilst Elena was awaiting George's arrival she didn't sit idly by, but went out and found herself a job.

She had been examining household furnishings in a shop-window when it struck her that the domestic scene she was looking at wasn't complete and that the interior would benefit greatly from improved soft furnishings and especially lampshades, which would match the curtaining. Boldly, she went inside and asked to see the manager. She made her suggestion about the lampshades and offered her services to make them. He asked her for a sample, which she duly produced, and she was given more orders. The designs which were in particular demand were her shades depicting the Beatrix Potter characters.

George's leave was granted and he flew to Pretoria and then entrained for the Cape. Elena had been beside herself hearing his voice again when he landed in Pretoria. She had missed him dreadfully. Her cheerful optimism, the company of her sister and little Jacques, and her employment, had helped to keep fear and uncertainty at bay but she did have moments of anxiety.

On the day of his arrival in Cape Town she awoke with much anticipation and thudding heart. Off she went to meet him at the station in Simonstown.

Standing on the platform, she eagerly scanned all the windows as the train puffed into the station, but failed to see him. As she watched the passengers disembark, she still couldn't see him. Panic began to ooze its way through her veins: had she got the wrong day? Was there a later train? Had something happened to him?

221

She was about to find the station master when she saw a man striding along the platform towards her. There was something vaguely familiar about him but she couldn't think what it was – perhaps a South African she'd met in Italy? Surely not someone who had been sent to give her more bad news? And then he smiled and she knew it was her George!

She hadn't recognized him – it was the first time she had ever seen him in mufti!

Her embarrassment was quickly dispelled by being swung off her feet and clasped to his chest. To see him in front of her again, to be able to touch him and smell him again, created an odd mixture in her chest of the relief of dear familiarity and the welling, thudding excitement of a brand new romance.

They were very hopeful that within Elena's period of grace in South Africa, his divorce would come through. They even went out and bought a wedding ring from a little jewellery shop in the middle of Cape Town. The shop was owned by an elderly Jewish man who was enthusiastic in his felicitations and wanted to know the course of their courtship. No doubt he was intrigued by the Elena-George combination. They were an arresting couple and Elena's accent and creative use of languages must have piqued his interest. How to begin explaining their circumstances? That was far too complicated so they gave him a much-simplified version and went on their way with his blessings.

George's divorce failed to materialise and, as his leave drew to a close, they realized that they had better accept the inevitable and make plans for Elena to return to Europe.

A week after his arrival, they travelled back to Pretoria together by train. Even this journey wasn't without incident. The train broke down at De Aar, 800 kilometres from Cape Town, in the middle of nowhere. This was the railway junction which represented much childhood misery for George. They were stuck there for many long, hot hours.

Once in Pretoria, George was required to report for duty and had to take up a temporary post. Elena's revised deportation date was the 27th of July 1946. She managed to get this extended through devious means. She, George and dear old Speedy Botha came up with a desperate plan: Elena would apply for an extension to her stay on the grounds that she was engaged to Speedy Botha.

Off she and Speedy went to the government building which housed the relevant official. Although Elena had pulled her fair share of stunts to bend the rules for her own ends throughout her youth, she was terribly nervous. Speedy stayed downstairs at the entrance and Elena made her way to the office she needed. She was introduced to a good-looking young man who shook her hand and smiled warmly. He invited her to sit down and listened attentively to her story. She felt that she was making great headway, especially when the official said that he knew Speedy and if Speedy didn't marry her, he would be delighted to marry her himself. He gave her an extension and wished her and Speedy luck. As he was seeing her to the door of his office he said, "Oh, and by the way, do give my regards to Captain Jennings!" Elena scuttled down the stairs and out of the building as fast as she could go!

It would be five months before the authorities finally caught up with her and enforced her deportation in January 1947. This was way beyond the extension that she had wangled with Speedy's help. One wonders if the official who gave her the extension hadn't somehow secretly continued to lend a helping hand.

These were five glorious months but they were threaded with the tension of waiting and hoping that George's divorce would come through in time for Elena to avoid being sent back to Italy. His divorce hadn't been finalized by the time the authorities paid her a visit and she had to leave the country.

She was to fly from Waterkloof Air Force Base to Cairo. This was yet another tortuous parting. She was beginning to feel like a frayed, old tug-of-war rope, getting nowhere and under constant tension. As she took her seat on the plane, she scanned the people standing alongside the runway until she spotted George's dear, familiar figure. He was waving at the plane energetically but there was something disconsolate and weary about his posture. She craned her neck to watch him for as long as she could as the plane gathered speed on take-off and lumbered into the air.

On landing in Cairo, once again she only had one contact number. This was the number for a man she had never previously met. He came to meet her at a designated hotel. Fortunately, he had the forethought to ask her how much money she had on her and realized that she didn't have enough to pay for accommodation at that hotel or any other respectable hotel. He took her to a boarding-house run by a friend of his. This establishment was specifically for women in transit, like Elena. The proprietress was a charming woman who chatted to Elena about her day and then realized that she had been out all day and was probably desperate to go to the loo – which she was. Behind the toilet door was a notice which tickled Elena: "Thank God for this relief!"

From Cairo she flew to Malta and then to Rome. When she arrived in Rome she was told that the train for Florence departed at 2 p.m. but that she should go straight to the station and book her ticket immediately as the train would be very crowded. It was only 10 o'clock in the morning. She managed to get a ticket and then sat on the platform waiting and watching as other travellers arrived – and they arrived and arrived and arrived.

In her compartment the passengers were jammed up against each other on the seats, and lined up in the space between the seats. The corridors were packed with standing passengers and even the toilets held standing passengers. In addition to this suffocating overcrowding the two- to three-hour journey took eight hours!

Elena became quite frantic to go to the toilet but there was absolutely no chance of getting through the crowd, even if the toilet itself hadn't been occupied. A fellow passenger told her how, on a previous trip to Florence, when the train had been equally crowded, some poor woman had become so desperate that he and another man had hung on to her arms while she suspended her rear-end from the window in order to solve her problem. There was no way that Elena was going to subject herself to that indignity. Perhaps her resistance to drinking water stems from such uncomfortable moments. Even now she refuses to drink water unless it comes in the form of soda-water and is mixed with her whisky. (No amount of nagging from Margaret or Lynette can persuade her that water is good for her: she claims that all the research into the health benefits of drinking water has been done by charlatans who have never produced any real proof.)

When the train finally pulled into Florence at midnight, Elena stumbled off and made a dash for home. She rang the doorbell and her befuddled parents, who had no idea that she was on her way home, shouted "Who's there?" A pitiful little voice replied "It's me! It's me! Let me in!" Their feelings of shock, bewilderment and delight at the return of their prodigal daughter were cut short as she dashed past them and up the stairs to the loo!

* * *

Elena stayed with her parents until George's return a short while later. She and George then went back to Genoa where they were accommodated in a requisitioned flat. This abode was spacious and beautiful, in the main square, the Piazza Manin. They shared this flat with a friend and were also provided with a cook and a maid. She didn't take up any formal employment but did continue to act as George's interpreter and secretarial assistant.

And so the life she thought she had left behind forever was resumed, in large part. Fortunately Elena was not particularly concerned about her marital status or lack thereof. She viewed George as her partner for life and felt that a marriage certificate would make no real difference to either of them. It would, however, be an essential requirement for her re-admittance to South Africa and so was a problem that couldn't simply be ignored. She still ponders, though, how her parents felt about her living with George and is troubled by the pain and worry she must have caused them. Amazingly, they never once castigated her.

Elena was free now to accompany George on his travels. They spent some time stationed at Lago Maggiore and this beautiful lake provided them with great pleasure and fun.

George commandeered an outboard motor boat from the local Italians. George and Elena, often accompanied by others, spent a great deal of time on the lake - sightseeing, skiing and fishing. Elena wasn't an experienced skier and her skiing was done on a board which George had made for her.

George also practised his photography and was fascinated by the play of light on water. He took pictures of some spectacular sunsets and water-wakes and interesting, somewhat seductive, posed pictures of Elena.

One afternoon they went 'fishing' with tall, strong Sergeant-Major William Bates, the lad from the Free State who had the terrible stammer. It was his job to light the stick of dynamite to blow up a shoal of fish for a quick and easy catch. Elena said to George, "Please don't make William count before he throws." William may have stuttered but he had a quick comeback for her: "M-M-Meidjie, m-m-moenie worrie nie – ek gooi eers en dan tel ek." *("Meidjie, don't worry – I throw first and then I count.")* Explosion safely over, they scooped up masses of fish for the barracks. The rest was grabbed by the local Italians who had started to row out to them as soon as they had heard the explosion.

Lago Maggiore is situated on the border between Italy and Switzerland. George was well aware of where the Swiss border lay but, as always, he felt compelled to 'test the waters', 'push the boundaries' and, of course, when they 'crossed the line', the Swiss opened fire on them.

Elena was scared witless and was wildly angry with him, but George wasn't going to admit to his foolhardiness, or to having made a mistake, and claimed that he had simply been checking to see if the Swiss guards were awake.

Another of George's hair-raising escapades involved a rickety wooden suspension-bridge. The roadway consisted of planking and the bridge was only intended for foot traffic. It spanned a very deep and wide gorge. When George said that he was going to drive across it, Elena didn't believe him. Then she thought he wouldn't be able to fit the Jeep on to it. He proved her wrong, although the wheels on the left side of the vehicle had to ride on a low barrier rail. She wasn't prepared to risk her neck in this bit of idiocy and insisted on getting out and walking across the bridge ahead of him. Even this made her uneasy. She did pause for a moment though, before starting off, to take a picture of what George was up to.

On the same day they needed to cross a river where the bridge had been destroyed. George walked into the river and then decided that it would be safe to cross in the Jeep. However, the water was deeper than he had anticipated and the Jeep broke down half-way across. He was forced to re-enter the swirling, freezing water and was able to dry the plugs and start the engine again but he paid for his foolhardiness later. That night he came down with a nasty relapse of malaria.

They were able to take a number of sightseeing excursions, as George's photographs show, and spent some time exploring the Alps on the Italian border. His pictures include the Matterhorn, Monte Rosa and Monte Bianco. On Monte Bianco they found a cable-car which had fallen into disrepair and was very dilapidated with many missing pieces. Practically no floor remained. However, it was still operational. George seized the opportunity and insisted that Elena accompany him. He enjoyed the scenery but she was utterly terrified. The absence of a floor provided a bird's eye view of the mountain which she didn't want to see.

They even made it to Venice. After a day of viewing and photographing the Piazza San Marco, the Campanile, the Church of St Agnesa and the Bridge of Sighs, Elena persuaded George to take an idyllic gondola ride. They selected the smartest gondola, which was upholstered and lined in black velvet with gold trimmings. The two had just settled into a romantic snuggle when George started to leap about and swear – the gondola was swarming with fleas.

Some of George's working hours confined him to an office and administrative tasks. At such times Elena acted as his unofficial secretary and receptionist. One entertaining incident from this period involved a young South African serviceman who had married an Italian woman without first obtaining his commanding officer's permission. He was summoned by George and arrived in a very nervous condition. When he told Elena why he was so agitated she added fuel to the fire by telling him that he was in big trouble and he'd better brace himself for the captain's wrath.

Elena heard George's raised voice but it quietened down towards the end of the interview. When the young chap came out he was chuckling. She asked what had happened. He said that the captain had been very angry and had given him a thorough dressing-down but had finished up by telling him to make sure he didn't do it again.

*   *   *

On the 24th of April 1947, George sent a message to Elena, who was at home in their flat in Genoa, that he had just received the news that he was to be repatriated the following day. In the preceding months George's divorce had been finalized so they were able to marry. However, this news about his repatriation meant that they needed to be married immediately or Elena wouldn't be allowed to return to South Africa with him.

When he arrived at the flat to pick her up he was accompanied by another couple who also needed to get married in a hurry. She was a South African nurse and he was a German doctor, a radiologist, who had been a prisoner of war. This looked suspiciously like a marriage of convenience so that he could get into South Africa.

This couple did make it to South Africa where he rewrote his exams and then opened a practice in Pietermaritzburg. The marriage didn't work and after they were divorced, he married a reputed beauty and they settled in Cape Town. His second wife was killed on the beautiful, but infamous, Chapman's Peak and he married for a third time.

The doctor and his prospective first wife said that they knew of a church in Rome where they could be married at short notice and they were confident that they would not encounter any problems.

However, it wasn't a simple matter of travelling straight to Rome. First they had to go via Florence to pick up a letter from Elena's parents, granting her permission to marry. This was standard Dutch practice: all women under thirty had to have their parents' written permission to be married.

They arrived in Florence very late in the day, having driven as fast as they could from Genoa. They had only paused on the journey for the barest essentials. There was certainly no stopping for a meal or a snack and they made do with eating dry pasta in the car.

Of course Barend was happy to oblige with such a letter and there seems to have been much excitement in the household during their short visit. Lucia made plans to meet the train carrying them from Rome to Venice the following night, as it passed through Florence, to say a final farewell.

Letter secured, they set off for Rome again. They arrived in Rome very late and what was left of the night they, rather quaintly, spent in separate hotels, Elena and the nurse sharing a room. The next morning, at ten o'clock, they set out in high spirits to find the church where they had been told they could be married.

A very nasty shock awaited them: it was the 25th of April, the public holiday which celebrated the end of the Second World War for Italy. The church was locked up and there was no sign of the priest. This wasn't as urgent a problem for the other couple but it was potentially disastrous for Elena and George.

Not knowing what else to do, and needing to gather their wits about them, they went to a hotel near the railway station. This hotel was a gathering point for military embarkation and George left Elena there, surrounded by all their bags and baggage, while he went in a desperate search for someone to marry them.

At this point the ever-optimistic Elena was suddenly overwhelmed by hopelessness and she started to weep. She couldn't believe that they had come so close to being married, and finally, permanently, together with no arbitrary law to separate them, only to have their plans scotched again. For so long they had buoyed themselves up with their optimism but there had also been so many tearful partings, plans gone awry, fresh starts, and crazy plans to overcome the obstacles. At one point they had even considered marriage by proxy. Although Elena had, in the past, shed so many tears of frustration that she thought she had no more to shed, this seemed like the last straw.

She really couldn't see any way forward. This was her moment of crisis of faith in their future together.

She became aware of someone hovering at her elbow and when she looked up it was to see a South African officer whom she knew. In the crowded vestibule he had spotted her and come over to find out what was wrong.

She poured out her story and he listened sympathetically. Then he told her that help was at hand and it was right there in the hotel.

Behind them in all the melée, was a NAAFI queue with men lining up for their monthly allowance of alcohol. In the queue was a Scots Presbyterian minister who was also an army chaplain. He was waiting for his whisky ration. Her South African pal was sure this man could, and would, help them. Off he went to talk to him, anxiously watched by Elena who was trying to read the clergyman's body language. Her relief was palpable as the minister finished listening to the sad little story and looked up smiling. He couldn't have been more obliging and said that if they could be at his church by two o'clock that afternoon, he would marry them.

Elena waited anxiously for George's return. Of course, he was exploring every possibility that came to mind and was reluctant to give up and go back to the hotel with nothing positive to report. When he eventually arrived, he couldn't believe that Elena had found a solution without moving an inch from the hotel lobby. But time was running out. And they had to sprint. George grabbed Elena's hand and ran so fast her toes barely touched ground.

They arrived, completely out of breath, at a multi-storeyed building which didn't look much like a church. This architecture was a condition stipulated by the Roman authorities in the 1920's when permission was granted to the Scottish Presbyterian Church in Rome to build a church – that it could not look like a conventional church. It is a three-winged building which borders a courtyard, the fourth side of which is closed by a wrought-iron palisade fence. Today the courtyard appears to be used for parking but during the war it was a pretty garden. The building looked, and still looks, like any other office block.

It was the garden, however, that redeemed it. Covering the fence and archway was a magnificent tangle of white roses. George picked one of the roses and threaded it through the buttonhole of her jacket – the sum total of her bridal flowers. Her beautiful wedding outfit, the pure wool dress and coat (made of the fabric given to her by Bruno with his love and blessings), and matching hat and shoes, were packed in her luggage and there had simply been no time to change. She was wearing her tailored brown suit and the red, leather walking shoes.

The only witnesses to their marriage were the organist, (so they did have music – very kindly arranged at the last minute on a public holiday by the minister) and two officers. These men were acquaintances of George whose assistance he had commandeered in the hotel lobby. Frantically hurried and conducted in a tempest of emotions, it was, nevertheless, a joyous and special event for all involved and the minister certainly seems to have had a sense of humour.

The Scottish Presbyterian Church in Rome is still in operation and seems to have a small but vibrant multi-racial congregation of people. The cascade of white roses is no longer there but other than that it looks today, very much as it must have looked then. The chapel itself is unadorned and plain but has its own austere, typically Presbyterian, simplicity and beauty.

Now it was a sprint back to the hotel to collect their luggage and board the train by five o'clock.

The train was, of course, very crowded but they managed, at least, to wangle a coupé. By no stretch of the imagination was this luxurious honeymooning accommodation. As was normal for train travel immediately after the war, the compartments were in desperate need of restoration and cleaning. The leather seats were cracked and broken and leaking horse-hair everywhere. This was not kind to tender skin and Elena says she had a mighty sore bottom the next morning.

Lucia had bought pastries in anticipation of a final farewell. Lucia, Barend, Agnese and Barend's cousin, Tante Sally, were waiting at the station in Florence at midnight for the Rome-to-Venice train to pass through so they could make their congratulations, have a kind of impromptu reception, and say goodbye but their touching plans were circumvented as the train by-passed Florence and travelled via Bologna.

When they pulled in to Venice the next morning and detrained, all the inconveniences and discomforts of the previous twenty-four hours paled into insignificance as they were greeted by the wild and ribald cheering of a trainload of servicemen.

Again they were separated for the night, the military authorities having accommodated the men and women who were waiting to be repatriated, in separate hotels.

From Venice, they sailed to Cairo. On board, once more, men and women were put in separate areas of the ship so there was no shared cabin for the honeymooning couple. Elena had to share accommodation with an Italian woman who held distinctly Fascist views.

When the captain asked Elena, at dinner one night, how his honeymooners were enjoying their cruise, she said it was lovely but that their accommodation prevented them from spending much time together. He couldn't believe this oversight and immediately arranged for Elena's roommate to be moved elsewhere so that George could move in with Elena. The woman was furious and made her displeasure very clear to Elena and anyone she could get to listen. However, there was nothing she could do and she met with little sympathy, especially from Elena who was of the opinion that she owed a former enemy nothing – and she didn't like the woman anyway.

They remained in Cairo for about a week in a tented camp. Conditions were quite primitive but their needs were well attended to by a batman who was a German prisoner of war. Elena was tickled at this role reversal. Despite the inconveniences, there was a relaxed, holiday atmosphere quite well suited to their honeymooning status.

The men entertained themselves with rugby and cricket games, fancying themselves as Springbok representatives of the homeland. The onlookers were, perhaps, not sufficiently respectful of their international sporting status and found considerable comic entertainment in watching these 'heroes'. Many of them had lost their peak physical condition brought on by active service, and had grown quite paunchy in the previous two years.

Elena was also learning new things every day. She had never seen a game of cricket before. Besides being mystified by the incomprehensible rules and jargon, items of equipment like the box were extremely challenging to explain to her.

From Cairo they were flown to Waterkloof Air Base in Pretoria where they were met by a very large police contingent. They never found out why there were so many policemen about but their presence didn't make Elena feel very comfortable, especially with the unfortunate record of her previous arrival in South Africa.

As she descended the steps of the plane, though, a surprised and cheery voice rang out especially for her: "Meidjie, what are you doing here again?" to which she shouted back, waving her left hand, "I'm married! I'm married!"

CHAPTER 20

Finding accommodation after the war was not easy and to start with they lived in a hotel. This was a smart establishment with a number of luxurious amenities.

In addition to being very thin, Elena found that her skin was extraordinarily dry. This wasn't helped by the dehydrating Highveld climate. In desperation she paid a visit to the resident beautician who gave her a piece of advice she still uses today. The beautician told her that she could sell her any number of expensive preparations from the shelves in her salon but the best thing she could recommend was 'Dawn' skin lotion which contained lanolin (the pink bottle). This advice solved Elena's problem and it is all she has used ever since. She has a most remarkable complexion for a nonagenarian and especially for someone with such a fair skin, which tended to freckles, and was accompanied by strawberry-blonde hair.

A little later they moved into a residential hotel. This was the Essenby Hotel in Beatrice Street near Church Street. Their room looked out on to a small garden which was for their private use. Elena decided to do some home-making and attempted to plant a garden. This was something about which she knew nothing but she was enthusiastic and thorough.

Off she went and bought some seeds and then dug a bed. Thinking that her flowers would benefit from a good deep bed, she dug the bed down to a depth of about eighteen inches – and then planted the seeds at the bottom of the hole! She waited and waited for the seeds to germinate and show some sign of life. When she complained to George that nothing was happening, he questioned her on exactly what form her horticultural practice had taken. On discovering what she had done, he decided that he should take over and went out and bought seedlings. She wasn't allowed to touch them and was only permitted to water them when he told her to. She never developed into a gardener and from then on George always took care of their gardens.

After the residential hotel they moved into a boarding-house where they had two rooms – a bedroom and a sitting-room. The sitting-room included a kitchenette. They shared a bathroom with other residents. This was a perfectly satisfactory arrangement and they were in no hurry to move.

Elena continued to work on her English and Afrikaans and quite frequently got herself into embarrassing fixes. This wasn't new to her. In Italy she had had many misunderstandings. Clive Bullock of the Indian Division, had one day suggested that they go for a swim in the Arno. Elena said no, no, she couldn't do that: she had too many "beans" in her body. Clive was mystified and asked her if she'd eaten too many beans. What she meant, of course, was that she was too thin and bony to be seen in a costume.

On another occasion, she told Clive that her canary had "made eye". He thought she was trying to tell him the bird had winked at her. She then tried to explain herself by making a hen's clucking sounds. Eventually she resorted to her English/Italian dictionary. This was also a painful means of communicating because she'd have to find the word in Italian, and then the English word, and then get her companion to read the word himself because her pronunciation and heavy accent created further difficulties. What she was trying so valiantly to tell Clive was that her canary had laid an egg.

A Scotsman, who was a regular guest, decided that he would sort out her accent and told George to leave the problem to him. He began work on the [th] sound in 'mother' and 'brother' which Elena pronounced as [d] (and still does). He was also bothered by her inability to say [u] as in 'cup' for 'mother' and 'brother'. She didn't have to master "the rain in Spain" – her nemesis was "The mother of my brother has another brother: the other 'udder' is the udder of a cow". She never got it right and the Scotsman soon admitted defeat, just as her singing teacher had done years before.

Some of her linguistic efforts in Pretoria were even more disastrous. She needed sewing thread and Speedy Botha accompanied her to a general dealer's store. This was a day on which she decided to practise her Afrikaans and she greeted the assistant with a confident and cheery "Goeie môre." That went well enough but when she was asked what she wanted, she told the assistant that she was looking for "draad" (wire) and was directed to the electrical department. Realizing that she hadn't been understood, she elucidated with "Ek wil draad koop om te naai." (*"I want to buy wire to sew."*) Unfortunately, 'naai' not only means 'sew' but is also the crude colloquialism for 'fornicate'. Speedy left the shop in a hurry.

A little later she went into a department store and, in her best English this time, asked the assistant for "hang coaters". Again there was mystification until she explained and demonstrated that she wanted those things on which one hangs clothes. "Oh, you mean 'coat hangers', Madam?" Yes, yes that's exactly what she meant. The assistant then said, "Madam, may I laugh?"

She also had a penchant for making up her own words. One such word was 'squosen' for 'squashed', which entertained George no end.

George had involved himself in the world of athletics again. Sadly, he had had to give up the javelin because of his chronic spondylitis which flared up badly with the twisting motion of throwing the javelin. He continued to help with the training of other athletes, though. He was particularly involved in the training of a friend who was a sprinter and advised this man to take a supplement. Elena was at an athletics meeting and sitting in the grandstand cheering on the athletes she knew. When it came to this chap's event she made full use of her legendary voice to urge him on. In her best Afrikaans she yelled, "Het jy jou pilletjies ('tablets' - or in course colloquial Afrikaans - 'testicles') gedrink?" Someone dashed off to find George to tell him to shut his wife up and explain a few things. In bad moments, George took to saying, "Elena, just don't talk!"

George had returned to South Africa with every intention of resuming his military career but it didn't take long for him to realize, along with many other returning servicemen, that the political scene was changing dramatically with the rise of Afrikaner nationalism. This was having a serious spillover effect on all state institutions, not least of which was the army. Having an English surname had become a distinct disadvantage to promotion. He had completed all the training and examinations to qualify for the rank of colonel and had applied for a promotion to Tempe in Bloemfontein. When yet again someone with the surname of 'Van der Merwe' (literally, in the last instance), who was less qualified, was promoted over his head, he reached the end of his tether.

Resentment about such promotions was particularly marked when said men had not gone away to fight. His resentment boiled over at an important officers' dinner one evening. This was quite an occasion with wives and high-ranking dignitaries present. George's rage had been building for months and something finally triggered it. He stood up and launched into a scathing attack. He concluded by telling the hierarchy that while good men had been fighting to preserve a civilized world, "You bare-breasted bastards drank our whisky, fucked our wives and took our jobs! I'm getting out!" In the hush that engulfed the entire gathering, George took Elena's hand and they left the assembly, along with George's military ambitions.

George had long been interested in medicine and looked into the possibilities of qualifying as a doctor. There were schemes in place to assist returned servicemen to study and qualify themselves. Elena was wholly supportive of the idea and George thought that if he could take on some form of part-time employment, they might be able to manage. He saw an advertisement for a caretaker of a block of flats. This would have suited admirably because their accommodation would also have been provided. Unfortunately he didn't get the position and concluded that studying medicine was not going to be practicable in his circumstances.

Speedy Botha had also left the army and he was working as an estate agent. He had seen an advertisement for a guest farm of 125 acres which was available on a ten-year lease in a little-known place called Munster on the South Coast of Natal. He thought that this might be just the thing for George and Elena. They signed the lease and thus had an exciting plan for their future.

*   *   *

They had concluded the lease agreement without viewing the property so had little idea of what to expect. Neither was George a Natal lad, so he hadn't grown up in subtropical climes. His experience was of the desert-like Northern Cape and much drier Eastern Cape. Nothing daunted, they set off for Natal.

Hendrieka, George's mother, accompanied them and agreed to keep Elena company for the six months George still had to serve before getting his army discharge.

Their journey from Pretoria to the Lower South Coast was, in itself, an experience for Elena. She was enthralled by the changing landscape that unfolded before her.

She had grown used to the relative aridity of the Highveld. The pleasant summer climate of hot days and cooling afternoon showers built into each day a sense of promise and reward. She didn't enjoy the notorious Highveld thunderstorms though. The cracking thunder never ceased to frighten her – too reminiscent of the bombs dropping on Florence. The biting winter chill didn't bother her: it was nothing compared to the cold she had known and it heralded a spectacular Pretoria spring of jacaranda blossom which entranced her. The cloud of purple up and down the streets of Pretoria seemed like the earth's recompense for the drab brownness and dust of late winter when hands and lips were constantly chapped and everything looked in need of a good hosing down. What stayed with her, above all, was the memory of the sharp, thin light of the Transvaal which gave the landscape a special clarity.

On the day of their move they left Pretoria very early and the sun was rising as they crossed the Vaal River into the north-eastern Free State. Elena had expected this part of the Free State to be much the same as the Transvaal but she noticed subtle differences. The countryside seemed to roll on in wide expanses in every direction, the gentle rise and fall of the landscape sporadically marked by an isolated hill.

As they approached the edge of the escarpment, these hills began to change into clearly defined mountain chunks with sandstone edifaces set atop screed-dotted slopes and capped with a verdant covering. The closer they got to the

Drakensberg the more these mountains resembled inverted funnels. She had already encountered the Basutho hat and was sure the hat had been inspired by these mountain shapes. She was fascinated by these varying sandstone formations. The crags and folds seemed to hold an ancient mystery. What impressed her most, though, as they travelled through the Free State, was the enormity of the sky. Illogical, she knew, but to her the sky just seemed much bigger than elsewhere.

There were more surprises in store for her as they reached the top of Van Reenen's Pass. Here they pulled off the road at a viewing-site and had their breakfast halt of flasked coffee and rusks. Ever after, Elena would associate the combination of coffee and rusks with that astounding view. Backed by craggy heights of grey stone, she looked down in wonder at diverging valleys dipping precipitously before her and then opening up and rolling away into the plains of Natal. The dense vegetation of the southern slopes of the Berg rapidly smoothed out into sparser, thorny acacia vegetation. This sudden drop into Natal presented a wholly unexpected new world to her. The Highveld took on a new perspective as though it existed on a plain of its own, underpinned by a completely separate layer, like a table standing on an exotic carpet, at least in Elena's imagination.

They spent the night in Pietermaritzburg. With mounting excitement, they pushed on early the next morning.

Durban flooded Elena with memories, especially as they passed through Umbilo and Elena caught sight of the harbour and dark green wall of the Bluff behind it. The day she had disembarked from the Samnes had been too traumatic for her to remember any details about Durban but the harbour and the Bluff were imprinted on her mind. Now, on her way to yet another new beginning, and safe in George's company, she could look back on her first arrival in the country with wry amusement. Her English had improved sufficiently for her to be able to tell George about her 'sale'/'salt' mistake. He chuckled and shook his head at yet another example of her creative use of language.

Leaving Durban, as they chugged south, the undulating fields of sugarcane were interspersed with pockets of dense, lush bush, the cane fields gradually giving way to more bush the further south they travelled. This bush seemed to crowd the narrow road in places, sometimes a little threatening as trees towered above with creepers and aerial roots draping their tendrils luxuriantly into the lower-growing shrubbery of the forest floor.

And then the tangle would give way to a view of beach or bay that left her enchanted: a caramel strip of smooth sand running between the dense green and the white frill of foam at the edge of the intense blue of the Indian Ocean. Most of these little bays are punctuated at either end by a jumble of rocks which George would assess for their fishing potential. It hasn't mattered how many times Elena has travelled that road, even after the freeway came into existence, but the sudden revealing of those beach scenes has never ceased to fill her with surprise and delight.

Along the route there were tiny settlements and holiday resorts. These were usually in the thatch-roofed rondavel style – unsophisticated and inviting - placed in close proximity to beaches and lagoons. Beyond Port Shepstone the area was sparsely populated with the road between Port Shepstone and Munster being little more than a sandy track.

When they arrived at Munster and turned off the road at Palmleigh-on-Sea, there was only a narrow sand track encroached upon by tall stands of reed, rank grass and clumps of iSundu, or wild-date palm, the palm-like wild banana, and lalapalm. Outcroppings of rock dotted the grassland and wherever these occurred, cabbage trees had sprung forth, often sharing their space with the wild-date palms.

The track was very difficult to negotiate in all weathers, as Elena was to discover: when it was dry one got stuck in the sand and when it was wet one got stuck in the mud. Perhaps to take the edge off what must have looked like a very daunting prospect, George announced, "Meid, we're home!"

As they crested a slight rise, there lay before them their new home, backed by a magnificent view of the ocean. Beyond the house the land sloped down to rocks and beach.

There was too much to take in as they stood surveying their new kingdom – house, bush, grass, sea, sand – wilderness. George and Elena stood for a moment, resting against the bonnet of the car, George's arms wrapped around Elena as she leaned back against him and gazed at this strange new world, neither saying much as they soaked it in.

At last the ever practical mother-in-law couldn't stand the hanging about any longer – there were things to organize and she wanted her tea. Waspishly she got them moving. They picked their way to the front of the house where George unlocked the door on to the enclosed verandah. As he pushed the door open, they were engulfed by that familiar, nostalgic, musty odour of seaside cottages left locked up for too long.

The whole establishment had been unoccupied for a long time and nothing had been maintained on either the land or the buildings. Inside the house no sweeping had been done in years and dust and sand had accumulated in the corners and their feet left tracks across the floor. The verandah roof showed signs of leaking in several places. The sea-facing windows were so begrimed with salt-laden deposit they lent a misty gloom to the room.

The wide, enclosed verandah extended across the width of the house. This created a very large room. It, in time, would be used as a lounge by the guests. On either end of the verandah was a bedroom, one of which was used by George and Elena as the main bedroom. In the centre of the house, and backing on to the stoep, was a very large dining-room. An archway led into a passage off which there were two more bedrooms to be used by guests. Strangely, but conveniently, the kitchen was accessed from the main bedroom. This was an enormous room with a huge wood-burning stove. One would have expected a stove of this size to have given off unbearable heat in the summer but it was never a problem because of the size of the room. Seeing the stove was like meeting up with an old friend for Elena: this was one piece of domestic equipment she knew exactly how to tame. There was also a verandah attached to the back of the house. This wasn't enclosed and would provide guests with a very pleasant sitting-out area.

Separate from the house was a row of four rooms under one roof and there were a further four, very large, thatched rondavels. Away from the house, and on another rise above the house, was the garage. There were two more rooms near the kitchen that could have been used for guests but they reserved these rooms for their female domestic helpers.

There were two bathrooms and two toilets situated outside the house which served the house and all the guest-rooms. The hot water for the kitchen and the bathrooms was provided by a donkey-boiler outside the kitchen. For the uninitiated, a donkey-boiler is a 44-gallon drum mounted on top of a three-sided brick base. A wood fire is lit inside the base, beneath the drum.

Exploration finished, it was clear that masses of work lay ahead of them - commented on in a continuous stream of critical grumbles from Hendrieka. None of this bothered Elena. She had danced her way through the rooms, delighting in the space and the potential she could envisage. Once they'd decided on sleeping arrangements, Elena began pondering how they would furnish the rooms. Hendrieka's bark stopped her in her tracks: unpacking came first.

The next couple of hours flew by. A few pieces of furniture had been left behind and George undertook the making of the beds while Elena wielded duster and broom in their bedrooms and the kitchen. Hendrieka organized the kitchen, telling Elena where things should go. She had little argument from Elena who was only too happy to let her mother-in-law get on with it.

Their water came from a spring above the house and gravity-fed into a tank. However, the water that fed into the house was brown with rust from unused pipes. George set off with buckets to the spring to collect water for their immediate use.

At last Hendrieka was satisfied that they could take a break. While she brewed her tea on a primus stove, Elena and George made their way down to the beach. This was not an easy stroll, as yet. What would later be a lovely sloping lawn reaching right down to the sea, was still thick veld grass. There was a row of casurina trees on either side of the house. As they looked back at the house they envisaged the scene they would create within the frame provided by the casurinas. The stone steps led from the verandah on to a broad terrace where someone had built a fountain. In this area, George would later build his braai.

Amongst the rocks they discovered a rock-pool, perfect for safe swimming. It was a tidal-pool so it was kept fresh by regular tidal flushing. In the smaller pools was marine life neither had previously encountered: strange anemones, shells, tiny hermit crabs and even a very alien-looking nudibranch which looked like a large, over-stuffed, speckled sausage. George found a rock formation he thought would be an ideal fishing spot – a site which would provide him with many pleasurable hours. There was little time that day to spend exploring this new adventure-ground but there was great satisfaction and contentment in knowing that it would all still be there for them tomorrow and tomorrow.

After a picnic-supper they sat on the steps watching a magnificent moon silver a path across the sea towards them. They celebrated their arrival with the whisky George had brought in their luggage and even Hendrieka deigned to have a small glass.

Hendrieka retired early to her room with a basin of water for her ablutions. George had a more romantic plan for washing away the grime and salty humidity of the day's exertions. He had rigged a bucket, suspended by a rope, to the branch of a milkwood tree. This was to be their outdoor shower. Stripped, they soaped themselves and then took turns to tilt the suspended bucket over the other's head. Naked, in the gleam of the moon and the balmy air, they felt akin to Adam and Eve in the Garden of Eden.

Later, lying in George's arms as they drifted off to sleep, Elena was overcome by the wonder of it all – the sights she had seen on their journey and this new place, filled with their hopes for the future. She found it hard to assimilate all the twists her life had taken.

The following morning, full of energetic eagerness, she was up before dawn. As she sat on the steps drinking her coffee, she watched the sun reaching up over the horizon of the sea and contemplated the work that lay ahead.

There was a tremendous amount of restoration work needed. Elena says she didn't need a rain-gauge. All she had to do was see how much water had collected in the bucket under one of the leaks in the roof over the enclosed stoep. The entire roof of the four attached rooms outside had to be replaced. All this necessitated the employment of workers, the first of whom was Du (short for Ndumiso) Mpofu, also known as John or Johannes. Johannes would prove to be a great handyman, a loyal employee and a life-long friend.

Their spring water was stored in a concrete tank near the kitchen. From the moment he saw this tank, which rested on top of a very tall concrete base, George was most concerned as the whole structure was leaning precariously to one side, like the Leaning Tower of Pisa. This structure was also too high to demolish with ease and safety. Instead, he and Johannes installed a new galvanized tank next to the garage. All the fittings and pipes were plumbed in for the momentous occasion when the old tank finally collapsed of its own accord. One morning George dashed into the kitchen and told Elena that if she wanted to see a sight she had better come immediately. Outside the kitchen they watched as the tank slowly tilted. It leaned and leaned until finally the whole thing crashed over, sending chickens squawking indignantly as they flew in every direction.

Once the guest-house was operational, they employed a waiter, a maid and a washer-woman. Johannes had worked as a chef in a hotel but had given this up as he couldn't bear the heat of the stoves. He resumed this role and showed a remarkable talent for creating unusual and delicious salads.

Dora was employed as a domestic worker and also became a cook. She was an interesting character. Well educated and very hard working, she had one weakness: she enjoyed her dagga (*marijuana*) on a regular basis. She also had a sharp sense of humour. Whenever Elena asked her what she would be cooking she had a quick-witted response which generally implied that Elena should butt out. It was Dora who gave Elena her Zulu name – Maphephuka – a leaf blown about in the wind. This was an ambiguous name with positive and negative connotations. Did Dora mean that her mistress was spineless and erratic or was the name a reference to her slenderness and unceasing activity? We'll give Dora the benefit of the doubt. In any event, the bestowing of a Zulu name was in itself a compliment and a sign of affection. 'Maphephuka' became the name by which Elena was known throughout the Zulu community, a name she still cherishes.

Another interesting employee was Simon. He quickly found George's measure and learnt how to deal with George's temper. On one occasion he was helping George by holding a piece of wood while George was attempting to knock a nail into it. George accidentally hit his thumb with the hammer he was using. As his thumb was suffused with pain, he glanced at Simon who had realized that it wouldn't be wise to laugh or utter a sound. Simon didn't move a muscle. His expression was dead-pan and his eyes glazed over. He maintained this dead-eyed look as George glared at him. Eventually George was forced to laugh at himself and Simon's steadfast refusal to react.

Simon was quite a lad with the ladies. He managed to impregnate every young domestic they employed. Eventually he decided to get married. The labola (*payment made to the bride's family*) he'd agreed to pay was an extravagant eight head of white oxen. George asked him, as he was penniless, how he was going to pay the labola he had promised the girl's father. His response was, "Oh, let the old man think. In the meantime I'll fiddle."

Another of George's labourers contracted a dose of gonorrhoea. George got the penicillin to treat this from the pharmacist and asked the worker who he'd got the disease from. The man claimed the sea had given it to him.

All the heavy work in the first six months of their stay had to be done by George over weekends. He finished work in Pretoria on Friday at five o'clock. He would then get straight into his car and set off for Munster, a journey that would take at least fourteen hours. Arriving on Saturday morning, he would have a couple of hours' sleep and then start work with Johannes. Work continued all day on Sunday and then, as the sun was going down, he would pack up and begin his return journey to Pretoria, arriving there in time to start work by eight o'clock on Monday morning. He kept up this punishing regime every weekend for six months!

During the week, while George was away, Johannes carried out George's instructions and Elena and Hendrieka did whatever they could manage inside and outside the house. They had started taking in guests as soon as they could, before George had returned permanently, and this added considerably to their work load.

Hendrieka had been less than delighted at the thought that her beloved son was bringing home an 'Italian' bride. It didn't matter to her that Elena's racial credentials in her Dutch ancestry were very much the same as her own. Elena had grown up in Italy and in Hendrieka's book that made her Italian. She, no doubt, thought Elena was some hot-blooded Italian seductress who had lured her son into marriage. The prevalent Afrikaner suspicion of Catholics as the 'Roomse Gevaar' (*'Roman Danger/Threat'*) also played its role in her prejudice, as well as the all-too-common gentile distrust of Jews. Elena couldn't win and Hendrieka was often sharply critical of her.

When Elena and Hendrieka had been working for days on clearing land for a vegetable patch, Elena awoke one morning with a splitting headache and was barely able to get out of bed. Her mother-in-law had plenty to say about lazy, spoilt young European women who lacked backbone and staying power. The following morning, when Hendrieka woke up, also with a pounding headache, and found that she couldn't even get her head off her pillow, she had to reconsider her position.

There was only one doctor in the district and he was in Margate. Elena 'phoned him and he diagnosed tick-bite fever. The only pharmacy was also in Margate and they had no transport of their own. Fortunately, they had guests staying at the time. These people were going to Margate and were able to collect their medication.

Although the guest-house had come with a few items of furniture and bits of kitchen equipment, they had to source a great deal more. They also had no furniture of their own because everything that George had accumulated in his first marriage had been claimed by Lusty Lily. Slowly they began gathering what they needed by attending auctions and second-hand sales. George had managed to secure a loan from the army but they couldn't splash out and they needed a tremendous amount of stuff.

Elena bought yards of sheeting and towelling and made her own pillow-cases, and hemmed the sheets and towels herself. Her sewing-machine was an old, hand-operated Singer and sometimes her arm would get so tired from turning the wheel that George would have to turn it for her while she guided the fabric. She couldn't afford to buy new upholstery fabric for the lounge suites so she resorted to dismantling the old upholstery, cleaning it, and then reupholstering, using the reverse side of the material. This worked most satisfactorily.

The house was wired for electricity but there was no power supply and George installed a three-kilowatt diesel generator. The more power that was being drawn off the generator the more effectively and efficiently the engine ran, so when they were eventually able to switch on the power, the whole establishment was ablaze with lights.

They might not have been blessed with electricity to start with, but they did have a telephone. However, it was like no telephone Elena had ever encountered. It was a party-line 'phone connected to a manual telephone exchange situated at the Munster Trading Post. Elena didn't understand that each subscriber on the line had a distinctive ring pattern. Consequently, every time the 'phone rang she answered it, and then couldn't really understand what was being said to her.

Eventually Dulcie Sawyer, the exchange operator, yelled at her to stop picking up the 'phone. So she did stop - completely. Dulcie didn't explain, or wasn't able to explain, to Elena what her code was and so she didn't attempt to answer it again. When George tried to contact her during the week and he got no response, he eventually became very concerned that something had happened. He contacted the police stationed at Marina Beach and a policeman arrived on horseback, at her kitchen door, to find out if she was all right.

In the meantime their animal 'family' was growing. Elena always had a cat and it was always known as "Mienies", a name she still uses. First there was just plain "Mienies", then came "Mienie-Monkey" and later "Mienie-Voetjies". Suzie, a little brown mongrel, was acquired at an auction in Port

Shepstone when Elena and George were buying second-hand furniture. The sale had ended when Elena spotted a box of puppies. All the males had been sold but there was one little bitch left. She tentatively put the suggestion to George that they should buy her and was quite surprised by his acquiescence. The puppy cost the princely sum of ten shillings and so Suzie had found herself a home.

Elena made up a bed for her next to their bed but as soon as the lights were put out, there was a series of little whoof-whimpers. Elena couldn't help herself and lifted her out of her box and placed her on her chest. Suzie snuggled into her neck, gave a contented sigh, and fell fast asleep. From then on Suzie had herself ensconced in their bed. A later arrival was Tilly, a brown and white Great Dane, with a lethal tail. She was a very loyal and much loved lass, but truly a dumb-blonde – Dilly Tilly.

They acquired three dairy cows and free-range chickens - in the truest sense of the term. The chickens were free to roam all day and then at night retired to the wooden chicken-coop George had made for them.

George and Elena also took to incubating their eggs. This was an activity which gave Elena endless delight. Turning the eggs twice a day was no inconvenience and the greatest wonder was to lean over the incubator at hatching time and peer in through the glass lid, watching, as first one, and then another, and another, shell was cracked open and the chicks began to make their acquaintance with the world. George constructed a moveable wire run of about a metre wide by three metres long and half-a-metre high. He also had a wooden brooder at one end with a shallow ramp which the chicks could negotiate. The whole contraption was easily moved about on the lawn.

The chickens were divided into two groups: the 'talking' chickens and the 'non-talking' chickens i.e. the chickens they allowed themselves to talk to and those that were intended for the pot. George used to comment on how dreadful it was "to eat one's own young".

Before they had electricity, Elena couldn't refrigerate the eggs and had to pickle them to preserve them for guests. She continued to do this even after the advent of power so that the eggs didn't go to waste and so that they would be well stocked when they were fully booked. She also became a dab hand at separating the milk and making butter. George had cut one of the walls off some old tyres and these were used as containers for the separated milk which they fed to the chickens. He did the same thing to a much larger tyre which provided a neat pond for the ducks.

Fresh fish was available every day and an umfaan (*young boy*) arrived every morning with a catch of crayfish. Elena would spread them out and select the crayfish which were still moving. The umfaan charged her the princely sum of a tickey a crayfish!

Before George's discharge Elena and Hendrieka had no transport to go shopping. The only butcher was at Banner's Rest, a distance of about fourteen kilometres. Once a week, one of the domestic workers would leave the guest-house at five in the morning to walk to Banner's Rest to collect their meat order, which she would carry on her head. On her return journey she would call in to Monty Sawyer's trading post at Munster to collect any other groceries that were needed. All her purchases would then end up in one parcel borne on her head.

Once George had arrived to stay, and had completed the most urgent of the maintenance jobs, he went on to develop the lands. He began by establishing a banana plantation. The cost of putting in a plantation was high and he sourced his culms from farmers further afield by collecting the secondary culms, or stems, which they were discarding. He planted two culms in every hole.

Barend's wedding present to them had been a gift of £250. If Elena had had hopes of spending this on any luxury or wedding-gift to be treasured through the years, her hopes were dashed. The money was spent on chicken manure to fertilize the new banana plantations. Her caustic remark on the matter when she was telling me about it was: "You know what my wedding present was? Chicken shit!"

Marketing produce from so far down the coast was always a problem because of the distance and cost of transport. Someone bought a truck to transport the bananas to the station in Port Shepstone. Here they were bought by

Indian distributors who railed them to Durban for further distribution. A number of local farmers made use of this service including the Nielsons and the Kaisers.

George also decided to plant dry-land rice, possibly inspired by what he had learnt about rice-growing in Italy. Somehow it fell to Elena to plant the rice. She had a group of women to help her and decided to inspire them to plant more quickly by giving them each a row to plant and creating a sense of competition, based on South Africa's most famous horse-race, the Durban July Handicap. It became a race to see who could reach the end of her row first and Elena competed as hard as any of her companions. Local farmers thought they were quite mad to be trying such a crop but it did well. Rice was a fairly scarce commodity after the war.

Elena refers to this time as their 'beachcombing years'. They were never flush with money, and often completely broke, but they both found life most satisfactory. It was always difficult to make the guest-house pay, again, as transport was a problem. People could travel as far as Port Shepstone by train but beyond that there was no public transport.

Many of their guests were friends and relatives and as much as the Jennings loved entertaining, a good number of these visitors didn't seem to realize that the business was their livelihood. Feeding such visitors three times a day was a financial drain in the Jenningses' already straitened circumstances.

Sometimes things became very difficult but their natural optimism, especially Elena's, the love of what they were doing, and the pleasure they took in their surroundings, kept them buoyed. Lying on the lawn at sundown, looking over the sea and drinking their wine (when they could afford it) gave them pleasure Elena has never forgotten. When they couldn't afford wine, they resorted to cane spirits and when they couldn't manage this, they had to go without.

They delighted in their surroundings and made good use of the beach at the bottom of their garden. George was a keen and accomplished fisherman and Elena also did a bit of fishing.

Sharks were plentiful and once when George hooked a large one, he handed the rod to Elena so that he could fetch his gaff. The creature was too much for her and she found herself sliding down the rocks towards the water. She certainly didn't want to be pulled off the rocks into the water with that beastie on the end of the line. Neither did she want to let go of George's precious tackle. She yelled blue murder for George and he managed to get back to her just in time to grab her around the waist to stop her perilous slide into the water.

The wildlife all around them on land, in the air, and in the sea was an endless source of entertainment and wonder. George loved bird-watching and used his photographic skills to great effect. Dolphin- and whale-watching were also enriching pastimes. One season a whale gave birth in Aunty's Bay and they had the pleasure of watching her and her calf for a week before they disappeared. It was a pleasure they couldn't share with anyone else. Whale-hunting had been resumed after the war and the factory was in full swing in Durban. A reward of five pounds was paid for every reported sighting if the subsequent hunt was successful. They were fearful that if they told anyone, and the word got about, not everybody would take such joy from the presence of the whale and her calf.

While George was still in Pretoria, Elena had a few hair-raising encounters with the wildlife. She was working in the kitchen one day when she heard the plaintive cry of a baby. She rushed outside looking for the source of this distress. There was nobody there apart from Johannes. He laughed at her confusion: the anguished cries were the call of a crowned hornbill. She came to love their ungainly, comic flight as they homed in on a favourite tree.

Another disturbing creature was the water leguaan or Nile monitor. She stumbled across this fearsome-looking character in the kitchen drain. He was a huge chap of close on two metres in length. Trapped in the drain, he reared up on his front legs, hissing loudly at her. She leapt away and he clambered out of the drain. As he scurried off, swiping his tail angrily from side to side, she was intrigued by the incongruous scattering of yellow spots on his rather drab body. She discovered later that younger leguaans sport rows of much more impressive bright yellow spots on their darker skins. Sometimes on a rainy summer evening she would hear a continuous, high-pitched, thin, screeching sound. She found it eerie and disturbing until Johannes identified it as the leguaan's mating-call.

Monkeys were plentiful and she never tired of watching their antics and the interplay of their family relationships. A favourite time for her was sunrise when she'd sit on the stone steps, drinking her coffee and watching the tiny mpitis, or blue duikers, at the edge of the bush. They were often in the company of the monkeys and seemed to have a happy arrangement with them: as the monkeys foraged for fruit, especially in the wild-date palms, the mpitis would eat anything dropped to the ground by the monkeys.

The mpitis were very shy little antelope which would dart away at the slightest movement. The larger bushbuck were a fraction bolder and would sometimes wander right out into the open to nibble at the lawn. If they sensed a movement they would stand for long moments, gazing in one direction. This gave Elena time to admire them, especially the males with their impressive striping, as long as she remained completely still.

It hadn't taken long for them to be accepted by the tiny human community, the members of which generally co-operated with one another and depended on each other. They were also good at creating their own entertainment and any community event was eagerly anticipated and well supported.

Every now and then George and Elena would take an evening stroll along the beach to the Glenmore Hotel for a sundowner. This was a convivial spot and particularly useful for the Jenningses when they wanted to get out but their dilapidated Jeep was out of commission, which it often was. Their dogs, of course, wouldn't allow themselves to be left at home on these jaunts and the hotel owners didn't object to their presence either.

One evening when they reached the uThongasi River, which separates the Glenmore Beach from the hotel, they found the river in spate and the bridge collapsed. George was not going to be put off by a flooding river or a broken bridge and grabbed a section of the wooden bridge to use as an improvised rowing boat. Nothing resembling oars was available but he did find a pole to punt across the river. He seated Elena in his contraption with Suzie, their little mongrel, at her feet. He also had his precious Leica with him which he entrusted to Elena's care.

By now quite a holiday crowd had gathered on the hotel side to watch proceedings. Off George pushed – and the vessel promptly sank. George swam across quite easily but Elena was encumbered with dog and camera, neither of which she could drop. There she was with both hands stretched above her, holding dog and camera, while she battled to keep her head above the water, walk where her feet touched base and do a sort of doggy-paddle/ treading swim to the other side. She made it with camera, dog and self intact, to the applause and cheers of the spectators. The owners of the hotel dried them off. They had their sundowners and dinner and then were driven home by the proprietors themselves.

The Glenmore Hotel and the Port Edward Hotel quite often held dances which very few people missed. On one occasion they were really looking forward to a dance at the Glenmore Hotel, then called 'The Green Dolphin', but a couple of days prior to the event the steering-column on the Jeep had snapped and George had rolled. This was the second time the steering-column of a Jeep had sheered whilst he was driving it, the first being during the war in Italy. On the first occasion, the Jeep rolled and he was dumped on his back in a rice-field. Fortunately it was a soft landing or he might well have broken his back. The accident did, however, contribute to his life-long back troubles.

The second time it happened the Jeep also rolled. This took place near Nicholson's Garage in Leisure Bay. He was rescued by Ludi Stoppel. Ludi took him to his home and Mrs Stoppel insisted on cleaning him up before Elena saw him so that Elena wouldn't be too alarmed by his bloodied and dishevelled appearance.

George managed to fix the steering-column but because the windscreen frame had been crushed and the soft-top canopy destroyed, the Jeep could no longer be used to take them on a 'dress-up outing'. A windswept Elena arriving at the dance was not her idea of the start to a glamorous evening.

The rare opportunity to dress up was very much part of the event, naturally. She thought they'd have to miss this one but George had other ideas.

When she expressed her reluctance to go, he disappeared for a bit and then called to her to see his handiwork. He'd rigged up a sort of cocoon over the passenger seat, out of chicken-feed bags, so that she could huddle down and not spoil her hairdo! It worked pretty well, if the smell of chicken feed could be ignored. Incidentally, Hendrieka had obviously overcome at least some of her reservations about Elena and generously made her some beautiful gowns which Elena loved wearing. Elena, too, was a handy dressmaker and was very good at restyling and recycling her clothing.

Cut off from the world at large they may have been in many respects, but they did often get the Sunday papers – delivered to their front door (almost). George had a friend from his army days, called Cecil Blake. After the war Cecil had become a pilot for the South African Airways. He often came to stay during the sardine run. Whenever he was on the Sunday Johannesburg-Durban-Cape Town flight, he'd drop the 'Sunday Times', weighted down with a bag of airline sweets, on to their front lawn as he flew by. He'd then do the same thing for the Port Edward Hotel.

He also made a habit of buzzing the guest-house. The noise of this was skull-shattering and the wind so fierce that the casurinas on either side of the house were bent double.

Once, when he spotted George kite-fishing from the rocks in front of the house, he deliberately severed his line. George wasn't going to let that go unchallenged. The next time the Dakota passed, George was waiting. He fired off a flare in front of the plane and waited eagerly for Cecil's telephonic response. When it came it wasn't quite what he had been expecting.

Cecil hadn't been flying the plane and might never have known about it. However, it was fortuitous that he did find out and was able to save George from some serious consequences. Cecil happened to come into the office as the irate pilot was telling someone that the plane had been fired on. When Cecil heard this he was immediately suspicious and when he established where the incident had taken place, he knew instantly that George was behind it. He told the pilot what had really happened and managed to get the man's co-operation in taking the matter no further.

In order to supplement their earnings and provide themselves with a steadier income, Elena took on the job of assisting Dulcie Sawyer as a telephone operator. Obviously her English had improved considerably and her fear of the telephone had evaporated. The irony of her new job didn't escape her and clearly Dulcie must have forgiven her for the number of times she'd irritated her when she first arrived.

CHAPTER 21

As their ten-year lease period on Palmleigh-on-Sea drew to a close, they had to start making plans for the future. The guest-house wasn't really paying and their often hand-to-mouth existence wasn't easy. And then the farm was sold. The name was changed to 'Greenheart' and what was Palmleigh-on-Sea now forms part of the Kérkira Eco Estate.

They moved on to a neighbouring farm and rented the outbuilding. This consisted of a large shed-like structure with four rooms that had been intended to accommodate labourers. The covered area in front of these rooms was used as stabling and storage.

Apart from a shower, there were no bathroom facilities. They used one room as a bedroom and another as a sitting-cum-dining-room. Elena had two gas burners on which to cook. George cleaned the place up and painted the rooms white and it looked quite respectable. It was very rough living but they managed happily and stayed there for about nine months. During this time George was occupied with planting up the valley between Munster and Palm Beach through which the highway now runs. A number of smaller properties had been bought up by one owner and George got the job of planting the slopes to bananas and other crops, including pineapples. An Italian ex-prisoner of war was employed to manage the crops once George had established the lands.

George was seriously considering a return to Pretoria and the possibilities of joining the police. The Deputy Police Commissioner in Pretoria, none other than Rocco de Villiers with whom George had become acquainted during his training college days, had offered George the position as liaison officer between the police force and the military.

Neither Elena nor George was keen on this option as they were so used to being in each other's company all day and working side-by-side. The thought of a nine-to-five job and the accompanying isolation for Elena held little appeal for either of them. An additional concern about taking up the liaison position was the changing role being forced on the army and police force by the National Party government's apartheid laws.

And then a post office job came up in Port Edward where a new post office had been built by Ludi Stoppel in 1948.

There were two positions going – those of postmaster and telephonist. An English couple had been running the post office but the post office authorities were becoming more demanding about their staff being bilingual. This didn't suit the English couple who had no intention of trying to learn to speak Afrikaans and declared openly that they would not speak that 'lingo'. They had accepted a transfer elsewhere. When Elena broached the subject of applying for the positions, George was not impressed. He reminded her that he had been an officer and he saw the running of a post office as a distinct come down. Eventually he saw the benefits of the position and they applied.

They had to go to Margate to fill in the application forms which were given to them by the Margate postmaster. The forms he handed them were in Afrikaans. Post office policy at the time was to alternate English and Afrikaans on a monthly basis to enforce bilingualism amongst the staff. This meant that one month everything had to be done in Afrikaans, including the filling in of all forms, the completion of reports and all correspondence. The following month all the forms would be in English. This was an Afrikaans month and Elena was soon defeated. Although her mother tongue was Dutch, she had never read it or written it. The kindly man realized she was struggling, took the forms from her and completed them himself. And so they got the jobs.

Johannes, too, was employed by the post office as a factotum.

They started work in Port Edward in August of 1957. There was very little in the village then: the beginnings of the Police Holiday Camp, the Port Edward Hotel, then owned by Ted and Gladys Weatherdon, a couple of stores, a few cottages, and no tarred roads. Most of the houses were holiday cottages and fishing shacks.

They rented a house in Port Edward near the country club. It needed a great deal of attention and George made a number of improvements, including tiling the verandah. When the owner saw the improvements she told George that because the house looked so much better, she was increasing the rent! George promptly removed the tiles he'd laid on the verandah and they moved to the 'Mousehole' which was in the main road opposite what is now the Silver Beach town house development.

The Mousehole belonged to a dominee (*Dutch Reformed Church minister*) who didn't have much money and couldn't afford renovations. It was agreed that if George would do the work, the dominee would pay for the materials. This arrangement worked very well for both parties. The work included installing a water-borne sewerage system and indoor sanitation to replace the long-drop, or pit-toilet, in the garden.

In 1961 they were offered a split-level house opposite Strawberry Lane business complex for £4000. The couple who owned the house had a general dealer's store across the road from the house where the bottle store is now. They had decided to move up to Rhodesia. When George said he couldn't afford this, they told him to make them an offer. As the Jenningses had been paying rent of R33 a month, they offered to pay this sum every month for ten years. The couple agreed to this with additional extremely favourable terms, including no deposit and no interest.

Again George had plenty of work to do and it was at this point that Phillip introduced himself. He was to be the gardener and George's assistant in the building projects. He arrived for his interview wearing shoes and socks but the effect was ruined by the fact that one sock was blue and the other was brown.

Phillip had no conventional education and couldn't speak a word of English. He had also had very little exposure to the ways of white men and didn't appear to be very bright. He was, however, a tireless and very willing worker, to such an extent that it could be a problem because he didn't know when to stop and never paused for thought. A prime example of this was what he did to the verandah extension George wanted to build off their bedroom. George had obtained a number of teak railway sleepers to use for the deck. He told Phillip to cut a piece off one of the sleepers. Teak being so hard, he imagined that this would keep Phillip busy for some time and would be a tiring exercise. When George returned at lunch-time he found that Phillip had cut every single sleeper. Consequently the verandah extension was a lot narrower than had been planned.

The house was not electrified and this was one of the jobs that George had to tackle. (Port Edward only received electricity in 1975.) All the walls had to be chased and the conduit piping installed. Hilda's husband managed to get the wire on the cheap but George did all the wiring himself and installed a generator. Phillip lived in the servants' quarters on the property and George decided to electrify his room too. This was too much for Phillip who couldn't get over the wonder of being able to pull a cord and have light.

Elena loved Phillip as a son and refers to him variously as "My wonderful Phillip" or "My glorious Phillip", and says, "Ag, I loved him so much". She often had to provide protection against George's wrath and Phillip had a habit of flinching and putting his arms up defensively when George approached, having taken numerous slaps around the ear-hole during his lifetime.

When George had completed his building operations some years later, he returned to his love of motor cars and their restoration. He had found an MGB advertised in the local paper and went to see it in Margate. He bought it on the spot. It was white with a red roof. The roof was a removable hard top. Some time later he found another. This one was red with a gold roof and black, leather upholstery.

The upholstery in the first car was in excellent condition but the body needed respraying. George took meticulous care with the duco, giving it six coats and earning generous praise from retired racing driver, Sid van der Vyver. Sid farmed on the Izingolweni Road and had become a great pal. He had made his fortune by inventing some part for Ferrari which made their racing cars much lighter. His esteem was greatly valued by George.

George had even gone to the trouble and expense of sending the engine to Durban to be chromed. When he took it for its roadworthiness test, he was most gratified by the interest and enthusiasm the inspector showed for every aspect of the car. The inspector insisted on a test drive and took the car out for two hours, leaving George at the testing-grounds wondering what had happened to his car.

One day, for some reason, George left the car outside the garage and told Elena not to worry, when he went off to work, as he wasn't expecting it to rain, but if it did, she was to move it into the garage. A little later Elena also went to work and thought nothing more of it. During the course of the morning it did start to rain and conscientious Phillip decided to push the car into the garage. Unfortunately, he pushed a little too hard and the car collided with the work-bench and vice at the front of the garage, crushing the bonnet.

Nothing daunted, Phillip set about repairing the damage. He found a container of body-filler and mixed this up with some water, to what he considered a suitable consistency, and then smeared the concoction on to the bonnet using his hands. When he adjudged the dent to have been filled to the right level, he proceeded to paint on the duco using a paintbrush. He was quite satisfied with his repair job.

When Elena came home at lunch-time Oliena, Johannes's wife who was employed as their domestic worker, said, "Madam, you had better go and see the boss's car." Elena told Phillip that he'd better take his belongings and run away because if the boss caught him he'd cut off his penis. Phillip wasted no time in making his escape.

Elena decided that the best form of defence she could adopt on Phillip's behalf was attack. As George walked in she launched, asking him how he could be so bloody stupid. He was quite taken aback and irritated that she should talk to him like that. To his, "What do you mean?" she told him that he had been stupid and asking for trouble to leave his car outside and threw in whatever other feeble argument she could think of. Their ensuing row did seem to take a tiny edge off George's shock and horror when he beheld his beloved car. It was some weeks before Phillip returned.

Astoundingly, this wasn't to be Phillip's only encounter with the little car. They had a paraffin deep-freeze and used to buy the paraffin in a tin which was stored in the garage. George had bought a new tin and told Phillip to put it in the garage. Phillip decided to roll it in instead of carrying it. In the process he managed to gouge a deep scratch along the entire length of the car as he manoeuvred the tin to the front of the garage.

Phillip remained for many years and Elena continued to contribute to his pension until his death two years ago. He contracted Aids and was hospitalized at Murchison Provincial Hospital. One afternoon Elena and I were trying to work out how we could get his money to him in hospital and ensure that it wouldn't be stolen from him, when Elena received a 'phone call from his nephew. This was to tell her that Phillip had passed away the day before and to thank her, on behalf of the family, for all she'd done for Phillip over the many years of their association.

George's work on the Strawberry Lane house included adding on an en suite bathroom and doing all the plumbing himself. He also built a rock-clad wall around the property. All the rock for this wall he collected from the Nielson's farm on the Pont Road. At that stage they had a little Fiat and George used this to cart all the rocks.

For this project he employed the services of a stone-mason to help him. This man was a real craftsman. Elena was intrigued to watch him testing each rock George had carted in by tapping it to see if it was sound. Every rock he disapproved of would be pushed aside with a muttered, "Condemned!" He did have some trouble with building the brick-lining for the wall. George had marked this out carefully using string to make sure all the bricks ran straight. This didn't mean much to the builder and, when George wasn't actually laying the bricks with him, they soon wandered off the line. It didn't take him long to learn though.

Sadly, this skilled man died of pneumonia whilst working on a project for Ray Harley.

George loved concrete spheres and wanted to finish the wall with these spheres placed at intervals. He persuaded Elena to 'phone someone who had a precast-concrete business near Trafalgar, to make enquiries. She put the call through from the post office and after greeting the owner cheerily and telling him who she was, she said, "Do have concrete balls?" There was silence on the other end of the line. The post office assistant started to giggle in the background and George began to fidget uncomfortably. The voice on the other end returned shakily and said, "Yes, Mrs Jennings, I do have concrete balls in a range of sizes." Elena was most indignant with George, the assistant and the owner of the business: how was she supposed to ask about those round concrete things? It took some persuading to get George to fetch his spheres.

It's gratifying to see that the wall, and George's balls, still stands today. They eventually sold the house for R32 000 when George found a brand-new build in the same street in which they had first lived in Port Edward, for R38 000. He built another wall around this house which he surmounted with more concrete spheres.

After George died, Elena sold this house and bought a town house at Villa Rica. On the day that she was to have moved she was very ill and incapable of getting out of bed. Before she knew it, her friends had loaded and moved her entire household of furniture (bar the bed she was in). They unpacked in her new house, hung the curtains and arranged the furniture and then delivered her to her new home.

She didn't remain in her new home for long as her great friend, Peter Farndel, had bought the Beau Geste property from Ralph Rock and wanted to develop it as a cluster-housing establishment. All that was on this site was a very large old farmhouse, which still stands today and which is now the number one unit. Peter and his family lived in this house. On the site where Elena's unit stands, Ralph's sister had a very old and derelict house which

Peter demolished. He used the rock from this house to build the retaining walls in the grounds. As an ex-Rhodesian he wasted nothing.

Elena had no trouble finding a buyer for her Villa Rica house. The dentist at the time was called David and his mother, Linda, was keen to have it. She was a bit flummoxed when she made an offer to Elena and all Elena did in confirmation of the deal was to shake hands. She wasn't interested in having a lawyer draw up an offer-to-purchase or any other document. Linda found this a bit unsettling and queried the safety of the deal with Elena's great friend Eleanor Wilcox, who was working as her son's receptionist. Elena was quite touched and proud to be told of Eleanor's response to Linda which was, "If Elena shakes hands, everything is fine."

* * *

The Jenningses settled into their new positions in the post office quickly and established a routine. Johannes also found his niche very quickly. His job included cleaning the post office and he took great pride in this. He was at the post office by four in the morning. His first task was to attend to the floors, which he kept washed and waxed to a gleam. In those days the fittings were wood and brass and these, too, he kept glowing. It used to irritate him no end when customers clung to the brass bars and left them grimy.

They also tried to beautify the outside of the post office. Johannes and George built flowerbeds and kept them planted up with annuals. A regular holiday-maker from Pretoria owned a large and well-known nursery and he brought them a wonderful collection of bulbs which created a spectacular display – and then someone stole all the bulbs! They replanted the beds but these bulbs also began to disappear. This time the culprits were four-legged. George was inspecting the garden when he noticed the plants just disappearing into the earth before his eyes: moles!

Post office regulations didn't extend to the amenities and their toilet was a long-drop behind the building. To add injury to insult, it was plagued with mosquitoes. George's method of combating this menace, if he had to spend any length of time there, was to take a newspaper with him – not to distract himself by reading but to light it and wave it about his head so that the smoke drove off the insects.

Initially, the postbag had to be collected from Munster as the railway bus only came as far as Munster. Johannes would take the outgoing bag to Munster and collect the arriving bag. The bags were transported in a wheelbarrow which he had to push along the sandy track, which represented the main road, a round trip of about twenty-four kilometres.

Eventually, when the bridge over the Umtamvuna River was completed in the early 1960's, the railway bus extended its route to Bizana in the Transkei. This made life much easier for Johannes as the bus then dropped the bag off every afternoon at the garage at the entrance to Port Edward. The bags were still transported to and from the post office in the wheelbarrow and Johannes could often be seen at the garage waiting for the bus and taking a well-earned nap in his wheelbarrow as he waited. Elena designed a stamp which read "Par Brouette" ("*By Wheelbarrow*") as opposed to "By Air" and wrote to the post office headquarters in Pietermaritzburg, suggesting that they make up the stamp for her use in Port Edward: the authorities ignored her request.

Another of Johannes's tasks was to return to their house at about twelve to prepare lunch for them at one. He also provided other services. One Saturday afternoon Elena was at home when George was on the golf-course. She was accosted by a drunk police guard who was becoming quite belligerent until Johannes came round the corner of the house, carrying a knife. He very firmly escorted the guard off the property.

George was also at work before five in the morning. He walked down to the post office every day, accompanied by his dog, a cross boxer-bulldog bitch called Bibi.

Bibi, too, had her daily task. This was to trot across the road to Owen Ellis's general dealership, called 'Our Stores', and fetch George's newspaper. She would carry it back to him, neatly rolled up in her mouth, and put it in his hand. One day he was deeply involved in conversation when she came back. He was aware of her hovering near him but he didn't stop talking. Eventually, when he had finished, he found that Bibi had disappeared with his paper. He discovered her round the back of the building, digging a hole and burying his paper – no more than he deserved for his rudeness.

Another of Bibi's peculiarities was that she had to have two Smarties every evening before bedtime and wouldn't go to bed unless she had had her Smarties. She was only given two a night – a coloured one and a chocolate, or brown, one. Amazingly, she would swallow the coloured Smarty and chew the chocolate.

It was a neighbour, Sylvia Minter, who had found an advertisement for bulldog-x-boxer pups in a newspaper. Sylvia was very keen to have one and, as the Jenningses were in need of a dog, they decided to have one too. Sylvia made the journey to the Port Shepstone Station to collect the pups. When she got there the puppies had already been offloaded and Bibi had made her escape from the crate. She was busily inspecting the platform when Sylvia arrived and was not the least disconcerted by her new surroundings. Her sister was still nestled in the box. The two dogs were able to maintain their sisterhood as they lived next door to each other. Bibi always left some of her meal as though she were keeping it for her sister's evening visit.

Bibi met her end, whilst on duty, in a sickening accident. When the road into Port Edward was sufficiently upgraded, the railway bus delivered the post right to the post office. Bibi objected to this monstrous vehicle disturbing the tranquility of the village and she would run alongside, barking at it. No one saw exactly how it happened but somehow she was crushed beneath the wheels.

She was buried behind the post office and Owen Ellis donated a Norfolk pine to be planted on her grave.

George and Elena decided that they would never own another dog because the loss of such a beloved member of the family was too painful to bear.

Post office administration demanded precision and allowed no room for personal preference. The regulations were the regulations. They had to be known inside-out and they had to be applied to the letter. George and Elena became adept at balancing the books at the end of each day and developed a sort of duel act in which, if they were having a balancing problem, they would both sit at the ledger, each taking the left- or right-hand page and scanning through their allotted side until they picked up the problem. The postmistress at Munster often called them at the end of the day because she couldn't balance, and they would drive across to give her a hand.

Other areas of administration were always a problem for Elena, the biggest problem of which was keeping her stationery cupboard in order. Everything in it had to be placed in a very specific spot. The problem lay in keeping it that way because it was a very busy point in the post office with every conceivable form and item used during the day, coming from this cupboard. In no time at all it would lose its parade-ground precision and head office spot checks invariably found Elena's cupboard in a mess, or certainly not in the required order. The cupboard was always the black mark on the report submitted on the Port Edward Post Office. Eventually she employed Sylvia's teenage son, during a school holiday, to organize her cupboard. She was so impressed and delighted with the results that she took a photograph and sent it off to head office in Pietermaritzburg to prove her good intentions.

Elena did try very hard to maintain post office protocol but there were some areas where she felt compelled to bend the rules. Her particular weakness was filling in forms for illiterate black people, and this was strictly against regulations. In addition to not being able to read or write, these people were faced by forms that were written in either English or Afrikaans and often they couldn't speak either language. Elena spoke little Zulu and Johannes acted as the translator. Somehow the two of them would manage to provide satisfaction.

Occasionally, Elena's grateful black clients would return with small gifts. One such old lady brought her two enormous whelks, measuring at least 20 centimetres each. Where she had found these shells is a mystery because we've never seen whelks of anywhere near that size on this coast. Elena still treasures them and has put them safely out of the reach of her new kitten.

Another area of contention was maintaining the two books (one in English and one in Afrikaans) in which all the rules and regulations of post office administration had to be recorded. These books were the post office 'bible' and were very carefully scrutinized by the officials. The books had to be updated constantly and whenever an amendment arrived in the postbag, George would announce its arrival and Elena would groan. The amendments had to be copied in by hand following a very rigid, prescribed layout. George handled the Afrikaans version and Elena the English.

Elena had no formal qualifications recognized by the post office authorities and George felt very strongly that she needed to get her school-leaver's certificate in order to secure her position. At forty-two, this wasn't a prospect Elena relished. Academic study was also something she didn't relish. The task was further complicated by the fact that she would have to write in English, a language in which she had not received any formal education. Even writing the Afrikaans paper wasn't that easy for her despite her Dutch background because she'd never done Dutch at school.

Her intelligence and experience stood her in good stead, however. Toly was also a great help in preparing her for the maths exam. Off she went to write amongst that year's crop of teenage school-leavers - who wanted to know what she was doing there – and she passed happily. Her exam-writing technique, though, was unusual: whilst pondering an answer she would gaze intently at the ceiling, visualising the answer up there. Eventually the invigilator approached her desk to ask what she was looking at.

To begin with, there were only thirty-seven telephones in Port Edward and surrounds. This gives an indication of how small the settlement was. The few businesses, including the garage, the butchery, the bakery, the bottle store, the hotel and two general dealers, had telephones. The remaining 'phones belonged to farmers and permanent residents. The few holiday cottages weren't furnished with telephones. The visitors made use of one of the two public 'phones at the post office. The second 'phone was reserved for black customers!

The postmaster had the onerous task of writing out the accounts by hand, making use of the switchboard operator's records. The householders' calls were recorded alongside their initials. The first task of Elena's day was to write up the accounts record book with the calls from the previous day. Abbreviations were used for the town to which the call had been placed, so these abbreviations had to be looked up, if they weren't known by heart, along with the charge-rate per minute of every destination.

The exchange itself was manual in every sense of the word. Of course the 'phones were all connected on a party-line system and each household had its ring-code of various combinations of short and long rings. The switchboard operator also had to turn a handle on the board to alert the person receiving the call. Eventually this aspect of the job was 'automated' – the telephonist was given a battery-powered handle! However, if the weather was chilly, the batteries didn't work. George solved this problem by placing a paraffin lamp near the batteries because there was still no electricity in Port Edward.

If there was a lightning storm Elena didn't answer the 'phone for fear of being shocked, a not-uncommon occurrence, but something a number of people didn't understand, or had given little thought to. Lydia Stevenson, from the garage, was one such person. During a particularly fierce storm she rang and rang and when Elena eventually answered, thinking that the storm was abating, Lydia was in a state of high dudgeon and very careless of Elena's explanation and warning. Elena had no sooner connected her than the line was struck and Lydia received a nasty shock. Elena couldn't have timed it better herself had she had personal control of the heavens.

Rural and primitive the whole operation certainly was, but it did give a strong sense of community. This was particularly evident with the farming community for whom there was a special emergency ring. This was especially useful when there was a veld fire. Someone would 'phone the message to Elena who would make the emergency ring on all the relevant lines, and then inform everyone who picked up the 'phone of the details of what was needed and where.

Not everybody had the same sense of community responsibility though. On one occasion Elena took a call from a heavy-breathing, salacious, foul-mouthed individual. She could have cut the connection but decided the fellow needed to be taught a lesson. She kept him on the line while she put a call through to the newly-opened police station. The police went round to the man's house, walked in, and tapped him on the shoulder. They didn't bother to charge him but did give him a severe dressing-down. The beauty of such a small place was that nothing remained secret for long and the story got around very quickly, along with the message that such behaviour could get you into a lot of trouble.

Elena operated the exchange until five in the afternoon and then she was relieved by a young woman who would continue the service until eight o'clock. This was a lonely and sometimes frightening occupation. One evening this young woman heard a repeated thumping on the roof. She was convinced that someone was on the roof and trying to find a way in. In a panic she called the police. They discovered her would-be assailant was an avocado pear dangling from the tree which overhung the building and which the wind was blowing about. On another occasion she was petrified by a snake which slithered out of a hole in the floor. She leapt up on top of the switchboard and there she was still perched when the police arrived to rescue her - again.

When telegrams had to be sent, the operator would 'phone Margate with the message from where it would be transmitted. Incoming telegrams were received by Margate and then passed on telephonically to Port Edward where Elena would have to write them out by hand. Elena hasn't confessed to any errors in this process but her English did play tricks on her on other occasions so one wonders if she was always accurate. After a visit to the doctor she told George that she would have to go into hospital to receive treatment for a 'fish-hook'. She meant a 'fissure'.

Eventually this hit-and-miss system was replaced by a telex machine. This sophisticated device was delivered to the post office and plugged in by the official who had accompanied it. Before he could make his escape, George stopped him to ask how to operate the thing. He said he didn't know and left.

A young woman at the Margate post office explained over the telephone. It involved pushing buttons to connect with the destination and then the message was typed in. The message was received at the other end on a gummed strip or tape. The narrow strips of message then had to be pasted on to a form which the customer would receive. If the tape broke during a transmission a raucous alarm went off. The first time this happened Elena got such a fright she bolted outside, thinking that they were under some kind of attack.

Telegrams were usually placed in the postboxes but if it was a very urgent message, Johannes would deliver it to the residence. Some holiday-makers were waiting for their son's matric results and when the results arrived, Johannes wasn't available. These people didn't have a 'phone, and neither George nor Elena could leave the post office. The holiday home was some distance away on a rise (near Silver Sands town houses). George took a large mirror outside and flashed a signal up the hill towards the house. The family caught on and came rushing down to collect the results.

The Jenningses often had to use their discretion and sensitivity in passing on messages and handling parcels. Someone in town had suffered the loss of a son to suicide and his ashes were sent in the post. Elena realized what the parcel contained and couldn't bear the thought of this man arriving to collect his post and discovering the parcel without forewarning. Her telephone operator assistant, Toekie Aukamp, 'phoned him to let him know, as kindly as she could, what awaited him.

For a number of years there was no police presence in Port Edward or any form of protection service. There wasn't even a permanent doctor. In a sense, the only 'official' establishment was the post office and so all sorts of extraordinary situations and crises ended up in the post office.

Victims of fishing accidents often arrived for George's attention and he was adept at removing fish-hooks from various body parts.

They were also called upon to give advice on family troubles and affairs of the heart. As in any small town, illicit love affairs soon became public knowledge and those that they didn't actually witness themselves, they were soon told about.

The post office technician, who was based in Margate, was a delectable James Dean look-alike. Being unmarried, he had few scruples about enjoying the attentions he received in Port Edward. Any new, young, female employee at the post office had to be inspected by him and his approval, or otherwise, he quickly conveyed to Elena. The marital status of his conquests was immaterial to him. There was one particularly good-looking married lady with whom he had a fling and when he visited her, he would position one of his workers at the top of a convenient telephone pole with instructions to ring him as soon as the husband was spotted on his way home.

A businessman in the town bought himself a brand-new Mercedes of which he was inordinately proud – until he caught his wife making merry on the back seat. He kept his wife but the Mercedes was promptly sold.

Another businessman who owned a store had quite a reputation for his philandering. When he took up with one particular woman, the two thought they were being very subtle when they worked out a code of gestures for when and where they would meet. His wife worked in the business with him so it would have been very awkward to make their arrangements for their trysts in the shop. His mistress would park near the shop and then he would come out and the gesticulating would begin – to the amusement of any witnesses in the know.

Of course his wife wasn't a fool and she soon realized what was going on. In desperation she discussed her heartache with Elena and George. George's advice was pragmatic and to the point. He reminded her that the money for the business had come from her family and the business was in her name. What she had to do was to confront her husband and tell him that if he didn't change his ways he would be out on his ear. It worked.

The Jenningses numbered two couples amongst their close friends and things became a little awkward when Mr X took a shine to the very beautiful Mrs Y. Mr Y was a very wealthy man and he informed Mr X that he was welcome to his wife but that he needed to know that he could never afford to keep her. Affair ended but friendship continued.

Another entertaining incident involved a man notorious for his philandering. He was paying a visit to his current interest, a woman who owned a boarding-house. His wife arrived looking for him and knocked on the front door. He bolted for the back door but his wife had anticipated this and had beaten him to it. As he hurtled through the back entrance she was waiting for him – with the traditional frying-pan at the ready!

George and Elena were also called upon to give advice on finance and investments. Dr McCusker was a retiree to Port Edward but he maintained a medical practice in Bizana. This was a cash business. He came into the post office one day with a huge roll of money. He handed it over to Elena and told her to invest it for him. When she asked how much he had given her, he said he hadn't a clue and left her to the task. He also entrusted his government bonds to her safe keeping.

Politics, of course, made its way into the post office. Being a state organization, the post office was often the recipient of regulations which were the offshoot of developing apartheid legislation. Elena's experiences of racial prejudice and discriminatory laws made her vehemently opposed to National Party policies. In addition to the devastation caused to the lives of individuals, families and communities, Elena couldn't bear the frustration and hurt inflicted by apartheid in everyday life.

George, too, had had his fair share of discrimination in the army and he was vociferous in his opposition. One of their customers came into the post office to do some canvassing for the National Party. He asked Elena who she was going to vote for and she told him that, of course, she would be voting for the right party. He was completely taken in, congratulated her on her wisdom, and left on a cheerful note. Fortunately George hadn't heard the exchange because he was busy in a back room. Had he heard the fellow he would have told him to take his filthy politics out of his post office.

The Jenningses were associated with a retired couple who were extremely parsimonious and who held very racist views. One of their economies was to avoid using their stove on a Saturday to save fuel. They didn't, however, refuse to eat, and made a habit of calling around to the Jenningses in time for supper. Elena got a bit tired of this and decided to put a stop to their visits – subtly, and by exploiting their racism. She instructed her cook to make sure that when he brought their plates of pasta to the table, he had his thumbs well embedded in the pasta. They never returned to share a meal.

Occasionally they would be confronted by horrific or heart-wrenching incidents. In the late 1950's there was a sudden spate of shark attacks on the South Coast heralded by the taking of a young girl's arm in Margate. No satisfactory explanation has ever been put forward for this situation. Port Edward, too, experienced a number of attacks, all of which were reported to the post office for George to notify the police.

Not all incidents were fatal. One man was intending to snorkel in the bay. When he dived off a boat he met a shark – head first! As his head went into the gaping jaws his snorkel jabbed the shark in the gullet. Sharky didn't like this and spat him out while his friends on the boat pulled him back on board by his feet. He was left with a ring of teeth marks around his head.

Other attacks were horrific and traumatic for all concerned. A honeymooner was swimming in the bay when he was taken by a shark. The bakery assistant, a black man, was fishing from the rocks nearby and very courageously went in after him. He actually managed to grab the victim's arm. This was a very unequal tug-of-war and the man disappeared in a swirl of blood in full view of his new bride. His body was never found.

A man, staying at the Police Holiday Camp with his family, went for a swim at sunset and simply disappeared. There was no sign of his body and eventually his poor family was forced to pack up and go home. Shortly thereafter the Indian barman, Jack, from the hotel, found a section of skin in a rock pool. He took his grisly find to George. It would appear that this hairy and fatty piece of skin had come from the unfortunate man's belly. George and the policeman who arrived in response to George's summons, decided that no good purpose would be served by making the family return to identify the remains and they had the remains buried.

Eventually the Nielsons generously decided to install shark nets at their own expense. These primitive nets were the strange contraptions seen so often in old cinés and photographs of South Coast beaches at the time. They consisted of upright wooden poles jutting out of the sea from which the nets were suspended and stretched. The poles were held in place by strong cables which were anchored to large metal rings set into concrete blocks. These concrete blocks were cast on suitably situated rocks. The blocks and rings can still be seen on Silver Beach. The nets were very ugly and created the impression that bathers were confined to a cage. They certainly spoilt the seaside ambience of freedom and ease. They worked though, and gave holiday-makers peace of mind. One wonders, too, if they weren't more ecologically sound than some modern methods of shark defence which so often result in the death of the shark.

An entertaining offshoot of the shark scare involved Stoffel Fourie and his ski-boat. Stoffel and Nellie Fourie came from Welkom and had bought a retirement cottage in Windsor Road, right on the shore, in 1950.

There seems to have been something of a ski-boat craze at the time with people getting their hands on all sorts of strange craft and often not really knowing what they were doing. Stoffel had found himself a metal boat with a tiny motor. He, Doc Wilson (who owned a holiday cottage in Port Edward and often visited from Underberg where he had a farm and a medical practice), Ray Harley, from Kokstad, and a chap I'll call 'Punch', who was seldom sober, launched from Silver Beach in front of a large audience.

Punch had gone to a lot of trouble to kit himself out and was resplendent in full waterproof gear – jacket, pants and sou'wester hat – in black. Stoffel was holding the rudder and as they hit the third wave the boat reared up and Stoffel's three crewmen fell out. Only Stoffel was left and he panicked and jumped out.

Punch started to yell, "I can't swim!" and Doc Wilson went to his rescue. He very professionally flipped him on to his back and began towing him. Ray Harley, in the meantime, had got to shore and when he looked back he began to scream, "Black fin! Black fin!" Doc saw the ominous triangular shape drifting in the water and redoubled his efforts. He kept going until he simply had nothing left to give, let go of Punch, and sank – to his knees:

he had been swimming in water no deeper than his kneecaps, which he discovered when he stood up! And then to add the final touch to the farce – the shark-fin was nothing more threatening than Punch's hat.

In the meantime, the boat had completed its arc and beached itself.

George, too, had a boat which he had built himself whilst living at Palmleigh. It was fourteen feet long and had a hardwood skeleton covered with marine-ply and then fibreglass. As he didn't possess an electric screwdriver, he had to screw in every one of the brass screws manually. Initially the boat was powered by an incredibly small three-horsepower motor and then later by a five-horsepower motor. George loved his boat and Elena enjoyed it for a time too. She was put off when they encountered a shark which was longer than the boat and which came close enough to slap the side of the boat.

Flood was another area of life in the district which involved the post office. The river which flows into the estuary at Silver Beach, the Inhlanhlinhlu, is at most times little more than a stream but when it comes down in spate it is a wild and dangerous torrent. It crosses under the present highway three times before flowing into the estuary. Even today it threatens the road with flooding and on the very rare occasion actually manages to flow over the bridges which are a considerable height above the river bed.

It flows through the bottom of our property, entering the property under the first bridge on the road and is then forced, by a ten metre high cliff or krantz, to make a sharp right turn. From there it flows north, parallel to the road. In full spate, the water is jettisoned under the bridge and hits the krantz with such force that it ricochets back across the river bed to hit the opposite bank and then continues along its more-or-less normal route. It behaves like a mad giant in control of a gigantic firehose. We have often worried about our pump being swept away because it is positioned a very short distance north of the krantz but the ricochet action is so violent that the water curves round the pump, missing it altogether.

Before the coming of the new road the bridges were all low-lying. In one such flooding a young couple on holiday tried to drive across and was swept off the bridge. The husband was trapped in the car and drowned. Somehow his pregnant wife was thrown out of the vehicle and was swept downstream where she was found washed up on Silver Beach.

Another victim was a travelling salesman but he was far more fortunate because he managed to open a window and escape from his vehicle as it was being submerged. He was also very lucky to have been able to escape without being hit by the debris which is usually washed down in such floods.

Sylvia Minter, who had taken the job as the switchboard operator at Munster when she was widowed, was still at work one night when George realized that flooding was imminent because it had been raining heavily. He became very concerned that she wouldn't be able to cross the bridges, or might take a chance as her son was alone at home. When George went to check, he found that the river had breached its banks. Sylvia came off duty at ten so he went back to the post office and 'phoned her to tell her not to try to come home but to spend the night at Nicholson's Garage. She did try to come home though, and was forced to spend the night in her car at the bridge, waiting for the water to go down.

Sylvia was a long-standing friend. Her husband was retired and they had come down from Rhodesia. They had a 'laatlammetjie' or 'afterthought'. Sylvia's husband was diagnosed with cancer of the bladder (strangely, the same form of cancer from which George suffered later on). Understandably, Mr Minter complained vociferously about his disease to anyone who would listen. One wag eventually said to him, "Well then, why don't you shoot yourself? But make sure you do it outside because it will make too much mess inside." Knowing the character who said it, it wasn't maliciously intended.

Sylvia was mowing the lawn and she heard a shot but didn't think anything of it. It was only a little later, when she went to the outhouse, that she discovered that her husband had shot himself behind the building. Her domestic worker arrived at the post office in great distress to tell George that he had to come quickly. He took over and did the necessary on that terrible day and thereafter. When it was all over, Sylvia needed a job and George managed to procure the position as telephonist in Munster for her. Her son was only about twelve at the time.

And then there were the two drunks who had been holidaying on the Wild Coast. On their return journey they came careering down the very steep incline on the southern, or Transkeian, (now the Eastern Cape) bank of the Umtamvuna River, aiming for the pont below. They were going so fast that they stood no chance of stopping and drove straight into the water. The Pont was, and still is, a popular recreational area and their escapade was witnessed by many. They managed to get themselves out of the car before it sank and swam to shore while their vehicle settled into the muddy depths.

They were taken to the Port Edward Hotel where the Weatherdons very kindly put the pair of them up free of charge. Of course, everything they had had with them, including money and clothing, was at the bottom of the Umtamvuna. It was a huge performance to retrieve their car using a crane.

The hotel was an important feature of life in Port Edward and the Weatherdons were good friends of the Jenningses. The two couples often found themselves in joint problem-solving ventures.

Dave Doig was one of their on-going, mutual problems. He lived at the hotel in a rondavel at the back of the establishment, for which he was charged very little. Dave had a terrible problem with alcohol. To quote Elena, "He drank like a bloody fish!" He also had a heart problem. Ted Weatherdon called Elena one night to 'phone Dr Feinberg, in Margate, to send an ambulance as he thought Dave was having a heart-attack.

The ambulance duly arrived and Dave was carted off to Port Shepstone where it was discovered that he wasn't having a heart-attack and was merely drunk – but so drunk that he needed to be hospitalized to be rehydrated. Dr Feinberg took the opportunity to dry him out and put him on the wagon but this didn't last for long.

Sending for the ambulance in the middle of the night for Dave became a fairly regular occurrence. Elena would rouse Dr Feinberg who would say, "The usual, Mrs Jennings?" to which she would reply, "Yes, Dr Feinberg," and neither needed to exchange any more information and the drill would roll forward. Poor old Dave died in his sleep one night after someone had had to tuck him in yet again.

Dr Feinberg was Elena's and George's doctor from 1949 to 1972 when he retired. He was regarded as an excellent diagnostician. It was he who diagnosed George's bladder cancer without any sophisticated equipment, to the amazement of the specialist in Durban who confirmed the diagnosis.

The hotel was a very tolerant establishment but behaviour did become particularly wild during the sardine run when fishermen arrived in their droves. Many of them didn't have much money, or any money, and couldn't afford the normal hotel rates. They were allowed to sleep in the outhouses free of charge. The trouble was that Gladys Weatherdon's turkeys often also roosted in the outhouses and they were not at all discriminating about where they muted. Usually the fishermen had had too much to drink the night before to notice the turkeys when they went to bed, or to feel the deluge during the night, but the morning light brought great indignation. They didn't get any sympathy from Gladys.

Two well-known fishermen amongst this lot were Lefty Schmidt (renowned for a record shark catch) and his brother, Boy. These two had a great following of fishermen and the season was considered particularly successful – and was inevitably wilder - if it was patronized by the Schmidts. It was at times like this that the local boys really got out of hand. Ray Harley fell prey to such a mood when it was declared that his chest was too hairy and the pub patrons decided to burn it all off.

Ted Weatherdon forbade the wearing of ties in his bar and if anyone was foolhardy enough to appear with one, he would cut it off and hang it up in the pub. One foolish fellow arrived in the midst of this mob in a suit! He was punished for his insensitivity to the standards of the establishment by being knocked down and used as a human mop.

There were times when even the benevolent boundaries of the hotel were over-stepped and Ted was forced to take action. George became Ted's unofficial bouncer when he was in the pub. Ted would look at George and give a slight jerk of his head in the direction of the door. This was George's cue to escort the patron off the premises – or remove him with a little more vigour if that was required.

Over weekends, when the post office was closed, the hotel became the first aid station. One Saturday afternoon an unfortunate fisherman got a hook through his lip as he was trying to tie it on to his line. He was brought into the pub where Doc Wilson happened to be. Doc had him laid on the counter and asked for the brandy bottle. Everyone, including the patient, assumed that he was going to dull the man's senses with it. Doc Wilson wasn't, however, the least concerned with his patient's pain threshold but he was concerned about infection, and the only brandy the victim got to taste was that which was sloshed on to his wound. Doc then called for the pliers from his own fishing box in the corner and completed the procedure.

* * *

In 1963, whilst going through old documents, George came across the papers relating to the golf-course which had become defunct. The land had been donated to the community some years previously for the purpose of building a golf-course and country club.

Ted Weatherdon had maintained the course and it was popular with locals and holiday-makers alike. However, Ted had had little support in the maintenance of the greens and eventually it just became too expensive for him to keep it going and it ceased to exist. People generally assumed that somehow the funds would come to light to resurrect it but nobody was in any great hurry to do anything about it. George discovered that there was a clause in the donation that stated that the land would be ceded to the municipality in two years' time if the community failed to use it for the purposes for which it had initially been granted. George loved golf and this really got his alarm bells ringing and he set to work.

According to Donald Dunlop, an old friend of Elena, the original piece of ground was donated by Fred North who made the donation when the township of Port Edward was proclaimed in the 1920's. Fred attached various terms and conditions to this donation, the most important being that the ground was to be used as a golf-course. Should it not be used as a golf-course for a period of twenty-five years, it was to be ceded to the local council to do with it as the council saw fit. The most likely use would probably have been to cut it up and sell it off for housing, especially as the course occupies a prime position within the township boundaries and has some lovely views.

Donald says that if he remembers correctly, the course was laid out before the Second World War, by Otway Hayes, Springbok golfer in the 1930's and father of luminary professional golfer, Dale Hayes. The course was in use up until 1940. The original first tee and the ninth green were situated where the bowling-green is today, the bowling-green having been built in the late 1940's.

When George made his discovery in 1963, he rounded up as many interested parties as he could find and this eventually boiled down to the convenient number of nine. It was agreed that each of these nine people would be responsible for a green and the following tee. The original greens were still visible, although very overgrown. Donald couldn't remember who was responsible for every green and tee but he did remember that Ralph Rock had the first green and second tee, Count De Tzerclass the fourth green and fifth tee, George had the seventh green and the eighth tee, Peter Davies had the eighth green and ninth tee, and Donald, himself, had the ninth green and first tee. Martin van Duyn, Charlie Stevenson, Andrew Henderson and Ted Weatherdon were also involved.

Count Tzerclass, who owned a holiday cottage in Port Edward and was planning to retire here but never managed to, donated a very old Ford tractor to mow the fairways. The intrepid group also managed to raise the funds to buy a slasher-mower for the fairways, a small mower for the green surrounds and a greens-mower. By the end of their first growing season they had all the greens playable and even their fairways, although not very wide, were cut reasonably short.

The Count also donated drainage pipes which were used to drain the valley in front of the fifth green (which is the fourth green now). Over time they were able to raise the funds to buy piping to irrigate all the greens and tees.

Their first trophy was donated by the SA Police and the attendant competition was played on New Year's Day. The first competition took place on the 1st of

January 1966 and was won by Peter Purchase with the best gross score. From the subsequent year the prize went to the best net score.

At the end of the 1960's it was decided to build a clubhouse. Up until that time Donald's house, which stands near the present entrance to the club and is now owned by Phillipa Makepeace, was used for players to change, and as a spot where they could park their cars.

Again the Count came to the fore and donated a large number of concrete blocks. He had been planning to build a house in front of the hotel. These blocks were stored in front of the police station, which borders on the golf-course, for a number of years before work on the building started.

The committee selected the site of the clubhouse and this necessitated moving the first green and tee. The tee was roughly where the present entrance is, and the green, which was a short hole, was where the tennis-courts were built. The green was dug up and replanted as the present fifth green. The tennis-courts are also no longer in use. This is a sad situation on two counts: the first being that country tennis is dying out owing to a lack of interest on the part of most youngsters, and the second being rampant crime because the tennis-courts are now used as a parking lot for club members as the courts are immediately in front of the clubhouse and an eye can be kept on the vehicles at all times.

Work on the clubhouse started in 1973/1974. Through the efforts of Sandy Payn, they managed to get a billiard-table from the defunct Flagstaff Club which had been forced to close down when the National Party government created the Transkei, a so-called 'independent' black state. While building was in progress they housed the table in the little house next door to Donald's general dealer's shop in Strawberry Lane.

Despite the immense enthusiasm of this little group, the number of players was never large and gradually dwindled. They found themselves short of funds and equipment which made the upkeep of the course very difficult. It was then that Barry Payn came on the scene and proved to be a tremendous help in keeping the course going.

*   *   *

Of course, strict racial segregation was practised in all post office dealings. Apart from the public having to use separate public telephones, they also had to use separate entrances and separate areas of the counter. The post office was divided down the middle by a ceiling-to-floor wooden partition.

The day finally came in 1971 when George received a message from head office to take down the partition. He was elated. Together with an equally delighted Johannes, the two set about tearing the thing down after closing time. They went at it with a vengeance and, like two naughty schoolboys, made as much noise and mess as they could.

By the following morning not a trace of the monstrosity was left, possibly making the Port Edward Post Office the first post office in South Africa to be rid of its humiliating and superfluous barricade. Their clients were astounded at the change the next morning – and a little perturbed too. Despite the disappearance of the barricade most customers, black and white, continued to use their accustomed entrances and sections of the counter – a reminder of William Blake's "mind-forg'd manacles"!

Elena had never grown out of her love of pranks and practical jokes and often couldn't help herself, even in her work place.

One of her favourite tricks, when she saw a customer opening the door to his postbox, was to reach in and grab the customer's hand as the post was being gathered. Her hands were usually cold and this added to the shock. The shrieks with which this trick was invariably received entertained her enormously.

Box 10 belonged to the garage owners, the Stevensons, and was situated at the bottom of the bank of boxes. Because the box was at floor level, it was awkward for the Stevensons to get a good view into the box and this suited Elena's purposes well. She put a rubber snake into the box between the letters and when Mr Stevenson opened the box there was a roar and an expletive that stopped all and sundry in their tracks.

Elena also had to endure her fair share of practical jokes at the hands of her customers.

Box 21 belonged to the Van Duyns and was at eye-level when Elena was sitting at her desk. Martin van Duyn would give an ear-piercing whistle if he spotted her, through his box, at her desk and concentrating deeply. She took to keeping a large syringe filled with water on her desk and managed to squirt him in the eye on a couple of occasions. When the post office inspector wanted to know what the syringe was for and she told him, she was informed very firmly that that sort of behaviour was not permitted.

The boxes were also used for some interesting exchanges. Lydia Stevenson had a lovely German shepherd and when George and Elena had lamb in their deepfreeze and cooked the shoulder, Elena would wrap the bone and put it in the postbox for the dog. George, too, made use of the postbags in unorthodox ways when it suited him: on one occasion he caught a huge barracuda and sent it to the Margate postmaster in a postbag.

April Fool's Day was never allowed to pass unmarked and amazingly her customers allowed themselves to be caught time and again. She 'phoned the butcher on one occasion and said that she was speaking on behalf of the technician who was with her and who was checking the lines. She needed the butcher to stand on a chair and sing 'Mary, Mary Quite Contrary'. When the butcher had obliged he asked, "Was that all right?" Her reply was, "Yes, for the first of April."

Dick Hooper came in one day and she told him she needed help measuring the outside of the post office with a length of twine. There was Dick circling the entire building with a piece of string in his hand. Then she left him standing for twenty minutes, holding the end of the twine, while she fiddled about with the so-called forms that had to be filled in.

She also managed to catch the hotel, the bakery and the restaurant in one go. She 'phoned them all and said that the health inspector was on his way. This unleashed a flurry of panicky activity in all three establishments.

The pranks which she regarded as her most successful usually had a political twist to them. At the height of public fear of Communist infiltration she put it about that a submarine, sporting a hammer and sickle on its turret, had been sighted off Splash Rock. The story spread like wildfire with an ensuing stream of people heading down the road to the beach to check the story. This was one prank that made it into the local paper, 'The South Coast Herald', and is still remembered today.

The tale that really got people worked up was when she put letters in everybody's postbox stating that the government had decided that, in order to solve the squatter problem, every property owner in an urban area would have to donate a certain percentage of his property for the erection of a shack to house a squatter. The note also announced the holding of a protest meeting and gave the time and place. She very nearly started a riot with that one!

Her other pranks were milder but gave her plenty of entertainment too. She glued 20c and 50c pieces to the floor of the post office and was entertained for most of the day watching people's varied approaches to trying to pick up the coins. Eventually George said to her, "Please, Meid, could you try to be a little more serious?" She also couldn't resist replaying her iced wooden cake trick (the one which she had developed and perfected on the South African colonel in Genoa) on uninitiated locals, including Barry Payn.

Her last big prank she put into action to celebrate her eightieth birthday. She announced that she would be marking the occasion by bungey-jumping off the Umtamvuna Bridge. She went as far as getting a medical certificate from Dr Hans Van Zyl declaring that she was of sound mind and in good health. She also obtained written permission from the police. Then she invited any interested spectators to meet her at the bridge at a particular time – which they did. Of course she had no intention of jumping and the joke was on those who had thought she would. This, too, got into the local paper and is remembered.

CHAPTER 22

In 1972 George was diagnosed with cancer of the bladder. He was given cobalt treatment at Addington Hospital in Durban and the treatment was successful in that it cured the cancer. However, it was administered with such vigour that his colon was burnt and he had to undergo surgery to remove a large section of his colon.

Shortly after the cobalt treatment and George's return home, he experienced excrutiating pain and Dr McCusker diagnosed a blockage in the bowel. George was desperately ill and the doctor feared that a road trip to Durban would take too long. He got Sid van der Vyver to fly George, and another very ill patient, to Durban from the landing-strip on Sid's farm.

An ambulance was waiting for them at the airport in Durban and they were taken to St Augustines. Dr McCusker had been right about a blockage but he hadn't known that the blockage had been caused by gangrene. George underwent surgery and returned home, only to have to go back a short time later for more cutting. By the time the surgeons were finished, half his colon had been removed. This left him with chronic and vicious diarrhoea which made it very difficult to conduct his life as he had always done. He had to take large doses of anti-diarrhoea medication every day.

During one of the emergency operations, George's front tooth had been knocked out. He had always taken great care of his teeth of which he was rather proud and not a little vain.

At the time there wasn't a dental practice in Port Edward but the retired head of the Faculty of Dentistry at the University of Pretoria lived in Port Edward, Professor Bob Dreyer. He had a small surgery at his home where he treated a limited number of patients, mainly friends. He offered to solve the problem by making a bridge. He achieved perfection, much to George's delight, and George's smile was returned. Occasionally he would forget to put the bridge in and if he happened to go out without it, he refused to smile.

George's battle with the diarrhoea did improve over time and eventually he was able to play golf again. However, the problem never completely disappeared and he was forced to take early retirement in 1973. Elena took over as the postmistress.

She loathed the title 'Postmistress' which, to her, sounded awfully prissy and schoolmistressy. Consequently, she took to calling herself 'The Postmaster's Mistress'. A new customer came in one day and asked to see the postmaster. Elena told him that she was the postmaster's mistress and could take care of his business. It took a while for the confused man to get her drift. Some time later she passed him in the street and he politely enquired if she was still the postmaster's mistress.

Because she was a woman, she was paid R1000 a month less than George. This was a substantial amount of money. A further injustice was that married women could not be placed on permanent staff. However, this had been rectified three years previously in 1969, when the postmaster in Margate was given permission to appoint three people to permanent staff and Elena was one of the three he selected. This was important to her pension and also enabled her to buy back pension.

Her first assistant or counter clerk was Ansie and she was succeeded by Toekie who worked in the post office for many years. The telephonists were Molly Walker and Dillys Frankish. The exchange closed in 1976 when automatic 'phones were installed. Elena recorded in the log book, or daily register, that this marked the end of an era. She, Molly and Dillys gave themselves a party to mark the occasion. A great relief to Elena was that she no longer had the laborious task of writing out the telephone accounts every month.

George wasn't able to sit about and do nothing and he found all sorts of activities to keep himself busy and make the inconveniences of his condition more bearable and manageable.

One of his initial tasks was to fit out the first of two Combis which could accommodate his special needs. He built a cubicle with a port-o-potty into the back of the Combi. This meant that he could travel a little further afield than Port Edward and was able to attend to business in Margate. What really tickled him was if he was caught short whilst parked in a Margate street, he would sit in the back of the Combi, and as people walked past, he would doff his hat in polite greeting. Passersby would respond with a smile, a wave, or a greeting, all the while completely oblivious as to what was really going on inside the vehicle.

He and Elena perfected their change-over routine in the Combi so that they barely had to slow down to change driver. George would announce that Elena needed to drive for a stretch and she would slide into the seat under him while he lifted himself out of the way. She would snake her right foot up under his right foot on the accelerator so that her foot was in place at exactly the moment when he lifted his foot away.

This technique did lead to a near disaster in Johannesburg traffic. They were travelling in the slow lane when George was suddenly taken short. As they were doing their change-over George became aware of a huge truck bearing down on them with horn blaring at them. George shouted at her to "Put Foot!" to which she shouted back that he'd better just "knuip" (*clench*) because she wasn't managing to get her foot to the pedal. Somehow they survived.

He also involved himself with the activities of the town board. In those days each little village had a committee which was responsible for administering the town and taking care of municipal affairs. Each board had a fair amount of autonomy and it was astounding how much voluntary time various individuals dedicated to the running of their hamlets. The responsibilities were not trivial and included water supply and sanitation. Although they didn't suffer too much interference, there were numerous by-laws and regulations which the board had to adhere to. Meetings of the chairmen of the various town boards were held in Port Shepstone.

George was elected as chairman of the town board in 1980, succeeding Owen Ellis. He was elected for a second term but did not complete this term and threw in the towel in 1985. This was partly owing to ill health but he was also tired of ongoing battles with two particular individuals. One was a cheap builder whose short cuts George wouldn't tolerate. The other was an individual who wanted to build a garage on his property for which there wasn't sufficient room without bending the by-laws. These two began putting rumours about and making accusations against George which he found unpalatable. One rumour was that every time George bought a new house he spent rate payers' money on tarring the road in front of the house. George was succeeded by the jerry-builder himself and it didn't take long before the town was abuzz about said gentleman embezzling funds. This man then disappeared from the district.

The position of chairman of the town board was a voluntary position and consequently the incumbent received absolutely no remuneration – an astounding situation when today's inflated salaries for municipal officials are considered. The only personal expense towards which a municipal contribution was made, was a payment of R10 a month for petrol.

He was assisted in the office by a secretary who was one of the paid employees of the board. This was Daphne Schauw. She had a reputation for being incredibly bossy. This was, perhaps, understandable as in most cases the secretary of a town board would have been responsible for the bulk of the day-to-day administration of the town because the chairman would have had permanent employment elsewhere: his board responsibilities would have been fitted into his spare time. George, however, treated his position as a proper job and spent every morning in the office or involved in board business. There were times when Daphne became too much for him and on one occasion he got up from his desk, took her by the arm, led her to the door and told her to "bugger off". She seems to have accepted this with good grace.

The other paid employees were cleaners, and a road gang and their superintendent. The board was responsible for the collection of rates, refuse disposal, water supply and road maintenance. When George took over, there were no tarred roads in Port Edward and this created great difficulties, especially in the rainy season. It was during his tenure that all the main streets were tarred. The greater municipal authorities did not provide the funds for this and many town boards had to raise loans. George avoided this through careful planning and budgeting and every stretch that was tarred was paid for in cash. He also made a point of meeting with the roads supervisor every morning to plan the day's maintenance. Oh, for a return to those happy days of well-maintained roads in this present potholed day!

All building plans had to pass through the town board office and be approved by the greater municipal authority in Port Shepstone. As there were no local architects or draughtsmen, Elena was often called upon to draw up plans. She was responsible for the plans for a number of the buildings and homes in the town, including my own house. When it came to designing a civic building for the town, which was to include a library and hall, George and Elena collected ideas on their journeys around the country by studying such buildings in the towns through which they travelled.

The result of their investigations is the building which now serves the town. Professional architects drew up the plans but the ideas came from the Jenningses. The journalist, Chris Bennet, who wrote for the newspaper which serves the lower South Coast, 'The South Coast Herald', had this to say in his weekly back page commentary: "*The Port Edward library, a fine and, I trust, thriving institution. It is also not a bad piece of architecture – to my eyes, anyway.*" He adds, "*The hall, for such it is … is cavernous, and periodically does duty for other community functions* (in this context Mr Bennet was talking about the collecting of chronic medications) *such as people lying on the floor and waving their legs in the air. I think it is called aerobatics or something.*"

* * *

On the 15th of November 1985 George and Elena had a horrific car accident. They were returning to Port Edward one evening and, as they neared the turning into Port Edward, Elena was about to take off her safety-belt. It was irritating her because it was a bit loose. She hadn't yet managed to unclip it when they were hit by a motor bike. The biker was travelling from the opposite direction and smashed into them head-on. The rider was killed instantly. He had been travelling so fast, and hit them so hard, that both front doors of their very solid Peugeot buckled outwards and couldn't be opened.

Their rescuers managed to help George out through a back door after lowering his seat. Elena's legs were trapped so they couldn't get her out the same way. They broke the window on her side and cut through her safety-belt. With a great deal of patience and effort they managed to free her.

In the meantime the hunt was on for the local ambulance drivers who couldn't be found anywhere. Eventually they were both tracked down to a pub where they had been imbibing for some time. They were in no condition to go anywhere and an ambulance had to be summoned from Port Shepstone. It was over an hour before it arrived. The result of this indiscretion on the part of the drivers was that the ambulance service in Port Edward was closed down.

George had a badly gashed face for which he needed fifty stitches, and a broken elbow. He had recently had treatment for skin cancer on his forehead and the impact knocked the large scab off, leaving him with a beautifully healed, shiny pink patch – and the rest of his complexion looking very leprous. Elena had a very deep gash across her shin, which still aches when the weather is bad, four broken ribs and whiplash. Her torso was black with bruising from the safety-belt but it had certainly done its job.

The motor bike rider was a chef at the Wild Coast Casino who had, reportedly, got himself well and truly stoked up on dagga after his shift ended. Elena says that it would have been far better if she and George had died together in the accident.

In 1986 George was diagnosed with lung cancer. He went into hospital to have a small section of the top of his lung removed. This proved to be a much larger section than had been anticipated.

He continued to play golf but this was a battle because he was too weak to manage the long walks between tees. Rina van Schoor's sister-in-law very kindly lent him a moped on which he could get around the course and this enabled him to continue for a while longer.

He had always enjoyed the fashion extravaganza made possible in golfing outfits and relished the shocking pinks and bright blues he would never have dreamt of wearing ordinarily. Phillipa Makepeace, who reports the local news for the 'South Coast Herald', described George in one of her pieces about a golfing event as appearing in all his "sartorial splendour".

He and Elena decided that they had to stop smoking and made a valiant effort in front of each other. However, they weren't entirely honest with one another. Elena arranged to keep a box of cigarettes in a friend's dress shop, which had opened in the Owen Ellis Mall, across the road from the post office where Owen had had his trading store. Anne Baxter kept Elena's cigarettes in the top drawer of the desk in the shop and Elena would slip in every day for a quick cigarette. George became suspicious and asked Anne if she ever gave Elena cigarettes. Truthfully she could say that she didn't – because Elena had had the forethought of forbidding her from ever handing them to her.

George, too, wasn't above such subterfuge. He used to have the occasional cigarette, or cigarillo, in the pub at the golf club. He made the mistake one day of asking Elena to fetch a spanner from beneath the driver's seat in the Combi - and what should she find but his stash. She didn't say a word. But she did leave a written message and sketch for him: "Kilroy was here!" – a remnant of the Allies' wartime tradition of leaving a graffito sketch of the little man with raisin eyes and a big nose peering over a wall, to mark every location they had captured from the Germans. Nothing was said.

It would be a false impression, though, to suggest that they never had rows. During a particularly acrimonious argument Elena decided that she had better shut up. George didn't like this silent treatment and said to her, "Meid, maak oop jou bek dat die russie kan reg smaak!" ("*Meid, open your trap so that the argument has some flavour!*") Elena, in her turn, often had recourse to saying, "George Jennings, don't you sergeant-major me!" When she asked him to do something for her he would say, "I'm not made of ballbearings!" or "My name is Samuel, not Samson."

George had firm views on their respective domestic roles and refused to help clean up the kitchen. His stock response to Elena's complaints about this was, "Meid, moet ek ook onder lê?" (*"Do you also want me to lie underneath?"*)

They were in the habit of putting the toothpaste on each other's toothbrush at bedtime, depending on who was in the bathroom first. When one was out of favour, the other showed disapproval by breaking the tradition. On the occasion that Elena had dinged the car, she put a large quantity of toothpaste on George's brush and tied a pink bow to the handle. George's response was, "Huh, you don't think that's going to help you, do you?" After a really huge row, Elena wrapped George's pasteless toothbrush in plastic: his comment this time was, "Now I'm in terrible shit!"

As George's illness progressed, their friends rallied round them and they continued to extract as much fun and laughter out of every day as they could. Doc Wilson's wife was called Yoli – Yoli of the beautiful eyes. She, too, was suffering from cancer and she told George just to take every day as well as he could and try to enjoy it. She died shortly before George.

Not long after she died, George persuaded Rob (Doc Wilson) to let him take him out to dinner to the Crayfish Inn, a favourite haunt of many South Coasters and holiday-makers. Rob wasn't keen and tried to sidestep the invitation by claiming that he hadn't brought any suitable attire with him from Underberg. George wasn't having it and even dressed him to go out. They also ended up having to share George's spectacles, but they had a memorable evening.

Rob remarried some time later. His second wife was a very attractive blonde but she didn't meet with local approval. The wedding took place in Underberg and many of the locals trekked thence. Their disapproval was further provoked by the fact that the reception was staged in Yoli's beloved rose garden on the farm. One of them said to Doc Wilson, "Rob, jy het nou 'n lat vir jou gesny!" (*"You've cut a switch for yourself now."*) The prophecy proved accurate: the blonde didn't last and they were soon divorced. Doc Wilson died in 2001 when Elena was in Italy. Eleanor 'phoned her to let her know.

When cancer was detected in George's other lung he was sent to Durban for chemotherapy. On their return journey from his first treatment he told Elena that he was going to refuse any further chemotherapy. She accepted his decision with a heavy heart but also with understanding.

As he grew weaker a number of people really came to the fore to help in many ways. Dot Hawthorn and Norma Payn were voluntary hospice workers who both provided enormous help in dealing with the pain and other distressing symptoms, including managing the choking, thick discharge from his lungs.

Dot is a remarkable lady whose husband had also worked for the post office. Dot had trained as a nurse and she and her husband retired to Port Edward. She is a staunch Methodist, gifted with much handiness and great helpfulness. Norma, too, is a very special breed of person who dedicated many years to helping women prisoners jailed in the Far East for drug trafficking – not a fashionable mission but one to which she felt great commitment, and not because of any family or personal involvement. Both of them were also responsible for starting the Shafts organization in Port Edward. Shafts collects all sorts of medical equipment, such as wheelchairs and crutches, and loans these items out, free of charge, to people who are unable to afford such items. In a community of many retired people, and one in which financial hardship is often evident, this is a very real help.

George's sister, Hilda, also came to lend a hand. Hilda was a hospital matron and a very formidable lady. She was very bossy and her injections were brutal. She had no tolerance for being kept waiting when George wasn't up to facing his shot. The set time for medication was the set time and the longer he kept her waiting the more brutal were the injections. Eventually George begged Elena to take over the job. They had to make sure that Elena administered the injection before Hilda's scheduled time in order to sidestep her. In a sense, Hilda still emerged victorious because there was no way George could avoid his medication under this system.

George had managed to get his hands on some potent pain pills which he knew could prove fatal if he took a certain number. He kept these in his bedside cupboard and made no bones about the fact that, if his illness became too unbearable, he saw no shame in taking matters into his own hands. The presence of the little bottle was helpful in its own way in the sense that it gave him a feeling of control in a largely uncontrollable situation.

The pills also came in useful after George died when Peter Farndell's dear old dog became very ill. She was very old and in a great deal of pain. Peter decided that he had to put the old girl down but wanted to avoid the stress to himself and her of taking her to the vet. He asked Elena if she still had any of the pills left so that he could do the job peacefully and painlessly. The dose would have been lethal for a man and Peter and his family said their farewells and then he administered them.

The following day, when Elena saw Peter, she asked him how it had gone. His answer was that it hadn't gone as anybody expected. Shortly after swallowing the pills, Buggalugs, as Elena called her, vomited them up, possibly because the dose had been so large, and proceeded to eat a large supper and then cavort about as though she had regained her puppyhood. The pills had obviously taken her pain away so that, for a short time, she could be her old self again. Sadly, this improvement wasn't lasting and Rhona, Peter's wife, undertook the unpleasant task of taking her to the vet a little later.

When Hilda discovered George's stash she had a fit and flushed them all down the loo. George was not impressed and Hilda was unrepentant. Somehow, he managed to obtain another stash.

Hilda was fortunate in the person who nursed her in her frailty and when she was dying. Her son-in-law, Pierre, took care of her and Hilda came to love him for his gentleness and kindness. The old martinet declared that no one could ask for a more compassionate and skilled caregiver than Pierre.

Another person whose dedication and kindness knew no bounds was Melt van Schoor. Melt came to the house every morning to help George bath and shave when he was no longer able to do it himself. If George was having a particularly bad day, and didn't have the energy to get going, Melt would sit and chat to him until he felt able to undergo the routine. George was always a fastidious man and this assistance went a long way to helping him retain his dignity and pride.

Melt lived in Port Edward for more than twenty years. In 2004 he moved to the premises of a trading store near Hole-in-the-Wall on the Wild Coast of the Eastern Cape. On Wednesday the 9ᵗʰ of September, 2010, during the evening, he heard gunshots and noticed suspicious people near his house. According to the 'South Coast Herald', he 'phoned a friend and asked him to call the police. Before anybody could arrive to help him, these people broke into his house and shot him three times. The shot to his head was fatal. The store was then robbed. Seven men were arrested.

The 'Herald' goes on to record Melt's great service to this community: *"During the years spent living in Port Edward, Melt van Schoor dedicated his precious spare time to the community by taking on the mammoth task of running the North Sands Bluff Surf Lifesaving Club.*

"The club was founded by the late Martin van Duyn who coached and mentored Melt who, in later years, took over the reins of the club, as well as nursing his mentor Martin, during his terminal illness.

"Melt provided Port Edward and all its tourists with a safe bathing beach through his dedication to the surf lifesaving movement and continuous struggle to keep the lifesaving club alive with properly trained, competent lifeguards.

"Melt was responsible for training not only the youth of Port Edward who enjoyed the opportunity to spend their vacations in a working capacity to serve the tourist trade, but also a number of older members, who, once qualified, dedicated their spare time to the lifesaving movement in support of Melt.

"Melt will always be remembered for his total dedication to the lifesaving movement in Port Edward, for instilling discipline in those members he coached, and his great sense of humour."

Rina, Melt's ex-wife, was the manager at Splash Spar until 2010, and she, too, was remarkably kind. When Elena was forced to stop driving, Rina would pick her up once a week and drive her into the village so that she could do her shopping at Spar, as she had always done, and attend to her banking business in the Owen Ellis Mall next door to Splash Spar. Rina continued to do this until Lynette and Pierre came to live with Elena. Now Pierre takes her shopping.

Elena gets great satisfaction out of these trips and is greeted by all and sundry in and outside the shop. Many of her post office customers remember her and she can always rely on an escort if she has to cross the road. She is greatly amused by the Neanderthal stares she gets at the picture of her arm being taken by a gallant black man. Elena has never used dulcet tones and returns the hailings she gets in the shop with equal gusto.

Martin van Duyn, who was a lifesaver at Amanzimtoti in his youth, was a great friend of the Jenningses. Just after the war he met a master builder who had emigrated from Holland. It was under this man's tutelage that he, too, became a master builder and made a substantial amount of money. With his fortune he was able to buy the Estuary, the beautiful Herbert Baker-inspired Cape Dutch style mansion on the estuary which flows into the sea at Silver Beach.

Today, the land surrounding the house has all been built up with the additions to the property, all of which form the Estuary Hotel. The press of development also includes privately owned houses in a stark imitation of the gentler lines of the original house. Before the changes it was a great treat to stroll along Silver Beach at dusk to view the house from the beach. As one rounded Tragedy Hill, there the gracious building stood with its lights gleaming enticingly and outlined by the dark and mysterious bush behind it. It was a sight many Port Edwardians took their visitors to see.

In the Van Duyn's day the house was backed by indigenous bush and trees which also encircled the lagoon. The bush was rich in wildlife. In the lounge at the hotel there is a magnificent painting of the estuary as one looks out from the hotel towards the sea. The picture captures the scene as it once was before any development took place and is a priceless reminder of an irretrievable past. Beryl, Martin's wife, underplanted the trees at the back of the house with azaleas which flourished in the climate and provided a spectacular display as one drove up to the rear entrance.

The house had been so positioned that, on moonlit nights, the moon would shine across the bay and the lagoon and, if the front and rear doors were open, its gleam would reach right through the house, reflected on the polished wooden floors. This was a magical sight. Now, unfortunately, the front of the house has been extended to accommodate the hotel restaurant so that magical sight is no longer possible.

The lagoon was always inhabited by a pair of fish eagles whose presence and eerie call gave their name to the hotel restaurant: The Fish Eagle Restaurant. A friend, Michelle Fourie, who was a teenager at the time, witnessed the demise of the last fish eagle to inhabit that spot.

Six months previously, the female had disappeared but the male continued to hang about. On a day in December of 2001 Michelle was swimming in the hotel pool, which overlooks the estuary, when she noticed the male soaring high into the sky. As she watched, he flew impossibly high and then plunged straight down at a terrible speed, into the waters of the lagoon – and was no more.

When Michelle and her mother investigated this behaviour they learnt that fish eagles mate for life and if one dies, after a period of about six months, the remaining bird will kill itself. Knowing that this is a documented behaviour didn't lessen the poignancy of the moment for Michelle or anyone who heard her story.

The Van Duyns and the Jenningses celebrated their wedding anniversaries at about the same time. For their twenty-fifth anniversary, Martin gave Beryl a large and beautiful diamond ring which she proudly showed Elena. She asked Elena what anniversary present George had given her. Elena replied that it was the best present he could possibly have given her: he had been declared free of the bladder cancer.

At about the time that George was diagnosed with lung cancer, Martin was also diagnosed with cancer. They were both very ill when Dick and Vina Hooper arrived at the Jenningses' house one morning and suggested that they pay the Van Duyns a visit to wish Martin a happy birthday. Off they all went.

Tea and coffee were served by Beryl, a sensible and responsible choice for two desperately ill men, and appropriate beverages for 10 o'clock in the morning. The men, however, were having none of it and George said to Martin, "Martin, ons gaan tog vrek: ons drink whisky!" (*"Martin, we're going to snuff it anyway: we're drinking whisky!"*) which they duly did and had themselves a memorable party.

After Martin died, shortly before George, Beryl sold up and moved to Grahamstown where she remarried.

Professor Dreyer also proved himself to be a loyal and dedicated friend in George's illness, and not only a brilliant dentist. He undertook to visit George every day to give him physiotherapy to loosen and clear the awful tar-like substance that clogged his lungs and airways.

Bob was always accompanied by his dog, a miniature schnauser. His routine was so well established that, on one of the few mornings when he couldn't see George, the little dog arrived any way. Elena told him that his boss wasn't there that morning and the little chap turned around and trotted home. Bob and his wife later immigrated to New Zealand to be with their son.

During his illness George told Elena that he felt great guilt at having removed her from her family and all that was familiar to her, to bring her to South Africa only to have to abandon her in death. He kept insisting that she ask Johannes Mpofu and his wife, Oliena, to come and see him. He wouldn't tell her why he wanted to see them and Elena assumed that he wanted to tell them about some sort of legacy.

Johannes was still working at the post office so could only make it on a Saturday afternoon. She overheard George saying, "Johannes, I'm dying. I leave Elena in your hands. Will you look after her?"

This they did by visiting her for many years despite their own burdens.

The Mpofus had only one child, a son, who didn't have his parents' work ethic or sense of responsibility. Alcohol got the better of him and he left a string of nine children for whom Johannes and Oliena had to care. After

Johannes died Oliena struggled on, trying to feed and educate this brood but she continued to visit Elena regularly.

By February of 1988 George was extremely weak. He was also in a great degree of discomfort, exacerbated by the mucus which now also coated and filled his mouth. On the night of the 20th of February he was desperately cold and asked Elena to "Lê lepel" (*lie as spoons*) as they had done for so many years. It was a breathless, steaming hot February night, the sort of weather so typical of February on the South Coast when, five minutes after a shower one is dripping with perspiration again. One tries to sit, stand, or walk so that one's own body parts don't touch. Elena lay close but nothing could warm George who was freezing cold.

The following day was no better for him. Wendy Warner, a nurse and Barry Payn's sister, spent most of the day with them and a doctor called to check on them. This was Peter and Anne Smythe's son-in-law who was holidaying here and very kindly came to give a hand because there wasn't a resident doctor available. Elena couldn't help but see the desperate pleading in George's eyes for it all to be over.

Norma Payn was sitting with George when he slipped away.

Elena has never shed another tear since that day. She says she was all cried out on that day.

George's service was held in the Methodist Church which was packed to capacity, and overflowed into the surrounding grounds. Elena was deeply touched by how many black people attended the service.

His ashes were strewn on the seventh hole, the hole which had been his responsibility to restore. When Elena moved to Beau Geste she gained a lovely view over the golf-course. Her entrance looks directly over the seventh hole. This is where Elena, too, wants her ashes scattered.

What happened to …?

Barend passed away from heart failure in 1959 and was followed by **Lucia** who died in 1975 from cancer.

Toly died from emphysema in 2004. Her husband, Ernst, lived with their daughter, Erna, and her husband, Rev. Harold Sadler, in Fishoek. He passed away on Sunday the 1ˢᵗ of June 2014 at the age of ninety-five. He and Elena talked on the telephone every Sunday until his final short illness. Jacques and his wife live in Pretoria.

Orso died of cancer in 1995.

Agnese lives in a Catholic retirement home in Florence where she is extremely happy. She and her elder son had a stint living in Brazil a couple of years ago but this was a miserable time for both of them. Agnese is currently writing her autobiography, much encouraged by her younger son, Sandro Krausz, and his family.

ACKNOWLEDGEMENTS

This project has taken a great deal longer than Elena and I ever anticipated. I am indebted to Elena for sharing her story, for her patience, her unflagging enthusiasm and, above all, her friendship. Then there is my husband, Greg, whose interest, encouragement, excellent spelling skills, Zulu knowledge and the cooking of many suppers, made the endeavour much easier. Eve Gower, my editor, gave many hours and a highly trained eye to correcting all those sneaky errors which so easily go undetected. Her faith in the story was also of inestimable value to me. My father, John Ward, has a memory for historical detail which most other people never knew, or have forgotten, and I often called on him. Agnese van Praag, and her astounding memory, was a resource of immense value as was Erna Taljaard Sadler who provided so much information about Toly. I also owe thanks to friends and colleagues who checked the non-English references: Ursula Flascas, Annette Haupt, Dale Salotto and Gudreen Mtshali. My gratitude, too, goes to Jean Swan and April Ross of Partridge Publishing for their gentle charm, efficiency and guidance in steering me through the publication process. Finally, there are my friends, Phillipa Rowney and Sarah Mellors: the former I thank for cracking the whip regularly, and the latter for her literary and history proficiency.

REFERENCES

Alhadeff, Vic. South Africa in Two World Wars: a Newspaper History. Cape Town: Don Nelson Publishers. 2013

Allan, Tony. Library of Nations: Italy. Amsterdam: Time-Life Books, 1985

Bulpin, T.V. Discovering Southern Africa. Cape Town: Books of Africa, 1970

Bulpin, T.V. Natal and the Zulu Country. Cape Town: Books of Africa, 1966

Butler, Guy (Editor). The 1820 Settlers. Cape Town: Human and Rousseau, 1974

Carr, Norman. Return to the Wild. First published in 1966. Reprinted in Three Great Animal Stories. London: Collins, 1971

Holland, James. Italy's Sorrow. London: Harper Press, 2009

Imperial War Museum. Great Battles of World War II. London: Marshall Cavendish Books, 1995

Joyce, Peter. The South African Family Encyclopaedia. Cape Town: Struik Publishers, 1989

Kubly, Herbert et al. Life World Library: Italy. USA: Time Inc, 1961

Morse Jones, E. Roll of the British Settlers in South Africa. Cape Town: A A Balkema, 1969

Rivett-Carnacc, Dorothy. Thus Came the English in 1820. Cape Town: Howard Timmins, 1961

Saunders, Christopher. Illustrated History of South Africa. Cape Town: The Reader's Digest Association South Africa, 1989

Encyclopaedia Britannica, 1971

Websites

American Friends of Italian Monnumental Sculpture: Projects@staglieno.com (Eugenio Baroni)

'The Annihilation of Freemasonry' by Sven G. Lunden': web.mit.edu

La Villa Novi Ligure: Trip-Europe Hotel and Travel Corporation

St Andrew's Presbyterian Church of Scotland: www.presbyterianchurchrome.org

Maja Einstein: www.einstein-website.de / neatorama.com/2008/12/20/maja-einstein

British 1820 Settlers to South Africa by Paul Tanner-Tremaine: paul@1820Settlers.com

Blaauwbank Historic Gold Mine and Resort: www.wilparkgroup.co.za/blaauwbank

South African Naval Museum: navpro@telkomsa.net

Robert Einstein family tragedy: www.telesanterno.com

Norman Carr: www.normancarrsafaris.com

James Jennings: www.geni.com / Site managed by Sally Ann McConnell

Wikipedia

Albert Einstein

Armistice of Cassibile

Baron Carl-Ludwig Diego von Bergen

Berchtesgaden

Daphné-class submarine

DELASEM

1820 Settlers

Foro Italico

Generale di Corpo d'Armata Paolo Berardi

Hospital of Santa Maria Nuovo

Kafue National Park

Lorenza Mazzetti

Robey Leibbrandt

Teatro della Pergola

W.O.J. Nieuwenkamp

Lightning Source UK Ltd.
Milton Keynes UK
UKOW02f0349271014

240642UK00002B/100/P